bangladesh
bhutan
india
maldives
nepal
pakistan
sri lanka

south asian
economics
STUDENTS**meet**

Economic Challenges to Make South Asia
Free from Poverty and Deprivation

Economic Challenges to Make South Asia Free from Poverty and Deprivation

Editors

Meeta Kumar and Mihir Pandey

ACADEMIC FOUNDATION
NEW DELHI

www.academicfoundation.com

First published in 2010
by

ACADEMIC FOUNDATION
4772-73 / 23 Bharat Ram Road, (23 Ansari Road),
Darya Ganj, New Delhi - 110 002 (India).
Phones : 23245001 / 02 / 03 / 04.
Fax : +91-11-23245005.
E-mail : books@academicfoundation.com
www. academicfoundation.com

Cataloging in Publication Data--DK
Courtesy: D.K. Agencies (P) Ltd. <docinfo@dkagencies.com>

South Asia Economics Students Meet (5th : 2008 : Delhi, India)
Economic Challenges to make South Asia Free from Poverty and Deprivation / editors, Meeta Kumar and Mihir Pandey.
p. cm.
Papers presented at the 5th South Asia Economics Students Meet , held at Delhi in March 2008.
ISBN 13: 9788171888146
ISBN 10: 8171888143

1. Infrastructure (Economics)--South Asia--Congresses. 2. Rural development--Government policy--South Asia--Congresses. 3. Economic development--South Asia--Congresses. 4. South Asia--Economic policy--Congresses. 5. South Asia--Social policy--Congresses. I. Kumar, Meeta. II. Pandey, Mihir. III. Title.

DDC 363.0954 22

Typeset by Italics India, New Delhi.
Printed and bound in India.

Contents

III
Improving the Quality of Physical Infrastructure

IV
Accountability, Institutions and Economic Growth

List of Tables and Figures

Tables

Figures

About the Editors/ Contributors

Editors:

Meeta Kumar has taught Economics at various colleges of the University of Delhi since 1990; since 1995, she has taught at Miranda House. She has also been visiting faculty at the Lahore University of Management Sciences (during the summer of 2006). She specialises in teaching the economic history of colonial India and development economics. She has been very actively involved with the organisation of several national and international debates, seminars and conferences for students, with a view to introducing inter-disciplinary perspectives in teaching and promoting intercultural interactions.

Mihir Pandey is Associate Professor of Economics at Ramjas College, University of Delhi where he has taught for 25 years. He received his B.A. and M.A. in economics from University of Delhi and a PhD in economics from Rutgers University. His research has been primarily in the area of international economics, focusing on India's trade policy. He has also worked on environmental issues in India.

Contributors:

Saher Asad, Lahore University of Management Sciences, Pakistan.

Manka Bajaj, St. Xavier's College, Mumbai, India.

M.S. Shanaz Banu, University of Colombo, Sri Lanka.

Rishi Chakravarti, Jadavpur University, India.

Asmita Ganguly, Jadavpur University, India.

Sanya Garg, Delhi University, India.

Nabaraj Gautam, Tribhuvan University, Nepal.

Fahim Hassan, University of Dhaka, Bangladesh.

Syeda ShahBano Ijaz, Lahore University of Management Sciences, Pakistan.

Abdul Rafeh Iqbal, Lahore School of Economics, Pakistan.

Shazana Ismail, University of Colombo, Sri Lanka.

Niranjani Kailayanathan, University of Colombo, Sri Lanka.

Amna Khan, Lahore University of Management Sciences, Pakistan.

Dulanii Liyanahetti, University of Colombo, Sri Lanka.

Sangeeta Nath, University of Dhaka, Bangladesh.

Jithmal Samankantha, University of Colombo, Sri Lanka.

Pramodha Samarasinghe, University of Colombo, Sri Lanka.

Shanuka Senerath, University of Colombo, Sri Lanka.

Nayantara Sarma, Delhi University, India.

Sameen Siddiqi, Lahore University of Management Sciences, Pakistan.

Mahjuja M. Taznin, University of Dhaka, Bangladesh.

Mezbah Uddin, Bachelor of Business Administration (Economics & Finance), North South University, Bangladesh.

Ranmini Vithanagama, University of Colombo, Sri Lanka.

Foreword

South Asia is home to the largest concentration of poor people in the world. But it is also the region that, for over a decade, has enjoyed the second fastest economic growth in the world. For the first time in its recent history, the region has a real chance of ending poverty in a generation.

A decade of rapid economic growth is changing the economic landscape of the region. Growth has reduced poverty substantially in most countries, and is bolstering both the political will to redistribute and raising public expectations that governments will use a deft policy hand to accelerate economic growth further, to sustain it, and to ensure that the growth is equitably shared. Having tasted the fruits of rapid growth, citizens are demanding more accountable government, particularly in the delivery of basic public services in health, education and infrastructure. The global financial crisis and the renewed focus on the role of government has only strengthened these expectations. And though growth has slowed down as a result of the crisis, a robust revival in the region seems to be on the cards.

These past few years have also brought heightened challenges for the region, home to a quarter of the world's population. The problems of poverty, deprivation, unemployment and security afflicting its poor people remain stark in their significance—some 400 million living in abject poverty, some facing violent conflicts, others confronted by corruption and confrontational politics, ill-health and illiteracy, child malnutrition, a looming water crisis and global climate-change impact of extraordinary proportions. And despite the shared history, institutions and cultures, the region remains the least integrated in the world. The gains from greater trade openness and cross-border FDI can be tremendous.

South Asia's potential and its challenges give the idea of the South Asia Economics Students' Meet, or SAESM, enormous significance. Bringing together some of the brightest young students of economics from within the region and allowing them the opportunity to present and debate their ideas on how to tackle the region's policy challenges can greatly help shape this future generation of political leaders and policymakers, business leaders and economics faculty and researchers. And it can help build the bonds of professional and personal interactions across borders that are so vital to a common understanding of the future of this region.

The organisers of SAESM are to be congratulated for investing systematically in this process over the five meets that have been held so far. I had the pleasure of participating in the 5th SAESM held at Ramjas College in Delhi in March 2008 on the theme of "Economic Challenges to Make South Asia Free from Poverty and Deprivation". The conference sessions on accelerating rural growth, investing in health and education, improving the quality and access to infrastructure, and addressing accountability and institutional problems in the region brought forth a rich discussion. I am now pleased to see this collection of papers from the 5th SAESM and want to congratulate the young authors and the editors of this volume for their commitment and hard work in bringing it out.

With my best wishes for the continued success of SAESM.

Shekhar Shah
Regional Economic Adviser, South Asia
The World Bank

Preface

South Asia has some of the highest trained professionals—engineers, doctors, scientists and economists—and yet there is little structured interaction among them. Although the nations have inseparable histories and shared heritage, social and political strife in the region has created barriers between the peoples during the second half of the 20th century. However, there have been changes in the region during the last 10 years. Economic growth rates have picked up and in fact, some industrial and services sectors such as software and pharmaceuticals have attracted global attention. There has been some effort at cooperation at an inter-government level, but it is possible to expand this to include the common people.

Against this background, a unique student initiative called South Asia Economics Students' Meet (SAESM) was initiated at Ramjas College, University of Delhi, India. Initially supported by three other partners, Lahore University of Management Sciences (Pakistan), University of Dhaka (Bangladesh) and University of Colombo (Sri Lanka), it was later joined by Tribhuvan University (Nepal). SAESM promotes budding economists of the region to foster intellectual bonding with other fellow students through student conference. The annual meet provides an opportunity for undergraduate students to write academic papers on topical issues in the region, to present the papers at the conference, to share their experiences, and to learn from each other, while promoting their knowledge on development and cooperation in the South Asian countries. The journey so far has seen a wonderful festivity of sharing intellectual space and making new friends at each of the stops—Delhi (2004), Lahore (2005), Dhaka (2006) and Colombo (2007). The first cycle of Meets has been completed. The 2008 Meet in Delhi was particularly significant as it sees the beginning of the second cycle of SAESM conferences. Each of the preceding Meets has been immensely successful, and proved beyond doubt the sustainability of the ideas behind the Meet.

I wish to express my appreciation and gratitude to Dr. Mihir Pandey (Ramjas College) and Ms. Meeta Kumar (Miranda House) who are the editors of this volume comprising a selection of papers from the 6th edition of SAESM jointly hosted by Ramjas College and Miranda House, University of Delhi in the spring of 2008 at New Delhi. I thank both the institutions for their support to the cause of SAESM. I would like to record a special thanks to all my fellow country coordinators of the SAESM fraternity for their commitment to SAESM. Finally, our gratitude to the World Bank, especially Dr. Shantayanan Devarajan and Dr. Shekhar Shah at the South Asia regional office and Dr. Rajni Khanna at the New Delhi office for making it possible through a generous grant to have this book reach the future economists of the South Asian region.

Deb Kusum Das
SAESM—Coordinator

Introduction

The papers in this volume were presented at the 5th South Asia Economics Students Meet, held in Delhi in March 2008. Two sets of reasons motivate these Meets. First, in an increasingly fractious South Asia, we believe the onus of effective strategies for regional peace and co-existence lies with civil society, and that inter-personal contacts among the young are a good place to start. The participants at these Meets are bright young students, studying for a Bachelor's Degree in Economics at some of the premier institutes in South Asia. They will, doubtless, go on to be important in shaping opinions, even policy, in their own countries. The second set of reasons is academic. Curricula in most of our universities are weighted, on the one hand, towards an Anglo-American approach, and on the other, to a narrow focus on each of our 'own' economies. Many of us believe that wider South Asian focus would enrich students' understanding of development issues in particular and economics in general. Each paper presented at the conference details a specific aspect of the presenter's home economy, thus providing participants with a rich smorgasbord of issues and perspectives around a pre-specified theme.

The theme for the Delhi conference was "Economic Challenges to Make South Asia Free from Poverty and Deprivation". The idea that poverty can best be tackled in the long run through inclusive growth has by now been fairly mainstreamed into our curricula. What this means specifically in terms of immediate, country-specific policies, however is subject to much debate. In order to focus the discussion, papers were invited on four sub-themes. Two papers from each country were selected for the final round of the conference. Ideally, we would have liked to include all of them, but space constrains us from doing so. Needless to say, choosing which ones to include was not an easy task. This book is divided into four sections—according to the sessions at the Meet. We have tried, as far as the quality of submissions permitted, to retain a balance across countries in each section.

Section 1: Accelerating Rural Growth and Empowering the Rural Poor

This theme was included to focus on the growth experience of South Asian countries which has led to the neglect of rural sector and a disproportionate persistence of rural poverty and inequality, as well as the deepening of a rural-urban divide. As a theme for our young contributors, this is both, very easy and very difficult. It is easy in that there is a wealth of material, both empirical and theoretical, that addresses the theme. But that is precisely the source of the difficulty. The material is vast and complex, even inter-disciplinary. It is also rapidly evolving. The papers submitted at the Meet largely focused on the scope of the non-farm sector in alleviating rural poverty, evaluations of rural poverty alleviation programmes, and the role of women's participation. Of the papers included in this volume, Ijaz's paper starts from the premise that the development paradigm adopted by Pakistan looked upon agriculture as source for extracting resources for industrial growth. She examines the effects of alternate pricing regimes on rural incomes and incentives in this context, and traces the low productivity in agriculture to inadequate investment in the sector. It is interesting that inadequate investment in agriculture is not viewed merely as myopic Government policy, but also a result of adverse incentives for private investment. She also suggests alternative pricing regimes that may ameliorate the adverse incentives, and stimulate investment, within the constraints of larger equity considerations. It is easy to generalise from this case to all of South Asia, allowing, of course, for differences in detail. Ganguly points out that the employment elasticity of farming is too low to generate adequate livelihoods for the large proportion of the Indian rural population. She emphasises the scope of the non-farm sector in ameliorating rural poverty and reducing the rural-urban divide in India. Ismail and Samankantha evaluates Sri Lanka's Samurdhi anti-poverty programme. To conclude this section, Fahim Hassan's excellent paper contains a survey on rural Bangladeshi women that reveals their social, economic and hygiene problems, as well as gender gaps in access to health, nutrition, employment, and participation in decision-making. It also uses an empirical analysis to examine the existence of a gender-poverty nexus. His results are inconclusive, but that does not detract from the paper. Between them, these papers raise a whole range of issues that have engaged economists working in this field for the last few decades. There are lacunae, of course. India's NREGA finds no mention, the scope of technology in promoting agricultural productivity and equitable growth in the subcontinent finds no mention. But that is the difficulty we referred to earlier.

Section 2: Investing in the Social Sector

This theme sought to take the discussion forward from the consumption *versus* investment debate, by focusing on the role of social sector investments in the sustainability of high growth in South Asia. In particular, papers were sought to focus on the role of health and education in simultaneously eradicating hunger and deprivation in the immediate run, and creating the capacity for faster growth in the longer run. Papers that were received focused on the importance of public and private sectors in investing in health and education; and the need and policies for revamping health and education systems in South Asia. The papers included in this section are those of Abdul Rafeh Iqbal of the Lahore School of Economics, Pakistan, Rishi Chakravarti of Jadavpur University, India, Mezbah Uddin of North South University, Bangladesh, Nabaraj Gautam of Tribhuvan University, Nepal, and Dulanii Liyanahetti and M.S. Shanaz Banu of University of Colombo, Sri Lanka.

Iqbal's paper examines poverty measurement issues in Pakistan, and contains an overview of Pakistani anti-poverty programmes. He examines the links between education and economic well-being, highlighting the issues in the context of Pakistan. He then looks at the health–development relationship before going on to suggest policy measures for alleviating poverty in Pakistan. Chakravarti's paper examines the role of education in eliminating poverty in general, and possible strategies for revamping the education system in India. After analysing the impact of education on economic growth and looking at the case of South Korea, he outlines the role of public and private sector investment in the education sector in India. Mezbah Uddin uses error-correction and Granger causality to estimate the elasticity of GDP growth with respect to education expenditures in Bangladesh, and with impressive insight, explains the low estimated elasticity in terms of the quality education that is delivered for a given level of expenditure on education. Gautam looks at health and education in the Nepalese context. He surveys the status of education, health, water and sanitation in Nepal, concluding that more investment is needed in the social sector by both the public and private sectors. Liyanahetti and Banu examine non-communicable diseases among the urban poor in Sri Lanka and examine the parallels with India. They look at the health systems in Sri Lanka and India, especially the role of public and private sectors in dealing with non-communicable diseases.

These papers illustrate issues that have gained foreground in the literature. They highlight that social sector investment is absolutely necessary to ensure high growth, while at the same time noting that it is not going to be sufficient without adequate attention to the quality of services delivered. The importance of both the public and private sectors in social sector investment is highlighted by all the authors.

Section 3: Improving the Quality of Physical Infrastructure

This theme focused on the infrastructural bottlenecks impeding the development of the South Asian region in various areas—transport, power, water supply and sanitation, irrigation. Public and private financing of infrastructure development was an additional issue discussed. Papers submitted examined specific sub-sectors and sought to suggest policies to address problems facing them in accelerating growth and improving service delivery. Four papers have been selected for this section, written by Mahjuja M. Taznin of University of Dhaka, Bangladesh, Saher Asad of Lahore University of Management Sciences, Pakistan, Manka Bajaj of St. Xavier's College, Mumbai, India and Pramodha Samarasinghe and Niranjani Kailayanathan of University of Colombo, Sri Lanka.

Taznin focuses on access to safe drinking water and sanitation in Bangladesh, examining its relationship with factors such as economic status, education, gender and location. Her analysis suggests that economic status is not a factor influencing access to safe drinking water and sanitation; it is other factors such as location and education that are significant, pointing to the lack of effective governance, inadequate infrastructure and inefficient delivery system. Asad examines the relationship between infrastructure and agricultural productivity in

Pakistan. Drawing upon previous studies from India and Nigeria, he looks at the impact of infrastructure availability on agriculture productivity as consisting of two effects. The direct or specialisation effect comes through access to markets by roads leading to product specialisation, and the indirect or intensification effect comes through increased use of irrigation, fertilisers, specialised seeds, etc. Asad's analysis of data from Pakistan confirms the findings from earlier studies that there is a significant positive relationship between infrastructure and agricultural productivity, and that the direct specialisation effect is stronger than the indirect intensification effect. In an interesting article, Bajaj looks at traffic congestion in Mumbai as a consequence of economic development. After establishing that economic growth leads to rising demand for urban travel, she examines the effect of increasing infrastructure supply on congestion. Concluding that increased public transport is the only sustainable method of dealing with this problem, she examines road pricing as a solution to reducing private transport and therefore, traffic congestion. Although used in many cities in different parts of the world, she notes that road pricing is regressive because it excludes those who are not able to pay. This becomes all the more important in the context of low supplies of public transport. Bajaj concludes by examining alternatives to road pricing to reducing private transport.

The final piece in this section by Samarasinghe and Kailayanathan is based on a case study of the Sri Lankan Railway. After analysing the structure and performance, they do a SWOT analysis. Recognising the importance of improving the railway system, the authors suggest policy measures by which the infrastructure can be improved.

Section 4: Accountability, Institutions and Economic Growth

This theme explored the importance of institutions in economic development. The session's focus was the debate surrounding market and government failures. It also looked at issues pertaining to governance and corruption in South Asia. As practitioners of the trade, we are all aware how amenable these issues are to polemic, and how easily debate gives way to jingoism. The maturity with which these have been dealt with by students is, to us as teachers, rewarding. Three broad sets of issues have been examined. The first: do institutions matter? Nath stresses the importance of governance for achieving growth. She uses Kaufmann and Kraay governance indicators, and GDP data in an empirical exercise to depict the causal relationship between governance (hence, institutional quality) and income. She then analyses Bangladesh's experience in this light. Nath emphasises the importance of fostering democracy, the free flow of information, eliminating corruption and strengthening local government in ensuring growth. But, does the form of government affect growth? Siddiqi details how democracy has not delivered good governance or lower corruption (and hence, higher growth rates) when compared to periods of non-democratic rule in Pakistan. Senerath and Vithanagama study the efficacy of setting up Provincial Councils in Sri Lanka under the 13th Amendment of the Sri Lankan Constitution. In another interesting spin on the issue, Sarma and Garg examine the 'rationality' of corruption, and thence best strategies for control of corruption. Finally, is privatisation an antidote to government failure? Khan's paper illustrates, through a case study of banks in Pakistan, how privatisation may not by itself improve performance or even profitability. We cannot resist quoting Nath, "Communism can never be a complete failure nor can capitalism be a complete success".

This collection of papers is special in several ways. The youth of our contributors is well compensated by their intellectual maturity. Apart from reiterating the capabilities of our students, it also reflects the quality of teaching and academics on the sub-continent. To us, it is the repository of the hope and effort that we have invested in our students, and in our future. We hope this will give the reader some idea of the capabilities of our 'future economists'.

I
Accelerating Rural Growth and Empowering the Rural Poor

1 Government Interventions in the Agriculture Sector of Pakistan

An Analysis and Suggestions

Syeda ShahBano Ijaz

Introduction

Pakistan is an agrarian-based economy with 70 per cent of its population based in rural areas and about 43.4 per cent of its labour force employed by the agricultural sector. Despite a gradual fall in its share in the gross domestic product from previous years, the agricultural sector still contributed a significant chunk of 20.9 per cent in the fiscal year 2006-07 (GoP, 2006-07). Focus on the agricultural sector is thus important, not only for bettering the livelihood of the rural population, but for the economy as a whole. Pakistan however, is one of those countries that considers agriculture's role in economic growth merely as that of a facilitator. Concurrent with the traditional views, the aim of development efforts has been to transfer resources from agriculture to industry.

The Lewis model discusses this dynamics by focusing on how development is a process of moving "surplus" agricultural labour, which has a marginal productivity of zero, to the urban industrial sector until wages in the two sectors are equated. At the same time, even economists like Johnston and Mellor, who wanted to highlight the importance of agriculture, focused merely on the contributions that the sector could make to overall economic growth, namely labour, capital, foreign exchange, food and a domestic market (Eicher and Staatz, 1998). Both these approaches sideline the importance of agricultural growth itself; they basically regard agriculture as a declining sector which needs to be squeezed to the maximum before it is finally allowed to reach a negligible, stagnant state. This paper discusses how pricing policies premised on this model have dwindled both profitability and incentives for further investment in agriculture. It goes on to conclude that given the need for increasingly liberal trade policies and diversification in food demand, the government needs to roll back intervention to a minimum and instead, encourage the role of the market to determine both prices, and hence subsequently, patterns of production.

This paper begins by providing a historical overview of the Government of Pakistan's policy with regards to agriculture; it then moves on to analyse the effects of this policy on profitability, output and incentives for future investment. The next section then provides a brief overview of the current wheat crisis and links it to the pricing policy being implemented in Pakistan. The last section provides alternative pricing policies, as well as the imminent need to focus on agricultural diversification with the aim to promote agricultural growth. It is important to note that throughout the length of the paper, the focus is on how to promote growth in agriculture as a means for rural growth, and not on how to utilise agriculture for the growth of other sectors in the economy. It is hoped that agricultural growth will reduce push factors in the rural areas and instead develop them on par with urban areas, thereby paving the way to rural empowerment.

Agricultural Pricing Policy in Pakistan

An Overview

Pakistan's policy towards agriculture has always been interventionist; although the degree and bias of intervention has differed, the government has always played an active role in determining prices and output levels. Although pricing policy has been developed to meet the objective of food security, this in itself presents an inherent paradox. Whereas ensuring an adequate supply of food requires the guarantee of high prices to farmers, ensuring availability to urban consumers requires the fixing of low food prices. Results however show that in this dilemma, the urban consumer has invariably won over the farmer, with food prices being set below levels that would signal the producer to invest more in agriculture and raise crop outputs.

During the decade of the 60s, interventions were largely indirect. An overvalued exchange rate favoured the industrial sector by supplying both capital goods and food at low prices. The mid-60s however, brought with them the issue of an inability to import enough food supplies which led to an increase in producer prices of most crops, and the initiation of input subsidies. This policy was reversed with the 1972 devaluation of the rupee and the establishment of direct controls which led to the development of parastatals and rationing shops; by 1972, the sale of sugar in the open market was actually banned. By 1976, all flour and rice mills and cotton ginning factories were nationalised. At the same time, the consumer subsidy on wheat amounted to almost 10 per cent of the government budget. Beginning in 1977 however, with the Zia government takeover, agricultural controls began to be gradually dismantled. Mills and factories were successively denationalised, and the sugar mills were allowed to sell some of their output in the free market. In 1981, the Agricultural Prices Commission (APCOM) was established which advised regarding the price-setting of all major crops (Nasim *et al.*, 1991). At the same time, input subsidies were phased out and the distribution of pesticides and to some extent, fertilisers, was transferred to the private sector. In 1987, the ration shop system was dismantled. Despite these measures, however, the government continues to play an important role in the procurement, storage, pricing and distribution of almost all major agricultural commodities (Chaudhry, 1995).

Table 1.1 shows that the result of this direct intervention has led to an under-pricing of most crops from 1984 till 1993 (exceptions being IRRI rice and sugarcane in some years), with the procurement prices being low relative to world prices. It is because of these low prices that the incentives to invest in Pakistan's agricultural sector have been distorted, leading to resource transfers from agriculture to industry.

Effects of Pricing Policy

Overall, low procurement prices have resulted in a reduction in profitability. Table 1.2 shows that according to a policy analysis matrix conducted by Ahmad and Martini (2000), the profit divergences resulting from agricultural pricing policy have been negative for all crops except for potatoes and wheat.

Table 1.1

Agricultural Commodity Prices Relative to World Prices GDP Deflator and NPK (Fertiliser) Prices

Description and Commodity Prices	*1984-85*	*1985-86*	*1986-87*	*1987-88*	*1988-89*	*1989-90*	*1990-91*	*1991-92*	*1992-93*
The Ratio of Procurement and Parity Prices at the Official Exchange Rate									
1. Wheat	0.524	0.648	0.533	0.544	0.539	0.478	0.682	0.597	0.615
2. Seed Cotton	0.694	0.878	0.930	0.568	0.639	0.423	0.470	0.632	0.645
3. Rice (Fine)	0.326	0.303	0.298	0.367	0.380	0.404	0.636	0.694	0.665
4. Rice (IRRI)	0.751	1.128	1.178	0.883	0.614	0.503	1.429	1.267	0.916
5. Sugarcane	1.721	1.193	1.528	1.848	1.438	0.582	0.740	0.859	0.896

Source: Chaudhary, 1995.

Table 1.2

Policy Analysis Matrix (PAM)

	Basmati Rice	*Wheat*	*Cotton*	*Maize*	*Potato*	*Sugarcane*
Policy Analysis Matrix	*Profit*	*Profit*	*Profit*	*Profit*	*Profit*	*Profit*
Private Prices	39060.14	1123.897	21705.04	8091.677	125400.4	4279.086
Social Prices	52284.14	-1103.033	28283.16	12924.33	111052.4	4545.913
Divergences	-13224	2226.93	-6578.121	-4832.65	14348.01	-266.8275

Source: Ahmad and Martini, 2000.

The cumulative changes in output due to price intervention has also been negative; on average, in the time period from 1963-1987, output fell for all major crops (including sugarcane, even though favourable pricing policies led to output increases from 1963-1975). In fact, during the 1990s, an under-pricing of agricultural commodities by almost 40-60 per cent led to output levels that were below the non-interventionist levels by almost 25-36 per cent per annum.

Rural incomes for farming households were also low compared to what they would have been in the absence of intervention, and even though non-farming households benefited from lower food prices, their labour-income would have increased in non-intervention due to higher output levels, and it could not be determined which effect would have been more advantageous.

Although fertilisers, an important input in agriculture were initially subsidised, the prices have shown a general upward trend even though world prices have been falling. This is because the amount of subsidy on natural gas has also been reduced, thereby increasing the costs of fertiliser factories. The price of urea has gone up from Rs. 295/50kg bag in 1995 to Rs. 350/50kg bag in 1999 (Nasim *et al.*, 1991; Ahmad and Martini, 2000). The result of low output prices and increasing input prices has thus been a resource transfer from agriculture to other sectors. Despite the offsetting effect of input subsidies, the net transfer from agriculture has been positive in all years from 1984 to 1993, with the contributing effect of pricing policy as opposed to an overvalued exchange rate, rising in importance post 1989-90.

Low prices, low output levels, low profitability and a successive net outflow of resources has thus, made the agricultural sector unattractive to investors. Agricultural development is thus impeded, with the sector being utilised only for surplus extraction and not as a means to push for rural growth and empowerment.

The Recent Wheat Crisis

Wheat constitutes the staple crop of Pakistan, being cultivated widely and resulting in output levels higher than that of any other crop. It contributes 14.4 per cent of the area cultivated in Pakistan and 3 per cent of the annual GDP (GoP, 2006-07). The government has always been active with regards to wheat policy, keeping in mind the importance of the crop; during the 60s, it was the only crop that was directly intervened in. Despite these precautions, however, the year 2007 saw the unfolding of a wheat crisis in Pakistan; wheat shortages led to price increases and many poor consumers found it impossible to purchase their daily requirements of the staple crop. This crisis came at a most unexpected time, considering that forecasts for the wheat harvest (which were later confirmed as actual output levels in the *Economic Survey of Pakistan*) were cited as 23.52 million tonnes. Pakistan's annual requirement for wheat however, is 21 million tonnes (Kardar, 2008). Despite this positive divergence, shortages shook the Pakistani economy in late 2007.

Linking this wheat shortage to the government's pricing policy, it can be seen that wheat output prices have always been kept below market and at border prices. Table 1.3 shows how the procurement price of wheat has often remained below the open market price.

Table 1.3

Average Wheat Prices and the Extent of Subsidy

Rs./Tonne

Year	*Procurement Price*	*Release Price*	*Import Parity Price*	*Open Market Price*	*Provincial Subsidy*	*Federal Subsidy*	*Total Subsidy*
					(Million Rs.)		
1990-91	2800.00	2550.00	3208.00	2687.25	2158.00	1609.00	3767.00
1991-92	3100.00	3100.00	4205.00	3085.00	1765.00	3671.00	5436.00
1992-93	3250.00	3400.00	4212.00	3608.25	979.00	2000.00	2979.00
1993-94	4000.00	3550.00	3804.00	3726.00	6006.63	1187.29	7193.92
1994-95	4000.00	4375.00	4874.00	4368.25	3352.44	2811.31	6163.08
1995-96	4375.00	4375.00	7718.00	4685.25	3565.08	6648.00	10213.75
1996-97	6000.00	6500.00	7572.00	7500.00	4282.65	5761.00	10043.65

Source: 1. *Economic Survey: 1996-97.*
2. *Agricultural Statistics of Pakistan: 1995-96.*
3. Ghani (1998).

With international prices higher than procurement prices, the wheat consumer has invariably been subsidised. During the past year, international prices have witnessed an even greater increase due to the shifting of demand towards high-value meat products, which in turn has raised cereal demand to be used as grain-feed for animals. With a yawning gap between domestic procurement/release prices and the import parity price (almost double according to some estimates (Kardar, 2008)), and a relaxation on export policies on wheat, large stores of the crop were smuggled out of the country, resulting in a shortage that immediately pushed up prices.

This shortage was further augmented by two factors: firstly, that the government itself had exported half a million tonnes of wheat and secondly, the huge financial subsidy given to wheat proved burdensome to the government coffers and made it even more difficult to import wheat at rising international prices and then subsidise it for domestic consumers.

The repercussions of the wheat crisis for the rural population were acute. The farmers had to contend with low procurement prices while the later hike in prices ended up benefiting the middlemen who had stocked up wheat. In fact, a lot of wheat mills that were provided wheat at low prices by the government, hoarded and sold it at a later stage, instead of actually processing it into flour. Those in the rural population belonging to non-farming households also suffered because the subsequent increase in the release price meant a fall in real incomes.

This crisis suggests that in face of rising world demand and international prices, it is no longer feasible for the government to excessively intervene in the agricultural sector through a pricing policy. Such a policy will only distort incentives, not solve the problem of agricultural growth and productivity.

Suggestions

Alternate Pricing Policy

The question now arises as to what needs to be done in order to boost the agricultural sector which may lead to increases in rural investment and growth. The first suggestion explores alternative pricing policies whereas the second talks about the effects of globalisation on the agricultural sector and what needs to be done to cash in on the changing world trends. The negative effects on investment and output of maintaining low prices through intervention indicates that in order to avoid crises as the one mentioned above, the free market should be allowed to play a role in determining prices. Given the current state of affairs, low procurement prices lead to low production levels of the crop, which lead to a negative divergence between release and market prices, hence not only creating disincentives for the agricultural sector but also pressurising government revenues. In the case of wheat, were the market allowed to function, the rise in prices due to shortage of wheat, and the ability to export and earn a high price abroad, would have automatically signaled to the producers to increase cultivation, thereby eliminating shortages. In a study conducted by Ejaz Ghani, two alternative pricing policy scenarios are assumed in the case of wheat. Scenario one discusses the effect of completely eliminating input and output subsidies, whereas scenario two analyses the result of phasing input subsidies gradually. The results are summarised in Table 1.4 (Ghani, 1998). According to the table, the output of wheat would fall in both scenarios (owing to the removal of wheat subsidies and a previously cited reason of wheat being a socially inefficient crop in Pakistan) whereas consumption would fall by a relatively much smaller amount (due to an almost inelastic demand for the staple crop). Retail wheat prices would therefore register a significant upward trend, and since this retail price would directly raise the price of wheat to farmers in the absence of government controls, farmer incomes would probably increase. At the same time, triggered by higher prices, farmers would have an incentive to increase cultivation efficiency and would thereby invest in better cropping and management technology.

Table 1.4

Percentage Differences: Baseline versus Other Scenarios

	Scenario One	*Scenario Two*
Production	–38	–24
Consumption	–1.84	–1.18
Net Trade	127.46	80.18
Area under Wheat	–18.64	–11.43
Wheat Yield	–23.9	–14.38
Real Retail Price of Fertiliser	9	4.29
Real Retail Price of Wheat	19.69	12.43
Per Capita Wheat Consumption	–1.84	–1.14

Note: Figures show the percentage differences between average baseline projections and projections associated with scenarios one and two for the period 1993 to 2000.

Source: Ghani, 1998.

Another alternate pricing policy may be for the government to implement a two-price scheme through using a targeted subsidy. It is true that because of widespread poverty in developing countries like Pakistan, eliminating all forms of government intervention would be socially undesirable, since without government support, many consumers would be unable to access basic foodstuffs at market prices. Given the hike in input cost and a rapidly increasing population leading to rising demand, the income of most rural and some urban consumers would be unable to keep pace with rising food prices. Government intervention however, need not be uniform across the board, but targeted towards those who actually deserve the subsidy. The common feature of any two-price scheme would be to allow the market forces to determine the price of all foodstuffs as dictated by demand and supply. This would fulfil one side of the food security equation, namely, adequate supply. In order to address the other side, that of the ability to access this adequate supply, the government could choose to selectively subsidise. It could either, as suggested by Shahid Kardar (2008), forward direct cash grants and transfers to the vulnerable and poor population of the rural areas, those comprising "generally the disabled, elderly, female headed households, orphans, widows and unemployed and unskilled household heads with large families." On the other hand, the government could ration the food at control prices to the poor population. This rationing mechanism would function on the basis of self-selection: only a few stores, utility stores in the case of Pakistan, would be forced by the government to sell at the lower ceiling price, the trade-off for which would be queuing for long periods as well as lower quality of food. The very poor and vulnerable, who would be entirely unable to avoid these disincentives of the lower price, would thus select themselves to avail the subsidy. By means of this two-price scheme therefore, dual objectives would be met: higher market prices would raise rural farm and non-farm household incomes (through higher wage-incomes as a result of high output levels) and at the same time, provide food at low prices to those whose incomes cannot keep up with the market prices.

Agricultural Diversification

Other than pricing policy, the Government of Pakistan also needs to take into account the larger international market. The signing of the Agreement on Agriculture in the World Trade Organization portends the decline of all forms of subsidies in the agricultural sector. Without this protection in place, the sector is likely to dwindle, leading to rising rural-urban inequalities, unless the sector is propped up by putting appropriate policies in place.

With the opening up of the agricultural sector to the international market, policy focus should shift towards those crops in which the country has a comparative advantage. For a labour-rich country like Pakistan, as dictated by the Stolper-Samuelson theorem, such crops are likely to be relatively more labour-intensive. Opening up to international markets also means that price variability, no longer restrained by government controls, is likely to increase. Furthermore, prices for high-value products such as meat, fruits and dairy are likely to be higher than prices for basic cereals. In light of these factors, the agriculture sector should diversify (to reduce the impact of price variability) into high-value products (in order to augment rural incomes) that are labour-intensive (which would increase non-farm rural incomes as well).

According to Qureshi *et al.* (2007), agricultural diversification does not simply entail a shift of resources from low-value to high-value agriculture, but also an increasing focus on non-farm activities such as processing and marketing as these activities also serve to augment the value of agricultural commodities. Figures quoted in their study show that the relative share of crops in the agriculture sector of Pakistan has actually declined, from 69.1 per cent in 1980-81 to 46.6 per cent in 2003-04. At the same time, the share of livestock has registered an increase from 26.4 per cent in 1980-81 to 49.1 per cent in 2003-04.

Agricultural diversification into high-level products is further triggered not only by increase in world income, but also due to an increase in urban incomes within Pakistan. Since high-value foodstuffs have invariably a higher income elasticity of demand than basic cereals, this is likely to increase demand for these high-value products. Furthermore, Qureshi *et al.* (2007), cite that the labour use of fruit, vegetables and fodder is higher than the labour use of food grains and oilseeds; cultivation of onions requires 553 labour hours/acre whereas that of wheat, even in the un-irrigated system requires only 77 labour hours/acre. Amongst food grains, only sugarcane requires very high labour-usage (415 labour hours/acre), yet even that is below the labour-usage requirement of onions. The ability to provide higher employment is thus also an advantage of agricultural diversification.

In order for agricultural diversification to take place however, the government needs to curtail direct intervention in the case of a few major crops; it needs to realise instead that food security can also be achieved by means of developing the rural sectors and thus increasing rural incomes. Government interventions should furthermore deal with facilitating this diversification, through establishing proper credit schemes, providing proper infrastructure (especially in the case of milk, meat and fruit storage), investing in agricultural research and extension specifically in the case of high-value products and encouraging vertical integration, thereby focusing on post-farm gate activities which play an important role in adding value to agricultural commodities.

Conclusion

Rural growth and rural empowerment, especially in a country like Pakistan, are both highly dependent upon development of the agricultural sector. This paper discussed how Pakistan's agricultural pricing policy has resulted in distortion of incentives in the agricultural sector, thereby hindering its growth. Although the government needs to intervene in order to supply urban consumers with foodstuffs at affordable prices, this bias towards the urban consumer, maybe even triggered by political concerns, has implicitly taxed the farmer and has thus deepened the urban-rural divide that already exists in the country. Low procurement prices have resulted in low output levels, lower rural farm and non-farm incomes, and net resource transfers out of the agricultural sector. This in turn has reduced the viability to invest in agriculture.

Across the board, price controls have also disproportionately benefited the middleman who is allowed to procure at low prices, hoard and then re-sell at higher prices during times of shortage. Also, input subsidies are more beneficial to large landholders since they are able to use their political clout to avail them. Thus, in order to allow the agricultural sector to develop, pricing policies need to be redefined, with farmers being offered the market price and the vulnerable and poor consumers being aided through targeted subsidies. Targeted subsidies can take the form, either of direct cash transfers or of a system of ration shops that encourage self-selection of the very poor of the population to avail the subsidies.

At the same time, the government also needs to take into account the entry of the international variable into the agriculture sector, due to liberalising of controls following the Agreement on Agriculture. In order to allow the rural sector to develop and achieve a standing of its own, the government should facilitate agricultural diversification. Increasing world demand for high-value agricultural commodities indicates that agricultural diversification will increment rural incomes; at the same time, diversification will help to dilute the effects of price variability in the international market. Increasing rural incomes will increase the feasibility to invest in the agricultural sector leading to further growth. At the same time, it will decrease push factors in the rural areas by developing them at par with the urban areas. It is therefore important to realise that equating development to industrialisation is faulty since it assumes that the agricultural sector will ultimately dwindle. Instead of allowing the agricultural sector to stagnate, it should actively be invested in to develop since this will achieve the objectives, both of reducing pressures on urban areas and of achieving rural development.

References

Ahmad, Salman and Roger P. Martini (2000). "Agricultural Policy Analysis in Pakistan", *CMER Working Paper* Series. Lahore: Lahore University of Management Sciences. pp.1-32.

Chaudhry, M. Ghaffar (1995). "Recent Input-Output Price Policy in Pakistan's Agriculture", *The Pakistan Development* 34(1): 1-23 (Spring).

Eicher, Carl K. and John M. Staatz (1998). "Agricultural Development Ideas in Historical Perspective", *International Agricultural Development*. Baltimore: Johns Hopkins University Press. pp.8-30.

Ghani, Ejaz (1998). "Wheat Pricing Policies in Pakistan", *Pakistan Development Review* 37(2): 149-166 (Summer).

Government of Pakistan (2006-07). *Economic Survey of Pakistan*. Islamabad: Finance Division. pp.15-33.

Kardar, Shahid (2008). "Economy: Understanding the Wheat Crisis", *The Daily Times*, 22 January.

Nasim, Anjum *et al.* (1991). "Pakistan", Krueger, Anne O. *et al.* (ed.), *The Political Economy of Agricultural Pricing Policy*. Baltimore: The Johns Hopkins University Press. pp.107-148.

Qureshi, S.K. *et al.* (2007). "Agricultural Diversification in Pakistan: Status and Opportunities", *Agricultural Diversification and Smallholders in South Asia*. New Delhi: Academic Foundation. pp.297-319.

2 Development of the Rural Non-Farm Sector in India

Asmita Ganguly

Introduction

The rural sector in India houses 70 per cent of the country's population out of which 40 per cent are estimated to be below the poverty line. Also, the existence of an urban bias with respect to government policy framework as well as public and private investment deprives the rural sector of basic infrastructure and civic amenities like roads, communication, electricity, health care and education. The need of the hour is therefore to promote public investment in the rural sector and empower the rural poor with skill formation, education and by extending adequate credit facilities for self-employment generation and also developing small-scale entrepreneurial ventures. The maximum scope of employment generation and thus poverty alleviation lies in the non-farm sector of the rural economy, as I seek to show in my paper. Even with adequate investment in agriculture, the employment elasticity in agriculture is very low. Statistics show that between 2000 and 2005, the employment in agriculture grew only by 1 per cent while that in the rural non-farm sector grew by 20 per cent. Statistics also show that there has been a definite shift from farm to non-farm employment in the rural sector in the past two decades.

In this paper, I primarily state the various problems faced by the rural population and how the non-farm sector can help solve them and help to empower the rural poor. I also discuss how the government, NGOs and the community as a whole can work together to develop the non-farm sector. As an example of the success of a non-farm industry, I discuss how Shri Mahila Griha Udyog Lijjat Papad has achieved phenomenal success and has become a highly effective means of income generation, social growth and mobility of women. This can be a viable model for successful rural non-farm industry. But there are also instances of rural non-farm industries, which in spite of having the potential, have failed to achieve desired targets, even in the presence of government and institutional support. I cite the example of the *khadi* industry, discuss the various problems faced by the industry and suggest some measures to eradicate those problems.

Before concluding my paper, I discuss various government schemes for developing the non-farm sector and state the extent of their success. I have also made some suggestions as to how these schemes could be improved.

Problems in the Rural Sector

- *Excessive Dependence on Nature:* Rural India is still heavily dependent on monsoons for irrigation and farm mechanisation, and risk reduction in agriculture in the form of multi-cropping and crop rotation are not widely adopted. Approximately, 53 per cent of the total agricultural land still remains to be irrigated and is at the sole mercy of rainfall.
- *Preponderance of Small Uneconomic Landholding:* The average size of operational landholdings in India was 1.55ha and has been declining since. It is estimated that farmers having less than 4ha of land are not financially viable, if they depend wholly on income from agriculture. Thus, 80 per cent of farms in India may not be financially viable.
- *Low Capital-Labour Ratio:* With its share of less than 30 per cent in GDP, agriculture bears the burden of more than 60 per cent of the workers. The gross capital formation in the rural sector has declined from 1.9 per cent of GDP in 1990-91 to 1.3 per cent in 2002-03. This is due to decline in public investment, which has diverted resources from investment to current expenditure on output prices and input subsidies. Also, banks acting along commercial lines fail to extend credit for the rural sector development in the fear of the loans becoming bad since past experience show that the risk of non-recovery is very high.
- *Low Factor Productivity:* Low crop yield has been the bane of India's agriculture for long. This is due to inadequate capital formation in

the sector. For example, yield of paddy in India in 2001-02 was 1874kg/ha whereas the world average was approximately 3000kg/ha.

- *High Incidence of Poverty and Unemployment:* Of the total 26 crore people below the poverty line in India in 1999-2000, 19.3 crore were in the rural sector. Similarly, the proportion of unemployment is much more in the rural sector than in the urban sector.
- *Inadequate Infrastructure:* Infrastructural facilities such as roads, communication, sanitation, provision of potable water, and also civic amenities like health care, education and legal security are either absent or inadequate in the rural sector.

The above problems of the rural sector set a sharp contrast to the urban sector, where credit, employment and access to adequate infrastructure are more easily available. Also, the real wages in urban areas are substantially higher than in rural areas, even after adjusting for cost of living differences. The natural outcome is migration from rural to urban areas. But cities and towns have limited capacity for absorbing excess labour from the rural sector owing to their own demographic pressures. Thus, rural migrants find themselves either unemployed or as casual labour, squeezed into slums.

To increase wages in agriculture and to shift workers to more productive areas, promotion of the rural non-farm sector is advocated. A growth in the rural non-farm sector is one of the main factors responsible for the reduction in poverty in the 1980s.

Role of the Non-Farm Sector in Eradicating Problems of Rural India

The rural non-farm sector encompasses all non-agricultural activities: mining and quarrying, household and non-household manufacturing, processing, repair, construction, trade and commerce, transport and other services in villages and rural towns, undertaken by enterprises varying in size from household own-account enterprises to factories.

Figure 2.1

Growth in Non-Farm Employment, State-wise

Source: Employment figures from National Sampling Survey Organisation (1973-1993).

Figure 2.1 shows that almost all the states have had positive growth in non-farm employment. On the other hand, farm employment has declined in 6 out of 14 states, increased substantially in 2 and has remained stagnant in the rest. This implies that the ratio of farm to non-farm employment can be seen as means to absorb the rural population growth and reduce rural unemployment in India.

Increase in income from non-farm activities offsets risks in agriculture and allows the rural households to diversify their sources of income. Income generated from non-farm activities can also be invested in agricultural production methods like multi-cropping and high yielding variety of seeds. Consequently, non-farm income acts as a stabilising force for farm income and indirectly as a source of productivity improvement in agriculture. The correlation of non-farm employment with poverty is negative in rural areas, since higher levels of non-farm activities is associated with higher economic opportunities leading to a reduction in poverty.

The percentage of non-farm employment exhibits a strong and positive relationship with indicators of social development. The states with high incidence non-farm employment reports high levels of literacy and also low infant and child mortality.

Table 2.1

Correlation Coefficients between Components of Non-Farm Employment and Indicators of Development during the Year 1999-2000 and also between the Changes in Variables during the Period 1983-1999

Variables	*1999-2000*	*1983-1999*
Construction & PCI	0	0.21
Construction & Population Density	0.15	0.57
Trade & Road	0.28	0.44
Trade & Literacy	0.67	0.42
Trade & Transport	0.91	0.43
Transport & Road	0.41	0.86

Source: Current Daily Status (CDS) figures of employment from NSSO and income figures from CSO, New Delhi.

The capacity of agriculture to absorb a large proportion of the incremental labour force in the rural sector is limited. The percentage of people below the poverty line among the agricultural rural household is very high. The Special Group on Targeting Ten Million Employment Opportunities Per Year (Planning Commission, 2002) has also come to the conclusion that despite significant investment made to develop rural infrastructure and marketing facilities, the employment elasticity in agriculture is likely to be as low as 0.01 as observed during 1990s. The only way that the incremental labour force can be meaningfully employed is through sector diversification. Industries and services that have high employment potential and are linked with other productive sectors help to create sectoral diversification by creating jobs at higher levels of productivity.

How to Develop the Non-Farm Sector?

The most important sectors in terms of share of employment in the non-farm sector are manufacturing, retail trade, personal services, construction, wood products and furniture, road transport and textiles. The total number of family based enterprises in rural areas is very large employing between 30-50 million people. Most of these enterprises depend on urban and semi-urban demand and are mostly a product of modernisation. There are also some unorganised and unregistered activities catering to rural demand like rope making, hand weaving and bullock cart making which are generally under-performed. To achieve growth, rural areas need productive activities, which produce rural exports, i.e., goods and services, which can be traded outside rural areas. The most important are agricultural products, natural resource extraction (forestry, mining and fishing), allied agricultural activities (livestock, bees, silk and aquaculture), rural tourism and traditional crafts.

Figure 2.2

The Share of Additional Employment Created by Different Sectors in Rural Non-Farm Sector during the Reform Period of 1993-94 to 1999-2000

(The Additional Employment created in the Rural Sector during this Period was 8.54 Million)

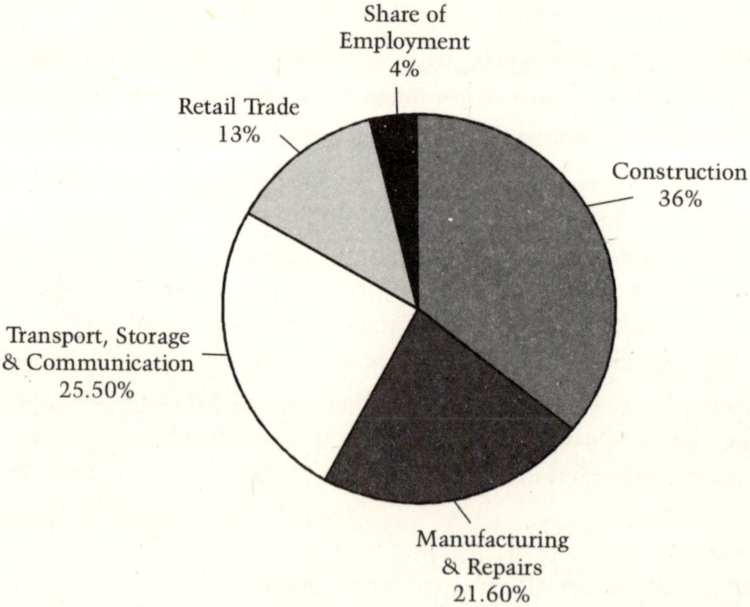

Source: *Economic & Political Weekly*, August 2001.

Competitive advantage is found in sectors in which:

- Primary activities, which are tied to natural resources (forestry, mining, tourism, etc.).
- Processing of resource is done close to where the resource is found (sugar processing, mineral processing).
- Employment of labour is cost effective, and
- The rural population has specialised skills.

The development of the non-farm sector is heavily dependent on the development of infrastructure, skill formation among the rural population and adequate marketing and credit facilities. Government efforts in this direction has remained limited due to high cost of administration leakages as seen in past experiences where their impact at raising household incomes have been marginal. Therefore, decentralising reforms by involving local authorities along with community participation can achieve desired results. An example may be cited of the Manjeri municipality in the relatively backward district of Mallapuram, in the state of Kerala with not much of a pre-existing industrial culture. In this area, the municipal authorities in collaboration with some NGOs and bankers, have succeeded in converting it into a booming hosiery manufacturing centre after developing the necessary skills and finance at the local level.

The rural sector in India has a large number of artisans. In this changing world, the demand for some products of the artisan's work has declined while some has increased. Government should conduct regular market surveys and assess the shift in demand. Post-liberalisation, there may be latent demand for artisan's work in international markets. Such markets should be tapped with the help of market professionals. Accordingly, government should encourage skill formation on a selective basis, i.e., promote skill formation in sectors whose products have greater demand.

Growth of the Non-Farm Sector in Rural India: The Evidence

During the past two decades, rural India has diversified significantly into non-farm activities and this has helped to bring India's cities much closer to the hinterland. During the past two decades, the rural economy in

India has grown significantly faster than the urban economy. During the past decade alone, the rural economy is estimated to have grown on average by 73 per cent compared to 54 per cent in the urban economy. The Central Statistical Organisation (CSO) figures show that the rural economy accounted for 49 per cent of India's GDP in 2000. This is a significant increase from 41 per cent in 1981-82 and 46 per cent in 1993-94. But agriculture grew only at 3.2 per cent on an average; so much of this growth is driven by the rural non-farm sector. As of 2000, agriculture accounted for 51.8 per cent of rural activity. This is a significant decline from 64 per cent in 1980s and 72 per cent in 1970s. On the other hand, services, which accounted for 21 per cent of rural activities in 1981 now accounted for 28 per cent. In addition, manufacturing, utilities and construction have nearly doubled their share in the rural economy from just under 10 per cent in 1971 to 18 per cent in 2000. Between 2000 and 2005, rural agricultural growth was as low as 1 per cent. In contrast, during same period non-farm jobs have gone up by 20 per cent.

Forward and Backward Linkages of Rural Non-Farm Sector with Other Sectors of Economy

In providing important inputs and services for agriculture, the non-farm sector can be thought of as another infrastructure that is essential for higher productivity in agriculture as discussed in Section 3. However, the difference between non-farm sector and other infrastructure is that the development of the non-farm sector is itself dependent on factors such as literacy, power, communication and also productive agriculture. But within rural areas, agriculture gets most of the share of the infrastructure outlay such as irrigation and research and development. Other types of infrastructure such as roads, communication, education and health do not get adequate attention.

As supply chains strengthen across the country, growing urban demand could provide a significant boost to the rural economy. Studies show that a 10 per cent increase in urban expenditure is associated with a 4.8 per cent increase in rural non-farm employment. Using an econometric approach spanning the past 26 years, it has been shown that a Rs. 100 increase in urban consumption expenditure leads to an increase of Rs. 39 in rural household income. Increase in incomes also lead to higher living standards. The parents send their children to school and avail medical facilities, thus boosting the education and health sectors. Demand patterns change as incomes increase, leading to more consumption of agricultural and industrial products. The channel through which this takes place is increased employment in the rural non-farm sector. Thus, a sustained urban household consumption growth rate, similar to that seen over the past decade could lead to 6.3 million non-farm jobs over the next decade.

Reviving a Sick Industry: The *Khadi* Industry

Over the years, the production of *khadi* cloth has been on the decline. It was 109 sq. metres in 1990-91 and declined to 98 sq. metres in 1998-99. Employment in this sector has also fallen from 14.15 lakh persons in 1990-91 to 13.85 lakh persons in 1998-99. As against the target of 20 lakh persons, as set by the Khadi and Village Industries Commission (KVIC), the total additional employment generated by March 1999 was 1.79 lakh only.

Moreover, the quality of employment generated from *khadi* production is very modest. Full time workers are estimated to earn only Rs. 40000 per annum while part time workers earn as low as Rs. 1500 per annum.

The basic problems with the industry:

- High cost of production.
- Product at the lower end of the quality range is not able to compete with mill produced fabric available in the market.
- Inadequate linkage between production and sales strategies resulting in accumulation of stocks.
- Low return on investment.
- Non-performing assets build up.
- Low production and shrinking employment of opportunities.

The above issues can be resolved through an overhaul of marketing strategies for *khadi* products. Product development and marketing need a professional approach. One way of addressing this issue is to leave the entire marketing and product development to the private sector. Also, to boost the demand for *khadi,* the government could try and promote *khadi* in the international market. Only a boost in demand would help to raise the employment in the industry to the desired target of 20 lakh and also help to substantially increase wages. And once the sector becomes viable, it will be able to avail bank credit instead of relying entirely on government allowance.

A committee on strengthening of the *khadi* and village industries was set up in November 2001, which recommended a special package for the development of the sector, which includes:

- Providing the option for market development assistance.
- Continuity for rebate for 5 years.
- Creation of database for the sector.
- Intensive marketing support so that the sector may fulfil objectives of generating rural employment and improving the quality of life of the rural people.

Shri Mahila Griha Udyog Lijjat Papad—A Possible Model

Shri Mahila Griha Udyog is a successful co-operative venture comprising female members. From an initial membership of 7 women, in Mumbai, the organisation now boasts of a membership of 42000 women across the country. Again, from a one stop organisation, today it has 63 branches and 40 divisions spread out in 17 states in India.

Lijjat has been a vehicle of social empowerment for women as also benefiting them financially by providing them sustained returns for their work. According to *Annual Report of 2003-04*, the accumulated profit of the Lijjat enterprise stands at Rs. 48.32 crore. The average monthly income to each worker is Rs. 3000.

Lijjat has engendered democratic principles through member participation as part of its administrative culture. In this respect, Lijjat was much beyond just an entrepreneurial venture, it was a symbol of women's strength. Many women who had little formal education were handling money and banking transactions and managing a business of around Rs. 300 crore annually.

The most remarkable aspect of Lijjat is the absence of an outside agency in starting the enterprise. It is truly a homegrown model, based on the intuitive intelligence and self-learning skills of a small group of poor women. It reiterates the widely held belief that the poor are highly entrepreneurial and only seeking an enabling environment to realise their potential. Lijjat is a voluntary organisation with collective ownership and trusteeship being practiced. A unique feature of Lijjat is that it has remained a member-owned and managed body resisting the rise of small managerial elite that normally takes control in all such institutions as they grow in size. This helped Lijjat become a highly effective livelihood generator, which also promoted economic and social growth and mobility of women.

One institution involved in promoting the growth of Lijjat was KVIC which recognised the value of its work and registered it under the "Processing of Cereals and Pulses Industry Group" under KVIC Act which helped them to access cheaper funds and enjoy tax benefits.

One of the key factors to Lijjat's success in terms of outreach and rapid scaling up is the policy of internal generation of resources and rotating working capital on a weekly or bi-weekly cycle. Marketing is on a strictly cash and carry basis; allowing for funds to be continuously recycled in the business profit margins were such that they enabled a rapid scaling up of operations through continuous expansion. The Sisters Savings Fund is also available to each of the Lijjat branches to tide over short-term cash deficits, in case of necessity. In addition to self-generated resources, borrowings from KVIC were resorted to as and when required.

During 1971-1976, KVIC had extended loans of Rs. 8.94 lakh under the "Processing Cereals and Pulses Industry Schemes" which was used for expansion of existing branches, establishment of new ones and for purchase of equipment for *masala* unit in Mumbai. The organisation scrupulously rejects charity and grants. Lijjat believes in running its business with acumen and professionalism on its own resources.

- Lijjat, since its inception adopted strictly commercial techniques of marketing instead of depending on government or semi-government marketing outlets. It appointed agents on a commission basis for marketing its products.

- Marketing is a centralised function in Lijjat. The branch office is responsible for setting a target for monthly production and marketing. Each Lijjat centre has a clearly delineated marketing territory to avoid competition among centres. Commission agents are attached to almost all Lijjat centres and they account for a major part of Lijjat sales. Another significant aspect of marketing in Lijjat has been the decision to export its products. Lijjat's export revenue in the year 2003-04 was Rs. 9 crore.
- Lijjat has grown and prospered with its strategy of forward and backward linkages. The setting up of various divisions for its input and output packaging needs has contributed to creating economies of scale in procurement as well as production.
- Lijjat has separate marketing, sales and advertisement divisions. The discounts paid were over half of the total expenses incurred by Lijjat during the year 2003-04. The advertisement expenses came to around Rs. 3.11 crore, which was 15 per cent of the selling expenses.
- The use of technology in production at Lijjat Papad would go against the basic principles of low skill production technique and decentralised production. As a natural corollary to its lack of upgradation of production technology, its outreach in terms of number of women it employs is very high. Thus, a successful balance has been achieved between scale, quality and employment.
- Lijjat has kept pace with the changing market place and has emerged as not just another profitable institution but a world leader in *papad* manufacturing. The uncompromising quality standard of Lijjat, its diversification into newer divisions to address its own growing needs better, the scale it has managed to achieve has helped it to achieve financial sustainability.

This model is a relevant example of how grassroot organisations can become vehicles of social mobility and empowerment of the poor even without the intervention of other institutions and proves beyond doubt that given an enabling environment small-scale enterprises can become means of generating employment, eradicating poverty and reducing gender biases.

Government Schemes

There are several schemes to promote the non-farm sectors mostly initiated by the Government of India. There are schemes to provide skills (TRYSEM, ITI)[1] and schemes to strengthen the gender component (DWCRA, RMK).[2] There are also schemes to provide wage employment (JRY, EAS, Food for Work)[3] on rural work programmes to achieve the twin objective of creation of rural infrastructure and generation of additional income for the rural poor, particularly during the agricultural lean season. But the various government-sponsored programmes have achieved only limited success because:

- Rural enterprises were not motivated enough to come out of their social and cultural stranglehold on the call of government agencies.
- Bureaucracy was not well equipped to take up the new challenge.
- The problems of multiplicity of schemes and agencies and the absence of any comprehensive coordination and follow-up mechanism.

IRDP (Integrated Rural Development Programme)

Since its inception in 1998-99, 54 million families have been covered under IRDP at an expenditure of Rs. 13700 crore. The average investment per family was Rs. 18377 during 1998-99 but this remained inadequate in generating income of Rs. 2000 per family per month as expected. Moreover, IRDP along with its allied programmes like TRYSEM, DWCRA, SITRA[4] and MWS[5] represented a matrix of multiple pragrammes without desired linkages and also, there has been lack of coordination among various departments. The programmes were implemented separately without keeping in mind the overall objective of generating sustainable incomes. Moreover, the programmes were wrongly based on the assumption that the

1. TRYSEM-Training of Rural Youth for Self-Employment; ITI-Industrial Training Institute.
2. DWCRA-Development of Women and Children in Rural Areas; RMK-Rashtriya Mahila Kosh.
3. JRY-Jawahar Rojgar Yojna; EAS-Employment Assurance Scheme.
4. SITRA-South India Textile Research Association.
5. MWS-Million Wells Scheme.

beneficiary possessed information and the skills to choose viable options, had access to raw materials and were aware of the nature of the product and factor markets. The disabilities of the poor, notably their exclusion from community decision-making were not taken into account. The IRDP loans are treated as a one-time affair. There is no provision for continuous refinance to enhance the capability of the poor. The administrative machinery to monitor local physical investment did not exist. This led to over-investment and non-repayment of loans jeopardising the financial health of the rural banking system.

TRYSEM (Training of Rural Youth for Self-Employment)

TRYSEM was a facilitating component of IRDP and aimed at providing basic technical and entrepreneurial skills to the rural poor in the age group of 18-35 years to enable them to take up income generating activities. The concurrent evaluation of IRDP (1995) showed that the rural youth trained under TRYSEM were only interested in the stipends and did not use the knowledge gained under the programme for furthering self-employment generation. TRYSEM had a weak link with the overall strategy for self-employment in rural areas or with industrial policy. The training was not related with aptitude or capacity of the trainees and was unrelated to the demand for concerned skills. It was not feasible for trained rural youth to run a self-employment enterprise with a poor technological base and uncertainty over availability of credit.

SGSY (Swarnjayanti Gram Swarozgar Yojana)

With a view to have more focused approach to setting up of new enterprises, to derive advantages of group lending and to overcome the problems associated with multiplicity of programmes, the IRDP and its allied programmes were restructured in 1999 into a single self-employment programme called SGSY.

The overall progress of the programme during the first three years of its operation has been rather slow. In spite of the shift in emphasis from individual assistance to assistance on group basis, individual assistance continued to be a dominating feature under the programme. The level of utilisation of funds, credit disbursement per family investment and credit subsidy ratio were also low. The SGSY is conceived as a credit-cum-subsidy programme with credit as the critical component and subsidy as the enabling element. But subsidy element in the programme is a major source of corruption and a disincentive to lend on account of low recoveries. Subsidy attracts the wrong kind of people who have little or no expertise or interest in setting up an entrepreneurial activity.

Suggestions for Improvement

- With the emphasis shifting from protective to promotional measures now, technological upgradation, market surveys, producer and design development should be undertaken as part of the central development programmes. And such activities should be well coordinated and routinely administered.
- Various programmes should be merged and implemented in coordination with leading NGOs of the districts. NGOs' participation will be advantageous as it will ensure better participation of the target groups and local NGOs will have better knowledge of the needs, skill base, labour structure and availability of the resources of the district and thus, make the programme more viable.
- SGSY should be transformed into a micro financing programme to be run by banks with subsidies phased out and lend adequate funds to viable projects preferably managed by self-help groups that would ensure generation of income for borrowers and repayment of loans.
- Funds should be provided by *gram sabhas* only when the beneficiaries contribute a substantial amount themselves.
- Grassroot organisations should be empowered and encouraged to set up new units. Also, incomes of women have to be increased by creating opportunities in higher productivity sectors since most of them are confined to agriculture.
- Special effort should be made to strengthen the economy of marginal and small farmers, forest produce gatherers, artisans, unskilled workers, etc. The poor should not merely benefit from growth generated elsewhere, they should contribute to growth. This would need strengthening of programmes based on skill and assets that the poor possess, and help them with credit and market support.

Conclusion

The Indian rural economy is infested with various problems of unemployment, poverty and low productivity of factors, which results in poor living standards. Sectoral diversification of the rural economy, that is, developing the rural non-farm sector can significantly help the rural population to not only come out of the vicious cycle of poverty and unemployment and raise their productivity, but also lead to development of the rural infrastructure and even agricultural development. There has been significant development of the rural non-farm sector in the past two decades but it still leaves much to be desired as certain traditional non-farm industries are on the decline like the *khadi* and handloom industries. Public investments in these sectors have to be increased substantially and also marketing, promotional and credit assistance have to be extended. Infrastructure and skill formation should also be developed for attracting private investment. Community participation along with the help of NGOs and local authorities can together achieve significant success in developing the non-farm sector.

References

Books:

Ellis, Frank (2000). *Rural Livelihoods and Diversity in Developing Countries*. Oxford University Press.

Kumar, Arun A.V. (1997). *Rural Industrialization in India: Aspects of Policy, Technology and Employement with Special Reference to Kerala*. M.D. Publication.

Ray, Debraj (1998). *Development Economics*. Princeton University Press.

World Bank. *India*.

Websites:

www.eldis.org/static

www.nabard.org/nonfarm_sector

www.blackwell-synergy.com

www.empowerpoor.org

www.esocialsciences.com

www.indiajournals.com

www.isec.ac.in/project1-2005.pdf

www.nri.org

www.hindu.com

www.ruralforum.info/papers/croxton.pdf

www.antiqbook.com

www.ingentaconnect.com

3 The Efficiency of the Samurdhi Programme in Accelerating Rural Growth in Sri Lanka

Shazana Ismail and
Jithmal Samankantha

Introduction

Poverty is the lack of some fixed level of material goods necessary for survival and minimal well-being. In most cases, it is associated with numerous characteristics like lack of assets, landlessness, unemployment or underemployment, illiteracy, malnutrition, high infant mortality, large family size, low productivity, low position in the social hierarchy, less access to publicly provided goods and poor infrastructural facilities and extreme vulnerability to natural disasters, disease and social conflicts. In economic sense, poverty may be understood as a condition in which a person or community is deprived of the basic needs for a minimum standard of well-being and life, particularly as a result of a persistent lack of wealth and income, or wealth and income disparities. Though Sri Lanka is widely cited as a country for achieving high levels of human development, the majority of rural people are living in a state of poverty. As a matter of fact, poverty is the major problem in the community development process in the country.

Thereby, there arises a need for the government to redirect its welfare policies and programmes to assist the poor adequately. The Government has made an effort by imposing poverty alleviation programmes to eradicate poverty, accelerate the rural growth and to empower the rural poor. Since Independence, successive governments have made an extraordinary effort to deepen its understanding of the nature and root causes of poverty in Sri Lanka, with a view to reassessing and reformulating its policy framework for reducing poverty. In order to alleviate poverty, they have implemented direct and indirect programmes. The Janasaviya[1] and the Samurdhi programme can be identified as two of the major income transfer-food subsidy programmes conducted by the government of Sri Lanka since 1948, which have sought to directly tackle the symptoms or causes of poverty. The purpose of this paper is to analyse the efficiency of the Samurdhi programme to accelerate rural growth and empower the rural poor in Sri Lanka.

The objective of this paper is:

- To examine the role of Samurdhi programme to alleviate poverty and accelerating the rural poor.
- To identify the inherent weaknesses in the Samurdhi programme.
- To propose remedies in order to overcome those weaknesses and to improve the quality of the programme.

This paper will follow an analytical approach drawing on published literature and data relating to the central theme. Further, it uses data from government documents and research reports prepared by various agencies.

The theme "Empowering the Rural Poor and Accelerating Rural Growth" is a broad theme which should be analysed from many aspects and involve the opinions of many experts. Thus, I had to limit its scope to an issue to test the efficiency of Samurdhi programme in empowering the rural poor and accelerating rural growth. Due to the conflict in the North and East, there have not been proper surveys conducted in order to collect the necessary data required. Thus, the lack of documented data relevant to the North and East is another grave limitation encountered in this study. This has necessitated restricting the scope of the paper to the rural poor, other than the people living in the North and East which stands as a major obstacle in the future, despite being an important area to be explored.

---

1. Janasaviya programme, a major poverty alleviation programme under the income transfer food subsidy scheme, was launched in 1989 by the United National Party (UNP). The dual objective of this programme envisaged short-term income supplementation and long-term employment creation to enhance the welfare of the economy. The programme promoted human capital development, income generation activity and infrastructure development with a view to lift the household above poverty line. However, an evaluation showed that the programme was unable to create sustained self-employment for most participating households (Gunatilleke *et al.*, 1997). This programme was virtually withdrawn with the appointment of a new government in 1994, led by the Sri Lanka Freedom Party (SLFP).

The five sections of the paper comprises an introduction in Section 1. Section 2 presents the role of the Samurdhi programme in Sri Lanka as an empirical case study. The impact of the Samurdhi programme in accelerating rural growth will be also discussed in Section 2. Section 3 presents the problems and the weaknesses of the Samurdhi programme. Section 4 presents remedial measures and suggestions to accelerate rural growth and to improve the efficiency of the Samurdhi programme, and finally the concluding remarks are presented in Section 5.

The Role of the Samurdhi Programme in Sri Lanka

The Samurdhi (prosperity) programme was initiated by the SLFP Government in 1995 for the reduction of poverty on a sustainable basis through the broadening of horizons and the creation of opportunities for income enhancement and employment. The main thrust of the poverty reduction strategy, as embodied in the Samurdhi programme, is to ensure the participation of the poor in the production process. That is achieved through increased access by the poor to resources for self-employment, enhancing their health and nutritional status, and improved rural infrastructure. Around 2 million households, most of these in rural areas, are beneficiaries of the Samurdhi welfare programme. This programme covers one-third of the entire population of Sri Lanka. By the end of 1990s, the Samurdhi programme was fully functioning in 21 districts in Sri Lanka.[2] Samurdhi expenditures amount to nearly 1 per cent of GDP. [3]

The Samurdhi programme consists of three components. The first component is the largest, claiming 80 per cent of the programme's budget which provides consumption grant transfer to eligible households. The second is a savings and credit programme operated through Samurdhi banks, and loans meant for entrepreneurial and business development.[4] The third component is rehabilitation and development of community

2. The programme is still not in full operation in Jaffna, Mannar and Killinochi districts.

3. Refer Annexure A-3.2.

4. Loan and credit programmes are listed in "Samurdhi National Programme for Poverty Alleviation" (1999). These include "Credit animators programme", "Samurdhi Development Loans (SASANA)", "Samurdhi Entrepreneurial Loans (SAVANA)" and Samurdhi leasing programme. SASANA and SAVANA disbursed 75 of all credit programme funds between 1996 and 1999 (page 28).

infrastructure through workfare and social or human development programmes. The Samurdhi programme also operates social insurance, funded through compulsory contributions of beneficiaries of the highest consumption grants. It was originally administered by the Ministry of Samurdhi and Youth Affairs and Sports. However, at present, it is administered by the Ministry of Samurdhi and Rural Development and Parliamentary Affairs.[5]

The programme is totally funded by the government intending to alleviate poverty and unemployment among the youth. Its characteristic feature is entrusting leadership to youth and encouraging them to have direct participation of the poor in the production process by increasing access to resources for self-employment, enhancing their health, nutritional status and improving the rural infrastructure. Thereby, it attempts to enhance the capacity of the poor to take initiatives to improve their quality of life. Thus, if this programme is practiced and imposed properly, it will empower the rural poor and accelerate the rural growth in the economy. However, it should be noted that the success of the Samurdhi programme in accelerating rural growth and empowering the rural poor primarily depends on the achievement of the following stated objectives:

- Expand opportunities for income enhancement and self-employment.
- Organise youth, women and other disadvantaged persons into small groups, and encourage them to participate in decision-making activities and the development process at the grassroots level.
- Assist persons to develop their talents and strengthen their asset bases through productive employment.
- Establish and maintain productive assets to create additional wage employment opportunities at the rural level.
- Support the really needy by providing social welfare assistance.
- Encouraging group savings, intra-group and revolving fund-based lending, maintenance of simple accounts and generation of report savings and credit at the group level.

5. Refer Annexure A-3.3 for structure and administration of Samurdhi.

Samurdhi has also established a social insurance programme, where the beneficiaries of highest consumption grants pay premium to finance a social insurance programme available to all eligible households. Further, the same beneficiaries contribute 20 per cent of the value of their stamps in lieu of "forced savings". These "savings" are unavailable for withdrawal for five years. One of the programme's specific goals is to create youth employment. These young men and women are hired as programme administrators and development officers and considered among the beneficiaries of the programme. Eight per cent of the Samurdhi budget is allocated to their salaries.

The Samurdhi programme attempts to enhance the capacity of the poor to effectively take initiatives to improve the quality of life of the family by implementing economic development projects identified on the basis of family needs, skills and assets, together with the financial, technical and management support provided by the government. The programme has a separate initiative for enhancing human capital development among the poor through investments in health, nutrition, education, extension services and vocational training. Thus, the programme strives to alleviate poverty on a sustainable basis.

The Samurdhi programme is implemented by the Samurdhi Balakaya, which comprises Samurdhi Niyamakas and other members elected at the village level. The members of the executive committee of the Samurdhi programme are youths aged between 18-35 years and permanent residents of the village. The Samurdhi Balakaya is the development task force at the village level.

The welfare component of the Samurdhi programme covers one-third of the entire population of the country, consisting of about 1.2 million families estimated to be at the bottom of the income scale. The beneficiaries of the Samurdhi programme receive a monthly welfare payment of between SL Rs. 100-1,000, depending on household income, which is intended to raise the income of a household to about SL Rs. 1,500 per month. The beneficiaries are also expected to use the payment to increase the household income from SL Rs. 1,500 to SL Rs. 2,000 per month through the self-employment activities. The beneficiaries of the Samurdhi welfare programme will exit from it when their income exceeds

Rs. 2,000 per month for a continuous period of six months, or when at least one member of the family finds employment.[6]

All Samurdhi beneficiaries are encouraged to save a part of the income supplement in order to develop a culture of thrift and savings among them. The accumulated savings can be used to finance new income-generating projects among the beneficiaries, either on an individual or group basis. The ultimate objective of the Samurdhi programme is not to perpetuate poverty and dependency, but to promote self-reliance on the basis of nurturing the saving habit and the development of income-generating self-employment.

Strengths of the Samurdhi Programme

- Eighty per cent of the programme's cost is incurred on grants on food stamps. The scheme guarantees the ultra poor at least 10 per cent of their food requirements. Thus, this ensures the satisfaction of their basic needs.
- Targeted families are encouraged to engage in productive activities based on a careful assessment of their capabilities and access to locally available resources. Thereby, this facilitates and supports one of the main objectives of the Samurdhi programme, reducing the level of unemployment thereby, reducing rural poverty.
- Strong established linkages with training institutions providing skills training. Programme ownership by the government as demonstrated by its full funding support to bear all the costs of training, provision of incentives to Samurdhi workers, seed capital for loans, infrastructure development and other social welfare components of the programme.
- Community ownership facilitated through the compulsory and voluntary savings scheme.
- Strong involvement of community leaders, workers and targeted families in decision-making, particularly in project identification, targeting and monitoring. This facilitates and supports in empowering the rural poor to certain extent.

---

6. Refer Annexure A-3.1 to see the Samurdhi eligibility criteria chart.

- Initiatives taken by communities are matched with government schemes through provision of technical, managerial and financial resources by various government sectors.
- Indigenous workers are employed as Samurdhi programme functionaries.

Opportunities to the Rural Poor

The Samurdhi Authority has made arrangements in improving the entry criteria and establishes the exit criteria. Further, it has better coordination with various government sectors towards an authentic multi-sectoral, integrated and holistic strategy; linkages with other successful government programmes such as the Participatory Nutrition Improvement Programme (implemented by the Ministry of Plan Implementation and Parliamentary Affairs with technical and financial support from UNICEF). The Samurdhi Authority is also making an effort in recognising the need to adopt a multidisciplinary approach to address poverty. The Central Bank report states that the Samurdhi programme was further strengthened in 2006. Further, the direct benefits were increased in 2006. This indicates the increased commitment of the present government in sustaining and strengthening the implementation of Samurdhi. Thereby, the government facilitates and supports the programme in achieving its stated objectives. Thus, it is clear that, if the Samurdhi programme is implemented and practiced in a proper manner, it creates opportunities for its beneficiaries in enhancing their income levels, reducing their relative poverty, increasing opportunities for employment, thereby accelerating rural growth and alleviating poverty.

The programme has already demonstrated its sustainability with funding support provided solely by the Sri Lankan government. It is a well established programme with strong support structures from national to village levels, foremost of which is the Samurdhi Bank, which on a continuous basis, extends loans to individuals or groups. Communities have been empowered to seek whatever technical assistance they may need. The macro policy environment is also supportive of Samurdhi.

Weakness of the Samurdhi Programme

Social assistance programmes can play an important role in reducing poverty. Sri Lanka has a long history of social programmes and of food subsidies in particular. Among which, the most recent poverty alleviation programme, Samurdhi, was introduced in 1995 which is the largest safety net programme. Sri Lanka has carried out consistently a series of costly social welfare programmes. However, rural poverty is a great phenomenon in Sri Lanka at present. Majority of the poor lives in rural areas where 80 per cent of the population lives in. This section presents the weakness of the Samurdhi programme and the causes for its weakness.

A large number of non-random targeting errors have been identified in the implementation of the Samurdhi programme. In 1998, the Central Bank reported that 50 per cent of the population of Sri Lanka is covered by the programme while the poverty rate was only around 20 per cent. This outcome indicates that many non-poor households receive Samurdhi grants, making the impact of the programme progressive. Thus, a thorough investigation of the design, operations and outcomes of the programme is therefore warranted. There still exist substantial and significant differences in the probability of being a Samurdhi recipient by ethnic status.

The unstable political economy prevailing in the country has been another reason for the large number of targeting errors which is not random. At present, politicians target the beneficiaries of the Samurdhi in order to influence voting and obtaining political power. Government officials and politicians are reluctant to adopt approaches other than a welfare approach for fear of political repercussions. Qualitative results suggest that other characteristics of households such as party affiliation or voting preferences also influence allocation of Samurdhi consumption grants. Thereby, this clearly indicates that the targeting errors are not random. Further, although the programme is modestly successful in reaching the intended beneficiaries, a large portion of its resources are being transferred to the non-poor than the needed. Thus, it indicates that the Samurdhi does not emerge as an efficient programme and would require extensive redesign to improve its efficiency.

When speaking of the efficiency of a transfer programme, the term 'efficiency' constitutes reaching the objectives of the Samurdhi incurring the least cost. Thereby, it should be transferred to the intended beneficiaries minimising the leakage to the unintended beneficiaries and the administrative cost. This requires proper targeting. Thus, it should be envisioned as a targeted system which should not prevent fair identification of intended beneficiaries. However, the cost of targeting increases with the accuracy of targeting, and targeting involves trade-offs between under coverage and leakage. It is well understood that administrative cost is an increasing function of the accuracy of targeting.

The Samurdhi incurs a targeting cost of 8 per cent which is a financial burden which must be covered by tax or debt. Thus, the inferior targeting outcomes of Samurdhi cannot be explained on the basis of saving administrative cost. Further, they can affect people's economic behaviour by distorting their incentives. In addition, it is important that the Samurdhi programme must compete with other government social spending and other government programmes that alleviate poverty.

A household with an income above Rs. 2000 lose benefits. Further, a household loses its eligibility upon employment of any household member. Thus, Sahn and Alderman (1996) demonstrated that participation in the food stamp programme in Sri Lanka reduced labour supply. The longstanding welfare approach adopted by the government has led to a chronic dependency of the people on the state.

The accountability of the Samurdhi programme is considered as weak. Samurdhi officers are accountable to two authorities, one of which is a local politician (Gunitalaka *et al.*, 1997). As a result, the people are of political influence and no external checks and balances are present to prevent them from acting on the demands of politicians. Politicisation is embedded in the design and influences of both the selection of Samurdhi administrators and authorities and beneficiaries. Thus, the programme lacks transparency and external mechanisms for monitoring and evaluation which is required for the Samurdhi to be an efficient programme.

Armed conflict with the Tamil Tigers restricts the implementation of the programme in certain areas. In addition to the above identified efficiency issues, the following weaknesses have also been identified:

- The welfare approach destroys the capacity of families to explore other indigenous coping mechanisms.
- The difficulty of linking the programme with other developmental activities, particularly those implemented by non-governmental organisations.

- In some areas, there is compartmentalisation of services rather than convergence.
- Lack of marketing facilities for products of income generating enterprises.
- For the ultra poor, financial support provided by the government is barely sufficient to meet subsistence requirements and thus, cannot be used for productive purposes.

Remedial Measures and Suggestions

Sri Lanka has carried out consistently a series of costly social welfare programmes and yet, the Central Bank of Sri Lanka states that a fifth of all households do not consume the minimum required caloric food energy (Gunaratne, 1987). However, it is certain that the poor in Sri Lanka would have been worse off without such programmes. Providing welfare is not the same as 'solving the poverty problem'. This section presents a few remedial measures to enhance the improvement of the Samurdhi programme in making it an efficient programme.

Large number of targeting errors was identified as a weakness in the Samurdhi programme. All potential beneficiaries are required to show up to a public meeting for community screening in order to improve targeting.

Political interference in selection of beneficiaries and the increase in corruption indicate that the targeting errors are not random. Thus, the government should improve the transparency of the programme and reduce corruption to ensure accurate targeting of beneficiaries.

Income and consumption poverty still prevails in Sri Lanka. Armed conflict with the Tamil Tigers restricts the implementation of the Samurdhi programme in certain areas in the North and East. Thus, extreme poor exist in the North and East due the large number of internally displaced people. Further, the high cost incurred for the war is around at least 7.8 per cent of GDP. This has constrained the investment of economic infrastructure in the rural areas. Thereby, finding a lasting solution to war is a major priority in accelerating rural poor and eliminating poverty. A path to peace is difficult and complex. Thus, a political solution is the only prospect for a long term resolution to the conflict. This will ensure the ability to practice the Samurdhi programme for the internally displaced people in the North and the East.

Another reason which limits rural development is that the economic growth benefits are not equally distributed. Growth in Sri Lanka is predominantly in the Western province where 85 per cent of the industry is located. Thus, the proportion of the rural poor families directly benefiting from employment in new garment industries is very small. Thus, the government should ensure that the growth benefits are distributed to the rural areas. Further, effective education systems should be implemented along with the facilities required in the rural areas in such a way that the education system geared towards public sector employment is matched by the job market. This will increase their higher education opportunities. As a result, it will reduce the level of unemployment and alleviate the poverty problem.

Conclusion

Sri Lanka enjoys the most extensive social protection coverage in the South Asian region among which the Samurdhi programme is the main safety net programme implemented by the government to support the poor to maintain their living standards, while also helping them to emerge from poverty. The Samurdhi programme was further strengthened in 2006 when the biggest capital allocation for the poverty alleviation programme was utilised in 2006. However, the Samurdhi programme needs to be further streamlined aiming at empowering the rural poor to extend their contribution to the development of the economy.

Various studies show that Samurdhi benefits are enjoyed by around 46 per cent of the population though the poverty level was 23 per cent. This highlights the need for improving the targeting of Samurdhi benefits. Thereby, based on empirical evidence, the paper reaches the conclusion that the targeting outcomes of Samurdhi are inadequate and the targeting errors are non-random. Thus, the patterns of targeting errors suggest that the programme would need extensive redesign in order to improve these outcomes. It should be redesigned in such a way so as to increase the transparency and accountability of the programme, reduce the impact of politicisation and accurately target the beneficiaries of the programme.

The Samurdhi social assistance programme was established to alleviate poverty and create opportunities for the youth and the disadvantaged. However, it does not appear to fulfil this contract. The impact of Samurdhi transfers on poverty alleviation is limited. Thereby, we can finally conclude that the Samurdhi programme is not inefficient solely within itself, but it is inefficient in the way in which it has been implemented. Thus, the programme requires sufficient redesign to improve its weaknesses.

References

Central Bank of Sri Lanka (1998). *Economic Progress of Independent Sri Lanka.*

———. (2006). *Central Bank Report*.

Centre for Poverty Analysis (2003). "Improving Capacities for Poverty Research Programme", *Toward New Empirical and Evidence: Poverty Issues in Sri Lanka*. Sri Lanka Association of Advancement of Sciences.

Glinskaya, Elena (2000). *An Empirical Evaluation of Samurdhi Program*. World Bank Research Paper.

Goodhand, Jonathan (2001). "Violent Conflict, Poverty and Chronic Poverty", *CPRC Working Paper* 6.

Gunaratne, L. (1987). "The Poorest of the Poor in Sri Lanka", in *The Alleviation of Poverty in Sri Lanka.* Colombo: Central Bank of Sri Lanka. pp.243-75.

Gunatilleke, R., R. Perera, R. Saliah and C. de Silva (1997). *The Samurdhi Programme: A Preliminary Evaluation*. Institute of Policy Studies.

Lakshman, W.D. (1997). *Dilemmas of Development*. Sri Lanka Association of Economists, Sri Lanka. *http://www.unescap.org/rural/doc/beijing_march97/sri_lanka.pdf*

Sahn, David E. and Harold Alderman (1996). "The Effect of Food Subsidies on Labor Supply in Sri Lanka", *Economic Development and Cultural Change* 45(1): 125-45, October.

Annexure A-3.1

Table A-3.1

Samurdhi Eligibility Criteria

Monthly Income in Rupee and Household Size	*Grant Size (rupees per month)*
Household Income<500 and Number of Members >=4	1,000
Household Income<1,000 and Number of Members >=3	500
Household Income<1,000 and Number of Members 2	200
Household Income<1,000 and Number of Members 1	100
Former Janasaviya Recipients	250

Note: Reportedly, the cligibility criteria changed from Rs. 1,000 to Rs. 1,500 in 1999.

Source: Ministry of Samurdhi, Youth Affairs and Sports. "Progress 1999, Programmes 2000."

Annexure A-3.2

Figure A-3.1

Samurdhi Recipients and Expenditure

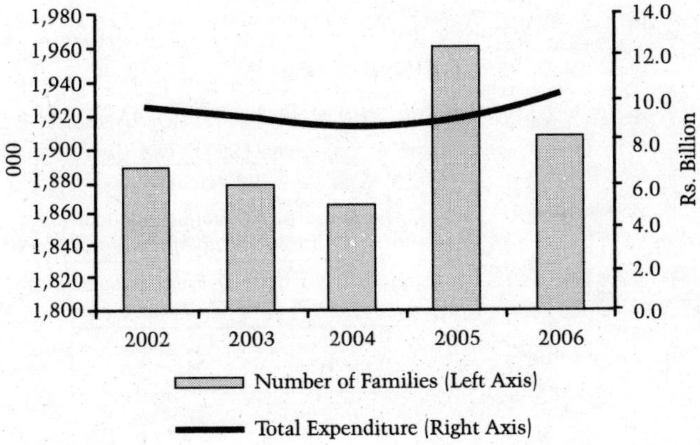

Source: *Central Bank Report,* 2006.

Table A-3.2

Samurdhi Welfare Programme Number of Beneficiary Families and Value of Grants 2005-06

Cash Grants Amount (Rs.)	2005 No. of Families	2005 Value (Rs. m)	2006(a) No. of Families	2006(a) Value (Rs. m)
Samurdhi Income Supplementary Programme				
Rs. 1,000 (Rs. 1,000-Rs. 1,500 in 2006)	7,115	85	7,902	106
Rs. 600 (Rs.600-Rs.1,000 in 2006)	655,092	4,717	645,354	5,517
Rs. 400 (Rs.400-Rs.600 in 2006)	330,725	1,587	449,646	2,407
Rs. 350 (Rs.350-Rs.400 in 2006)	347,323	1,459	308,866	1,324
Rs. 250 (Rs.250-Rs.350 in 2006)	267,843	904	180,550	542
Rs. 140 (Rs.55-Rs.250 in 2006)	352,566	592	321,250	690
Total	1,960,664	9,244	1,913,568	10,586
Nutrition Programme				
Rs. 200 (with effect from June 2004)	112,960	271	119,184	148

Note: (a) Provisional.

Source: Central Bank Report, 2006.

Annexure A-3.3

Samurdhi's Organisation and Administration Structure

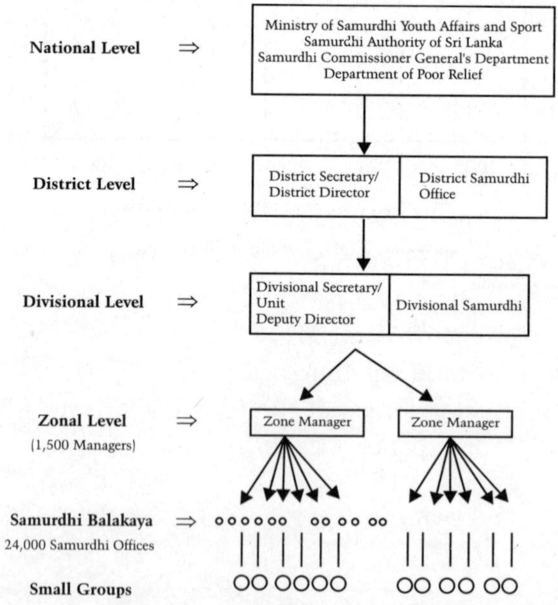

4 Evaluating the Poverty-Gender Nexus

A Review on Bangladesh

Fahim Hassan

Introduction

Poverty, by amplifying inequality, gives birth to numerous constraints and hindrances for development and economic growth. The inherently unequal society of Bangladesh reflects this imbalance in different aspects of life. Gender discrimination plays a significant part in preventing women from escaping the cycle of poverty. In rural areas, the case is even worse. In this paper, poverty is defined not only on the basis of income and consumption but also the lack of essentials for a minimum standard of well-being. It refers to various forms of economic, social and psychological deprivation among the people who lack adequate ownership, or sufficient access to resources for achieving a minimum level of living. While estimating the intensity of poverty in Bangladesh, the deprivation and the degradation of rural women is often overlooked. This paper, therefore, is focused on the link between rural poverty and gender discrimination, and examines whether women are more likely to be in poverty than men in rural areas.

The paper is organised in the following manner: after a brief discussion on existing literature, Section 3 and Section 4 briefly discusses the methodology used in this paper and the sources of data. Section 5 portrays how women in rural areas have a poor standard of living compared to men in terms of employment, health, mobility and property rights, and highlights the gender impact on poverty from empirical evidence. Finally, some policy recommendations are illustrated followed by the conclusion.

Literature Review

The legacy of gender discrimination is pointed out as a global phenomenon by the World Bank (2005). The report develops an index of gender inequality and concludes that women are deprived compared to their male counterparts all over the world. It also analyses the importance of strengthening women's voice and recommended various policies to be implemented, e.g., promoting greater gender equality through private sector development. Gender of the household head, education and household poverty and welfare are closely interlinked. In a study conducted in the context of Nigeria between 1980 and 1996, multivariate analysis showed that female-headed households were more likely to be poor. It also showed that education and household size have significant influences on household welfare and the probability of being poor (Okojie, 2002).

Urban and rural poverty have different causes and manifestations. This is because of the lack of infrastructural facilities such as gas, electricity and transport in rural areas (Khan, 2006). In addition, one of the main causes of rural poverty in Bangladesh is the erratic and extreme climate and the fact that a large proportion of the country is low-lying and susceptible to natural disasters. Many rural areas are subject to annual flooding that destroys crops and livestock. Eventually, people have to rely on local money lenders and get deeper into poverty due to high interest rate. Thus, poverty incidence is higher in rural areas than in urban areas. In rural areas, 29.3 per cent people are below the lower poverty line, almost 15 per cent higher than that of urban areas (HIES 2005, Annexure A-4.1).

The deprivation of women begins from birth and continues through the unequal provision of education, health care and nutrition till old age. In many countries, especially in the LDCs, 'women' are identified as the most vulnerable group facing degradation and humiliation in different aspects of life. Situations in the rural areas are even worse. Women are the poorest among the rural poor, especially when they are the sole heads of their households, such as widows or wives of men who have migrated in search of employment. They suffer discrimination because of their gender, they have scarce income-earning opportunities and their nutritional intake is often inadequate.

Methodology

The methodology of this paper includes a sample survey and an econometric model. The sample survey titled "Rapid Assessment Survey on Rural Women" was conducted to analyse the current status of the rural women. In the survey, the main purpose was to see the social, economic and matrimonial problems faced by the women.

Furthermore, a logistic regression model has been implemented to assess the impact of gender on poverty, to be more specific, whether female-headed households are more prone to be poor compared to male-headed households. In this regard, the state of being poor[1] is set as the dependent variable and household size, sex of household head, household head literacy, household head skill and landlessness are set as explanatory variables. The general equation evolves as follows:

$$SP = HHSIZE + D_1 HHSEX + D_2 HHLIT + D_3 SKILL + D_4\ LANDLESSNESS$$

State of being poor (SP): Poor = 1, Non-poor = 0

Household head sex (HHSEX): Male = 1, Female = 0

Household head literacy (HHLIT): Literate = 1, Illiterate = 0

Skill (SKILL): Skilled = 1, Unskilled = 0

Landlessness (LANDLESSNESS): Landless =1, Landowner = 0.

Description of Data

Both primary and secondary data are used in this paper to provide empirical evidence of theoretical arguments presented above. The sample survey, conducted in 2007, mainly covered two thanas[2], Kotowali and Burichong, under Comilla district. Randomly selected 50 women who lived in rural area were surveyed under a standardised questionnaire (Annexure A-4.2).

---

1. The state of being poor is defined according to the HIES (2000). A household whose income level is below 652 BDT per month is considered as moderate poor. This amount was derived through Cost of Basic Needs (CBN) method where it was calculated that it requires 652 BDT per month to acquire the basket of basic food and non-food items.
2. A thana is an administrative unit that is smaller than a district and consists of a number of villages.

The sources of the secondary data are Household Income and Expenditure Survey (2000, 2005), Labour Force Survey (1999-2000), Poverty Monitoring Survey (2004) and some other sample surveys conducted by different research organisations.

The data for the econometric model are drawn from HIES conducted by Bangladesh Bureau of Statistics in 2000. The survey includes 7440 randomly selected households. Among these, 5040 households are in rural areas, while the rest are in urban areas. The mean household size is 5.18 and average earner per household is 1.45.

Discussion of Results

This broad section contains an analysis of results obtained from examining the data. As a background study, gender discrepancy are pointed out in various sectors e.g., employment, health care, mobility, property rights and political representations. Later findings from the econometric model are presented to evaluate the vulnerability of the female-headed households.

Rural Women and Employment

The characteristics of the labour market vary by region and by gender. Female participation in the labour market provides women access to income and generates socio-economic empowerment. It can also play a significant role in the economic growth by changing the dynamics of the entire labour market. In Bangladesh, though the female labour force participation rate in rural area has gradually increased over time, it is significantly lower compared to male labour force participation rate (Annexure A-4.1).

The employment pattern of rural women significantly differs from that of urban women. In this section, this pattern will be illustrated through analysing the working status, unemployment rate and wage rate.

a. Stereotyped Working Status

In rural areas, work is typically divided along gender lines, with men being responsible for outside work and women for housework and child care. Often they assist in weeding or post-harvest work. Having fewer marketable skills and lack of social acceptance, women are mainly concentrated in unpaid household activities. Even if some manage to work outside, the double-shift burden affects their productivity. A study by CPD (2000) showed that in rural area, total working time in economic activities was 7.81 hours per day for a woman, that is lower than that of a man, 8.07 hours per day (Table 4.1). The interesting but predictable fact was that women spent almost 80 per cent of their labour hours in household work.

Table 4.1

Type of Activity by Gender

Type of Activity	*Hours Spent By*	
	Male	*Female*
Economic Labour	6.73	1.79
i. Agriculture	3.5	1.41
ii. Non-agriculture	3.23	0.38
Domestic Labour	1.34	6.02
Total Labour (average/day)	8.07	7.81

Source: Center for Policy Dialogue (CPD), 2000.

b. Higher Unemployment Rate

Fluctuations in unemployment rate are observed in terms of both region and gender. In rural areas, the unemployment rate has increased from FY 1995-96 to FY 1999-2000 and from then, it decreased gradually. Female unemployment rate declined drastically from FY 1999-2000 to 2002-03. Still it is higher *vis-à-vis* male unemployment rate in rural areas.

Table 4.2

Unemployment Rate in Bangladesh, 1996-2003

	1995-96	*1999-2000*	*2002-03*
Urban			
Total	4.8	3.9	5.0
Female	6.5	7.6	6.2
Male	4.4	2.9	4.6
Rural			
Total	3.1	5.8	4.1
Female	8.3	8.2	4.4
Male	2.3	5.0	4.0

Source: BIDS (2007). *Research Monograph 21.*

One of the major causes of higher unemployment rate of women is their lack of skills. Table 4.3 shows that in 2000, more than 90 per cent of the female labour force participants from rural areas were unskilled. Lack of appropriate market skills or technical knowledge reduces their job opportunity and also decreases their share in better paid jobs.

Table 4.3

Distribution of Labour Force by Skill, 2000

Area	*Sex*	*Skilled*	*Unskilled*	*Total*
Rural	Female	8.9	91.1	100
	Male	37.2	62.8	100
Urban	Female	11.9	88.1	100
	Male	34.6	65.4	100

Note: Age 15 and above.
Source: BIDS (2007). *Research Monograph 21.*

c. *Wage Discrimination*

Another dimension of gender disparity is wage discrimination. Women are discriminated against in terms of wage both in rural and urban areas. Table 4.4 shows that in 2002-03, a female's wage was only 60 per cent of a male's wage in rural areas. Ignoring the small fluctuation, it can be concluded that it has remained constant for the past few years. This phenomenon reflects the fact that in a same household if there are both female and male workers working on same field, the female is worse off due to wage discrimination considering the other factors remain same.

Table 4.4

Wage Discrimination between Male and Female by Area

Year	*Area*	*Tk. per Day*		*Female's Wage as a Percentage of Male's Wage*
		Male	*Female*	
2002-03	Rural	62	37	60
	Urban	75	42	56
1999-2000	Rural	63	35	55
	Urban	85	59	69
1995-96	Rural	44	25	57
	Urban	60	36	60

Note: Rural and urban consumer price index is applied using base year 1985-86 =100.
Source: BIDS (2007). *Research Monograph 21.*

Most rural women are self-employed and engaged in small scale businesses. These have minimal capital. Usually women rely on indigenous materials and use antiquated technology. To increase the productivity of these enterprises, technological advancement is obviously required. Besides these sorts of obstacles, women in rural areas also face some other problems which are different from the problems faced by men. Women have to balance both, wage earning activities as well as household activities. This load of 'double shift burden' hampers their working incentives and lessens their leisure.

Rural Women and Health Care

Rural women are more vulnerable when it comes to health care. Lack of proper diet, improper methods of contraceptives and poor sanitation increases their susceptibility. This sub-section thus reveals how rural women are deprived in terms of contraceptive usage, methods of treatment, sanitation and access to safe drinking water.

a. Usage of Contraceptives

The contraceptive prevalence rate is lower in the rural areas. This increases the possibility of unwanted pregnancy. The rate of condom users in rural areas is significantly lower than that of the urban areas. This increases the high risk of HIV and other sexually transmitted diseases among the rural women. In addition, frequent pregnancy creates antenatal and postnatal complications.

Table 4.5

Contraceptive Prevalence Rate by Method and Area

Method	*National*	*Rural*	*Urban*
Any Method	55.13	52.17	60.37
Any Modern Method	50.19	47.76	54.51
Condom	5.32	4.08	7.52
Oral Pill	32.35	31.70	33.49
Injection	9.96	9.43	10.89
Male Sterilisation	0.21	0.22	0.20
Female Sterilisation	1.84	1.84	1.84
Traditional Method	4.88	4.40	5.73
IUD	0.62	0.57	0.71

Source: BBS (2003). *Sample Vital Registration System*.

b. Methods of Treatment

The following table depicts that both in rural and urban areas, women have relatively less access to modern health care facilities compared to men. It also shows that the percentage of women who do not have access to any type of treatment has increased over time both in rural and urban areas. Moreover, the numbers of females who are going to quacks[3] in 2004 are significantly higher in rural areas (41.3 per cent) than urban areas (9.8 per cent). Also, the number of females who are going to quacks in rural areas has increased while in urban areas, the number has decreased.

Table 4.6

Distribution of Patients by Methods of Treatment in the Urban and Rural Areas, 2004 and 1999

Methods of Treatment	*Urban*				*Rural*			
	2004		*1999*		*2004*		*1999*	
	Male	*Female*	*Male*	*Female*	*Male*	*Female*	*Male*	*Female*
No Treatment	20.5	24.1	6.6	5.1	18.7	18.9	5.5	9.5
Govt. Hospital	18.2	18.7	13.7	5.1	13.0	9.2	13.1	12.8
Non-Govt. Hospital	5.0	5.0	4.1	5.1	2.0	2.1	2.1	1.8
Private Doctor	37.1	34.4	32.7	29.1	17.3	19.2	30.6	31.7
Quacks	7.9	9.8	28.7	30.7	40.7	41.3	38.0	38.8
Homeopathic	4.4	4.3	5.2	9.5	4.8	5.7	4.4	1.3
Kabiraji	1.6	0.1	2.1	10.2	1.4	1.5	1.6	1.2
Hakemi	0.2	-	2.8	-	-	0.2	0.3	-
Others	3.8	2.2	2.1	-	1.3	0.9	2.5	1.7
Own Knowledge					0.8	1.0	1.7	1.3
Total	100.0	100.0	100.0	100.0	100.0	100.0	100.0	100.0

Source: Poverty Monitoring Survey Report, 2004.

c. Sanitation and Access to Safe Drinking Water

Women's health is jeopardised in rural areas because of the lack of access to proper sanitation. Table 4.7 depicts the sanitary facilities that are available to all rural people in Bangladesh. Using open spaces as toilets is a major cause of waterborne diseases that affect males and females equally.

3. Quacks are doctors who practice medicine without any medical degree or formal knowledge.

Table 4.7

Access to Sanitation

Type of Toilet Facilities	*Percentage*
Flush Toilet	0
Sanitary	6
Slab Latrine	12
Katcha Latrine	54
None (Open Space)	28
Total	100

Source: *Rapid Assessment Survey on Rural Women, 2007.*

In rural areas, safe drinking water is not available as arsenic contamination is widespread all over Bangladesh. Ponds, canals and rivers are also not a hygienic source as the water is used for various purposes. Sixty per cent of rural women use tube well as a source of drinking water. Tube well and well are often likely to have arsenic contamination. Thus, ignorance and lack of awareness of rural women increase the risk of health hazard for the whole household.

Table 4.8

Sources of Drinking Water

Sources of Drinking Water	*Percentage*
Tap	10
Tube Well	60
Well	20
Pond/Canal/River/Spring	10
Others	-
Total	100

Source: *Rapid Assessment Survey on Rural Women, 2007.*

Poorer women get up earlier than men to queue up for water and take advantage of the dark while using communal or other types of toilets that lack privacy. Again, most of the women use traditional biomass fuels (e.g. cow dung) for cooking and sometimes for household heating in winter. As a result, they suffer from several respiratory problems and chronic obstructive pulmonary diseases due to continuous exposure to indoor smoke. As a result, they become more vulnerable to health hazards than men do.

Rural Women and Mobility

Women in rural areas have fewer income earning opportunities because they are less mobile than men (Paul, 1992). Expansion of female activity space is not encouraged by the traditional patriarchal society. Gender division of labour is frequently induced by cultural and religious restrictions.

The daily activities of rural women are usually concentrated at home or in their own neighbourhoods. This usually includes unpaid work like fetching water, cooking, washing dishes as well as income generating work, for instance raising poultry, paddy processing, weaving and growing vegetables in the backyard. Public roads, market places and open fields are more accessible to men. The presence of women in such places is usually acceptable only in proper dress and company. Thus, women may sometimes work with their husbands in the nearby fields. In remote villages, poor women with restricted mobility depend on the male family members for any entrepreneurial venture.

While surveying the rural women, a striking fact was noticed. Table 4.9 shows that 64 per cent of them had not been outside their village for the last three months. Only 36 per cent of rural women travelled outside for various purposes (majority of them went to the weekly village market to sell homemade products).

Table 4.9

Percentage of Women who Travelled Outside the Village during the Three Month Period (October-December 2007)

Frequency (Per Month)	*Percentage*
Never	64
Once or twice	28
2-5 times	6
More than 5 times	2
Total	100

Source: *Rapid Assessment Survey on Rural Women, 2007.*

For further inquiry, women were asked about their companionship when they travel outside their residence. The results are compiled in Table 4.10. Majority (70 per cent) of the women reported that they are accompanied by their husband. Very few of them (4 per cent) travel alone. Apart from their husband, they are often escorted by their neighbours or relatives for social acceptance.

Table 4.10

Persons Accompanying Women when they Travel Outside their Domicile

Person	*Percentage*
Husband	70
Children	10
Relatives	6
Neighbours	10
None	4
Total	100

Source: *Rapid Assessment Survey on Rural Women, 2007.*

Recently, the female activity space is increasing as the socio-economic pattern is gradually changing. Infrastructural development, industrialisation, spread of micro credit, and overall changes in social views are generating more space for women. But still, compared to males, women are less mobile. Consequently, they remain mostly as unpaid household workers. This is also one of the major causes of greater female unemployment rate compared to men as lower mobility results in fewer new job opportunities.

Gender Disparity in Property Rights and Political Representations

The Constitution of Bangladesh grants equal rights to women and men in all spheres of public life. However, when it comes to family matters such as marriage, divorce, custody of children and inheritance, matters that are viewed as the realms of private sphere, the law fails to protect the rights of women.[4]

4. Article 27 states that, "All citizens are equal before law and are entitled to equal protection of law" and Article 28(1), "The State shall not discriminate against any citizen on the grounds only of religion, race, caste, sex or place of birth". However, Article 28(2) states, "Women shall have equal rights with men in all spheres of the State and of public life", thus restricting family matters to the discriminatory laws of the "private sphere".

In Bangladesh, 89.58 per cent people are Muslims, according to Population census, 2001.[5] Muslim law is discriminatory towards women when it comes to inheritance and marriage.[6] Also women are usually not permitted to participate in the *salish* (local arbitration). In many cases, they are not concerned about their voting rights. In almost all cases, they are not considered as a witness in the marriage contract by tradition.

Gender-Blind Poverty Measuring Methods

To measure the incidence of income poverty, several methods have been used in Bangladesh over time. Among these methods, food energy intake (FEI) and direct calorie intake (DCI) were used by the Household Expenditure Survey (HES) (FY 1991-92). FEI method computes poverty lines by finding the value of per capita consumption at which a household can be expected to fulfil its calorie requirement. DCI method is used to calculate the incidence of absolute poverty where population or households fall below a threshold calorie intake (2122 kilocalories per person on a daily basis). Similarly, a person having daily calorie intake less than 1805 kilocalories is considered to be in abject poverty. In the HES conducted in FY 1995-96, the BBS for the first time adopted the cost of basic needs (CBN) method for constructing poverty lines which was also used in HIESs of 2000 and 2005. In this method, an absolute poverty line is defined as the value of consumption needed to satisfy minimum subsistence needs (food as well as non-food consumption).

All the three methods share a common imperfection: these do not take women's consumption pattern separately into account. Raihan and Razzaque (2007) showed that the normative basket chosen for measuring poverty does not represent the whole population. This is actually not a

5. BBS, *Population Census*, 2001.
6. For example, as per Muslim law, a widow gets a very inadequate treatment in comparison with that of a widower, such as in same condition the wife gets 1/8th and husband gets 1/4th. In addition, a daughter gets half the share of a son. In this context, it is seen that the very fundamental rights of a woman is violated for inheritance law regarding access to property. In the same condition, an uncle gets double that of the aunt. When divorce occurs, the wife gets only the dowry and the cost of living for three months as alimony from the husband. All the property earned by the couple goes to the husband. Most importantly, the rights of divorce are reserved only for the male.

typical basket. It even fails to differentiate the preferences between the rural and the urban areas.

The CBN method compares between the male-headed and the female-headed households. So there is a possibility that CBN non-poor male-headed households may have poor female members. The CBN method fails to mark them, as its measuring unit is 'household'[7], not 'individual'. The original representation will be revealed through measuring the intra-household resources distribution. Therefore, the gendered poverty estimation under the CBN method may portray an erroneous picture.

Empirical Results

The outcome of the logistic regression is presented below:

Table 4.11

Findings from the Logistic Regression Analysis

Explanatory Variables	*Co-efficient*	*Standard Error*	*P-Value*
Household Size (HHSIZE)	0.90	0.012	0.00
Household Head Sex (HHSEX)	.268	0.089	0.03
Household Head Literacy (HHLIT)	-0.949	0.057	0.00
Skill (SKILL)	-1.577	0.118	0.00
Landlessness (LANDLESSNESS)	.777	0.067	0.00
Constant	-.667	0.095	0.00

Note: Number of observations: 7440.

The above result shows that there exists a positive relationship between poverty (P=1, NP=0) and household head gender (M=1, F=0). This means a male-headed household is more likely to be in poverty than a female-headed household. This result derives due to the distribution of data. Among the 7440 households, only 667 are female-headed which is less than 10 per cent of the whole sample. This small number of female-headed households fails to show a greater impact on poverty. The substantial number of male-headed households virtually determines the

7. A household is formed by the persons living together and taking food from the same cooking arrangement. The persons may or may not have a relationship among them. Home servants who take food along with them is also included in a household.

effect of gender on poverty. The other outcomes meet the expectation, i.e., household size shows positive correlation with being poor. That means the bigger the household, the more is the probability of getting poor. Dummy variables like household head literacy and skill show that if the household head is illiterate or unskilled, the household is more prone to live in penury. The regression equation also lacks important variables like geographical location of the households or infrastructure. This can be another reason behind this result. Furthermore, there is a possibility that in this sample, the female-headed households may receive remittance from male members who work as migrant workers in distant cities or even in other countries that alter their financial status and made these households non-poor.

Recommendations

Based on the above findings, the following recommendations can be suggested:

- *Capacity Building Programmes:* Special training should be given to rural women to improve their technical knowledge. For instance, new production techniques as well as effective post-harvest activities should be encouraged. Entrepreneurship development programmes should be constantly implemented in order to improve their skill level.
- *Counselling and Professional Consultancy:* Potential women entrepreneurs should be encouraged to start their own business. Institutional help and guideline will be highly beneficial in this regard.
- *Increasing the Number of Female Teachers and Trainers:* More female teachers and trainers should be recruited. It will generate female employment. In addition, it will also help the older female participants to be more interactive and frank with the trainers.
- *Reducing Women's Dependence on Stereotyped Occupations:* Rural women are mainly concentrated in agricultural activities. Expansion of the non-farm economy will increase diversity in professions and lessen the typical risks (seasonal fluctuations due to drought, flood etc.) of farm economy.

- *Forming More Women's Association:* Women empowerment can be strengthened by networking (forming more associations, groups and clubs). Building linkage between other organisations will mobilise funds for further programmes. It will also help the women to raise their voices against disparities and inequalities.
- *Marketing Support:* Micro or small scale entrepreneurs lag behind in terms of packaging and marketing. Proper guidance and training will enlarge their access to the market.
- *Awareness Arising Through Traditional Events:* Consciousness among both males and females should be raised for having hygienic and healthy living. The media may not be able to play a major role as most of the people in rural areas are either illiterate or do not have access to TV or radio. Instead, social awareness may be spread through various events during festive times. If lyrics based on social issues (e.g. domestic violence) is sung by popular artists, it may draw more attention of the local people. Teachers should encourage students to perform dramas that portray health consciousness (using toilet, washing hands before eating etc.).

Conclusion

The above analysis concludes that in rural areas, women are more deprived and discriminated against in terms of employment, health care, mobility and social rights. Thus, the gender dimension of rural poverty requires further attention. In traditional methods of poverty estimation, these gender disparities are mostly overlooked. To reduce poverty incidence, as well as social injustices and oppression, is to raise the income level with participation of the women in the family. More gender-sensitive policies should be implemented to narrow this disparity.

References

Alamgir, M. (1974). "Some Analysis of Distribution of Income, Consumption, Saving and Poverty in Bangladesh", *Bangladesh Development Studies*.

Bangladesh Bureau of Statistics (n.d.). *Statistical Year Book*, various issues.

Bidani, Benu, and Martin Ravallion (1993). "A Regional Profile of Poverty in Indonesia", Policy Research Department, World Bank, Washington D.C.

CPD (2000). *CPD Dialogue Report No. 27: Fertility Behaviour in Bangladesh and West Bengal: A Comparative Study*. June.

Guhathakurta, M., S. Baden, C. Green and A.M. Goetz (1994). "Background Report on Gender Issues in Bangladesh", *Report No.* 26, prepared for the British High Commission, Dhaka.

Hashemi, S.M., S.R. Schuler and A.P. Riley (1996). "Rural Credit Programs and Women Empowerment in Bangladesh", *World Development* 24(4).

HIES (2005). *Report of the Household Income and Expenditure Survey 2005*, Bangladesh Bureau of Statistics.

———. (2000). *Report of the Household Income and Expenditure Survey 2000*. Bangladesh Bureau of Statistics.

ICDDRB. (2006). "Domestic Violence against Women in Bangladesh", *Health and Science Bulletin* 4(2).

Khan, A.R. (2006). "Rising Inequality in Bangladesh: An Analysis of Sources and Policies for Containment", from *Growth and Poverty: The Development Experience of Bangladesh*. Dhaka, Bangladesh: The University Press Limited. pp.4-20.

Khandker, S.R., M. Pitt and J. Cartwright (2003). "Does Micro-credit Empower Women? Evidence from Bangladesh", World Bank Policy Research *Working Paper* 2998.

LFS (1999-2000). *Report of the Labor Force Survey*, Bangladesh Bureau of Statistics

Okojie, C. (2002). *Gender and Education as Determinants of Household Poverty in Nigeria*. World Institute for Development Economics Research.

Paul, B.K. (1992). "Female Activity Space in Rural Bangladesh", *The Geographical Review*.

PMS (2004). *Poverty Monitoring Survey*, Bangladesh Bureau of Statistics.

Rahman, R.I. (2005). "The Dynamics of the Labor Market and Employment in Bangladesh: A Focus on Gender Dimensions", *Employment Strategy Paper*, ILO.

Raihan, S. and A. Razzaque (2007). "Intra-Household Distribution and Poverty Incidence: An Empirical Investigation on Bangladesh", from *Capturing Intra-household Discrimination and Poverty Incidence: A Study on Bangladesh*, Chapter 5.

Ravallion, M. and B. Bidani (1994). "How Robust is a Poverty Profile?", *The World Bank Economic Review* 8(1): 75-102.

Ravallion, M. and B. Sen (1996). "When Method Matters: Monitoring Poverty in Bangladesh", *Economic Development and Cultural Change*.

World Bank (2005). "Improving Women's Lives: World Bank Actions since Beijing", Gender and Development Group, World Bank.

Annexure A-4.1

The head count rate (HCR) of HIES (2005) for upper and lower poverty lines are given in the following table:

Table A-4.1

Head Count Rate (CBN) of Incidence of Poverty

Residence	*Upper Poverty Line*		*Lower Poverty Line*	
	2005	*2000*	*2005*	*2000*
National	40.0	48.9	25.5	33.7
Rural	43.8	52.3	29.3	37.4
Urban	28.4	35.2	13.7	19.4

Source: BBS, 2006; HIES, 2005.

Table A-4.2

Rural-Urban Dimensions of Poverty

Poverty "Type"	*Rural Poor*	*Urban Poor*
Transitory	Viable farmers, pastoralists and landless rural workers affected by sudden natural shocks or seasonal income losses; rural households affected by civil conflict.	Urban formal workers (and dependents) suffering temporarily unemployment or real wage declines.
Chronic Poor	Small holders, small herders or landless with limited or no access to productive assets or deteriorating asset base; rural communities isolated from markets and services; labour-poor households.	Urban informal sector with limited no access to productive assets, labour-poor households, especially female-headed households.
Chronic, Multidimensional	Marginalised cultural categories (ethnic or caste groups, marginalised indigenous communities); households with high dependency ratios, chronically sick and disabled.	Marginalised cultural categories; households dependent on anti-social activities, refugees, internally displaced persons.

Source: OECD (2001). *DAC journal*, Vol.2.

Table A-4.3

Labour Force Participation Rate (as percentage)

	Using the Usual Definition[8]					
	National		*Rural*		*Urban*	
Year	*Women*	*Men*	*Women*	*Men*	*Women*	*Men*
1983-84	8.2	78.2	7.7	78.8	12.1	74.3
1984-85	9.9	81.4	9.1	82.0	15.6	78.1
1990-91	14.1	79.6	14.4	80.6	12.7	76.2
1995-96	18.1	77.0	17.4	78.8	20.5	71.1
1999-2000	22.8	73.5	22.0	73.5	25.6	73.5
	Using the Extended Definition[9]					
1989	63.4	85.3	59.6	87.4	29.4	76.4
1990-91	58.2	79.6	65.1	80.6	30.1	76.2
1995-96	50.6	78.3	57.3	80.6	28.6	71.6
1999-2000	51.8	78.7	57.2	79.8	33.7	74.8

Source: BBS, *Labour Force Survey*, Various years.

Table A-4.4

Summarising Methods of Measuring Poverty

	Direct Calorie Intake	*Food Energy Intake*	*Cost of Basic Needs*
Indicator	Calorie intake	Expenditure (or income)	Expenditure (or income)
Threshold	2122 kilocalories/person	Expenditure level at which household members are expected to reach calorie intake threshold	Expenditure level at which household members are expected to meet basic needs (food and non-food)
Measure	Head-count or other	Head-count or other	Head-count or other
Strengths and Weaknesses	Indicator not representative: threshold consistent (for monitoring calorie intake)	Indicator representative: threshold not consistent (for real expenditures)	Indicator representative: threshold consistent (for real expenditures)

Source: *Bangladesh Economic Review, 2006*.

8. The usual definition of a person in employment refers to any person aged 15 and above who was either employed (worked at least one hour in the reference week) for payment or profit or with/without payment or profit or was unemployed during the reference period.

9. The extended definition includes own household economic activities (such as care of poultry and livestock, threshing, boiling, processing and preservation of food and so on).

Annexure A-4.2

Rapid Assessment Survey on Rural Women Questionnaire

Section 1: Personal Information

Name:
Age:
Profession:
Religion:
Marital Status:
No. of Children (if any):
Educational Background:

Address:
Village: Thana:
Zila:

Section 2: General Questions

[a] Are you a member of any credit programme?

(If yes):
Government:
Or, Non-government:

[b] What is the main source of your drinking water?

[c] How long does it generally take to fetch water?

[d] What type of toilet facilities do you have at home?

- ☐ Flush toilet
- ☐ Sanitary
- ☐ Slab latrine
- ☐ *Katcha* latrine
- ☐ None (open space)

[e] Did you voted in the last election?

[f] Have you ever been a witness in marriage?

Section 3: For Married Women Only

[a] What was your age at marriage?

[b] What is the age difference between you and your husband?

[c] What was your age when you had your first child?

[d] What was the place of your last delivery?

- ☐ Govt. hospital
- ☐ Private hospital
- ☐ By neighbour/relative/friend

[e] In your family who goes to the market to shop?

[f] Have you been a victim of domestic violence in past three months?
(If yes):
What type:

- ☐ Verbal abuse
- ☐ Physical torture
- ☐ Threat of divorce

[g] What was the main reason?

- ☐ For applying for credit/loans
- ☐ Preparing meals not to his liking
- ☐ For doing something which was prohibited by husband
- ☐ For dowry
- ☐ For arguing
- ☐ For refusing to give him money
- ☐ Influenced by in-laws
- ☐ Others

II
Investing in the Social Sector

5 A Quiet Revolution

The Need to Invest in the Education Sector in India

Rishi Chakravarti

Introduction

Education is the greatest hope for the survival of humankind and for the forward progress of civilisation. It is the most basic necessity after those that are vital to life itself—food, clothing and shelter. It is education that lifts people out of the state of chronic poverty in which they are constantly struggling to fulfil basic needs such as these. The direct link between poverty and lack of educational opportunities has been demonstrated many times over.[1] As Lyndon Johnson said during the "War on Poverty" in the 1960s, "Poverty has many roots, but the tap root is ignorance." Economic development is closely associated with poverty reduction in many countries. It is also believed that increased education lead to improved health, income level and living standards.

I discuss this paper in three parts: "The Rationale" addresses the need to invest in education; "The Vision", where I set achievable targets for education in India, and in "The Model", I suggest certain policy measures to achieve "The Vision".

The Rationale

The Domino Effect: Women's Education

> If you educate a man, you educate an individual, but if you educate a woman, you educate a family.

---

1. Those investigators who have used learning outcomes as a measure of education (Hanushek and Kimko [2000]; Coulombe [2004]) have found robust connections between education and economic growth. Such findings are consistent with micro-economic studies linking basic skills acquisition to increased productivity and earnings.

It is not a coincidence that the countries with the highest levels of human development also come closest to offering equal opportunity and gender equity in their societies. Many studies have shown that the most rapid and effective way to slow population growth in the developing world is through the education of women.

Education lowers fertility and improves maternal health. A mother's education has been shown to raise the probability of their own children attending school.

Women's Wages and Fertility Decline

There is a direct correlation between women's wages and fertility decline. Consider the following argument:[2]

There are necessarily two costs associated with child rearing: direct costs of children[3] and the indirect or opportunity costs of children that are measured by the amount of income foregone in the process of bringing up the child.[4] So the opportunity cost of children is roughly proportional to the growing wage rate multiplied by the number of hours spent in parenting. In societies where opportunity cost is high, fertility rates tend to be low. It is clear that as the number of children begins to rise, the income left for "other goods" will begin to fall. This trade-off traces out the budget-line 'AB' (Figure 5.1).

We assume, at this point, that children and "other goods" are normal goods.[5]

The point of tangency of the indifference curve with the budget line is the point where the marginal benefit equals the marginal cost from child rearing. Now, suppose the wage income of the mother increases due to

---

2. Assumption 1: Gender bias plays an important role in this. In India, it is presumed that women must allocate the bulk of their time to upbringing of children.
3. They need to be fed, clothed, kept in good health, looked after and schooled etc.
4. Time spent at home with the child is the time not spent earning income.
5. Assumption 2: In the model, the preference of a couple over the number of children it wishes to have and "other goods" are denominated in terms of money.

   Assumption 3: We neglect the exact form of preferences here, which are represented by indifference curves (IC and IC') in Figure 5.1 to avoid unnecessary complications.

Figure 5.1

Women's Wage and Fertility Decline

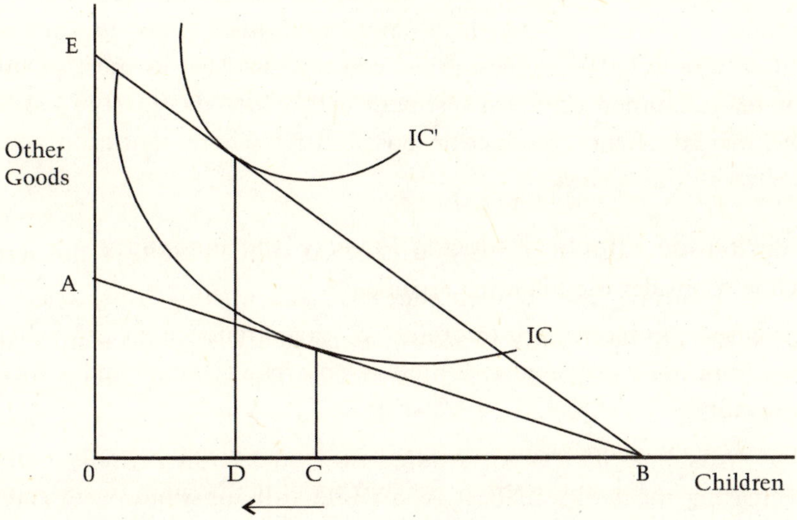

improved education[6], the budget line will swivel outward about B to the new budget line EB. Since the wage-income has gone up, the opportunity cost of children has gone up as well. This creates a substitution effect away from children and lowers fertility (from C to D). Thus, it is possible to lower the fertility rates, in India, through increased female wage rates as a result of improved female education.

Education and Human Productivity: Benefit to the Industry[7]

Education enables people to develop analytical skills and cognitive abilities.

Education increases human productivity in two ways. Firstly, it increases the worker's speed and quality due to increased knowledge and understanding of specific tasks. In addition, the worker makes better decisions about the allocation of resources, thus making him more efficient. Secondly, this acquired knowledge can then be utilised to innovate and to create technological developments. Positive changes in technology will improve the production of materials and the communication of

6. Annex A-5.2.
7. Annex A-5.1.

information. An educated labour force will be able to adapt to technology change.

Studies find that increases in educational attainment account for around 20 per cent of growth in output per worker. This, to some extent, reflects the fact that employers see educated workers as more productive. Therefore, human capital investment will reduce the costs of production and increase firms' production possibilities where education acts as a catalyst to this change.

Distribution Effects: Reducing Poverty and Inequality

The strong link between education and earnings[8], especially based upon the productivity interpretation, gave credence to the belief that education could play a powerful role in poverty alleviation and reduction of inequality.

Birdsall *et al.* (1995) studied how education actually helped in decreasing inequality in East Asia while still contributing to economic growth. They argued that a virtuous cycle can be established in which policies such as promoting high-quality basic education contribute to growth and reduced inequality, which in turn stimulates higher demand for education. Knight and Sabot (1990) argued that the well known Kuznets curve[9] of rising inequality in the early stages of rapid economic development need not apply to all situations. Rapid education expansion under the right conditions can lead to rapid economic growth and less inequality than would be implied by the Kuznets curve.

Effect on Agricultural Production

Primary education can enhance the productivity of farmers in India.

In India, the returns to primary schooling increased during the rapid technical progress, the green revolution. Increased schooling improved the productivity of farmers as well as helping them acquire knowledge about preventing resource degradation. The farmers were able to cultivate crops in a more scientific manner with the use of technology, thereby increasing

8. See Annex A-5.2.

9. A famous hypothesis, owing to Kuznets (1955), that inequality might rise and then fall as we move from lower to higher incomes through the stages of economic development.

farm output.[10] Rural incomes are positively affected by both education of the farmer and his wife.

It has been seen that four to six years of education is the minimum threshold for increasing agricultural productivity. Literacy allows farmers to adopt new agricultural methods, take risks and respond to market signals. A basic education also helps farmers gain title to their land and apply for credit at banks and other lending institutions. Primary schooling of farmers and that of neighbouring farm workers can raise crop production, suggesting an important externality.

Social and Political Arguments

"Only the educated are free."[11]

An educated population has positive outcomes for the Government economically with a larger tax base and socially through increased political involvement and democratic development. Education helps in fostering social cohesion by reducing social conflicts and poverty. In this regard, the need to impart value-based education to children at the early stages is essential. The essential elements of such education should be based on the development of concerns towards the need of society and the nation. Concentrated efforts to meet the basic needs of poor families, as well as strong programmes of education will instill a long term vision and teach people to be responsible in the use of natural resources. This will go a long way towards environment protection.

Rationale for Government Intervention

Differences between private and social returns are a cause of market failures or imperfections.

The purposes of government interference in the education market are:

First, there are positive externalities associated with investment in education.

It is important to make a distinction between the private and social rates of return to education. Private returns are the private benefits, after taking into

10. India saw annual wheat production rise from 10 million tonnes in the 1960s to 73 million tonnes in 2006. (*http://news.bbc.co.uk/1/hi/world/south_asia/4994590.stm*)

11. Epictetus (55 AD-135 AD). *The Discourses.*

account private costs, which families obtain from investing in education. Social returns are the social benefits and costs including private ones. The social returns exceed the private returns because of the positive effects of education on crime, fertility, improved citizen participation and on growth and productivity of the economy as a whole, which the society benefits. The social rate of return from an additional year of schooling of an individual is anywhere from 5 to 15 per cent.[12] The government should consider all benefits to make a Pareto optimal allocation of investment in education.

Second, there are information asymmetries, for example, when parents with little education do not realise the benefits of investing in primary education for children.

Third, there can be credit market imperfections that prevent low and middle income households from overcoming budget constraints by borrowing for primary education, even when the private rate of return is high.

Fourth, government tax and subsidy policies can alter the calculation of private versus social rates of return.[13]

Finally, primary education has more students from disadvantaged backgrounds and the lack of investment in primary education will increase inequality. Primary education is the starting point for the education system and is the key to connecting young people with education and providing equality of opportunity.

As Figure 5.2 shows, the society will under-invest (Sp<Ss)[14] in education because it fails to recognise the social benefits of education. This presents an economic rationale for some significant degree of public investment.

---

12. Psacharopoulos (1981, 1994) estimated social rates of return to education at the national level based on international data arriving at OLS (ordinary least squares) estimates ranging from 5 to 15 per cent.

13. Friedman (1955) argues that the state should subsidise those purchasing education and tax those that receive the benefits including external benefits, the welfare of both groups will be improved. This ensures a more equitable distribution of opportunities and is the least expensive way of enforcing minimum standards of education.

14. Sp = Private optimum schooling, Ss = Social optimum schooling.

Figure 5.2

Private and Social Optimum Levels of Schooling

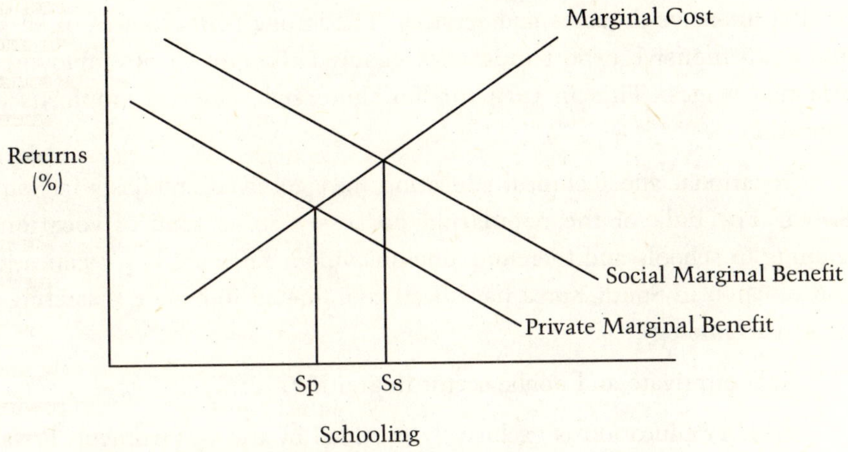

Lessons in Excellence: A Case Study of South Korea

South Korea's growth has been described as an economic miracle behind which there is an education miracle.

Even before the economic boom, South Korea started investing in education. Educational attainment in the labour force increased remarkably from 1945 to 1960 because of the strong growth of school enrolments. By the early 1960s, this early investment had given South Korea a human resource base; educational attainments of South Koreans far exceeded those of other developing countries. Teacher-pupil ratio in schools is 1:28 in South Korea, which is only half of that in many developing countries.[15]

The critical parameters of high-quality teachers, long school days, low repetition and dropout rates demonstrate efficient management of primary education.

The pattern of South Korea's economic growth:

In the first phase, South Korea pursued a high quality primary education, and once the knowledge base consisting of a well-educated labour force was formed, then an outward-looking economy emerged. In

15. In India, the teacher-pupil ratio is 1:42 (2005-06).

this phase, the exports were concentrated in labour-intensive manufactured goods. This gave confidence to the economy and investments were made in high-quality secondary education. It shifted its focus towards more capital or skill-intensive products and services. The strong performances of labour and skill-intensive export industries ensured the growth of employment and real wages. This in turn further increased society's emphasis on education.

Vocational and technical education have received emphasis in South Korea. The bulk of the population possesses some kind of vocational training in schools and therefore, unemployment rates are low.[16] Education and research in South Korea have been coordinated to ensure mastering of foreign technology.

Role of private and public sector in South Korea:

Primary education is exclusively provided by the Government. Private schools have a negligible role even in the case of secondary education, though there is some private secondary education but in Korea, higher education has been dominated by private institutes.

In Korea, a high school graduate earns 1.18 times the earnings of a middle school graduate and the ratio increases with higher levels of education. Thus, it is found that investment in human capital, especially in education, is more conducive to economic growth than investment in physical capital. The knowledge economy demands an extensive public and private vocational training system. Governments initiate it, and later on, private enterprises via different direct and indirect benefits support this initiation so that they can provide their own workers with training of good standards.

Where Does India Stand?

There is enough evidence in India to show that a high literacy rate, especially in the case of women, correlates with low birth rate, low IMR[17] and increase in the rate of life expectancy. The recognition of this fact created awareness on the need to focus upon literacy and elementary education programmes, not simply as a matter of social justice but more to foster economic growth, social well-being and social stability.

16. For South Korea, unemployment rate is 3.3 per cent while for India, it is 7.8 per cent.
17. IMR: Infant Mortality Rate.

India spent 4.11 per cent of its GDP on education during 2000-01 but about 44 per cent of its adult population still remains to be made literate.

Figure 5.3

Expenditure on Education in India

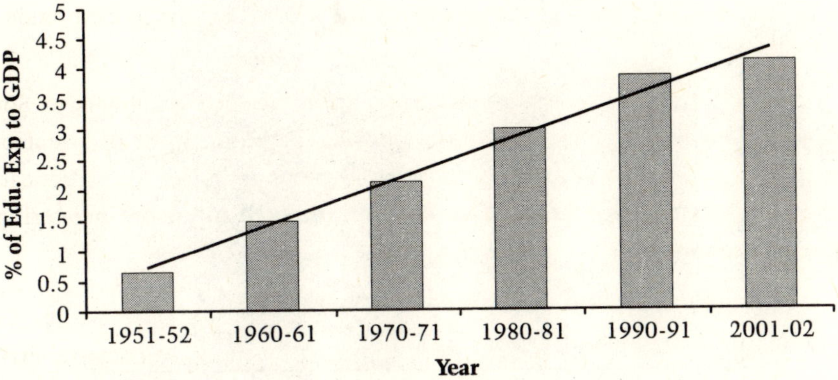

Source: National Accounts Statistics published by C.S.O.

The expenditure on the education sector was slightly less than 1 per cent of the GDP in 1951-52. It reached a level of 4.11 per cent in 2000-01.

Educational Indicators

1) *Gross Enrolment Ratio (GER):* is defined as the percentage of the enrolment in the primary and upper primary (classes I-VIII) to the estimated child population in the age group of 6-14 years.

Table 5.1

Gross Enrolment Ratios

Year	*Elementary*	*Classes*	*I-VIII*
	Boys	*Girls*	*Total*
1950-51	46.4	17.7	32.1
1960-61	65.2	30.9	48.7
1970-71	75.5	44.4	61.9
1980-81	82.2	52.1	67.5
1990-91	100.0	70.8	86.0
2000-01	90.3	72.4	81.6

Source: National Accounts Statistics published by C.S.O.

2) *Gross Dropout Rates:* represents the percentage of pupils who drop-out from a given grade or cycle or level of education in a given school year.

Figure 5.4

Dropout Rates (Classes I-VIII)

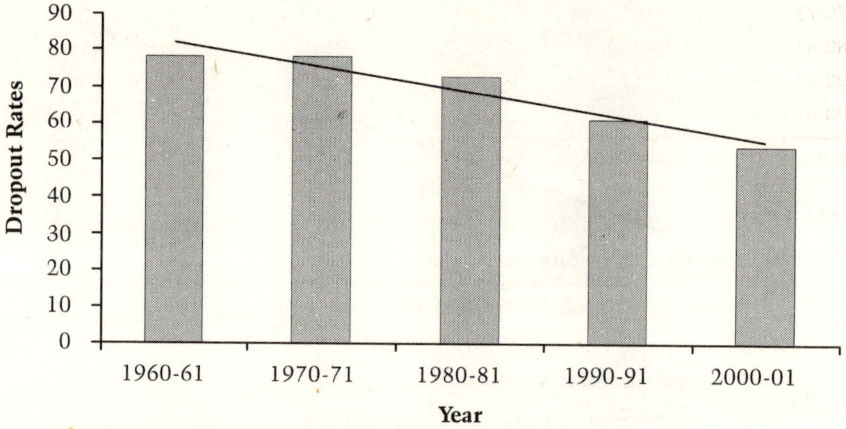

Source: National Accounts Statistics published by C.S.O.

3) *Teacher-Pupil Ratio (TPR):* on the basis of the school enrolment and number of teachers, the TPR is indicated in Table 5.2.

Table 5.2

Teacher-Pupil Ratios

Year	*Teacher-Pupil Ratio*
1950-51	1:21
1960-61	1:25
1970-71	1:25
1980-81	1:27
1990-91	1:31
2005-06	1:42

Source: National Accounts Statistics published by C.S.O.

4) *Number of Girls' Enrolment per Hundred Boys Enrolled:* a lot needs to be done in this field, even though the number of girls' enrolment has gone up significantly.

Table 5.3

Number of Girls' Enrolment per Hundred Boys Enrolled

Year	*Primary (I-V)*	*Middle (VI-VIII)*	*Secondary (IX-X)*
1950-51	39	18	16
1960-61	48	32	23
1970-71	60	41	35
1980-81	63	49	44
1990-91	71	58	50
2000-01	78	69	63

Source: National Accounts Statistics published by C.S.O.

5) *Literacy:* a person is considered literate if he or she can read and write, with understanding, in any language.[18]

Figure 5.5

Literacy Rates

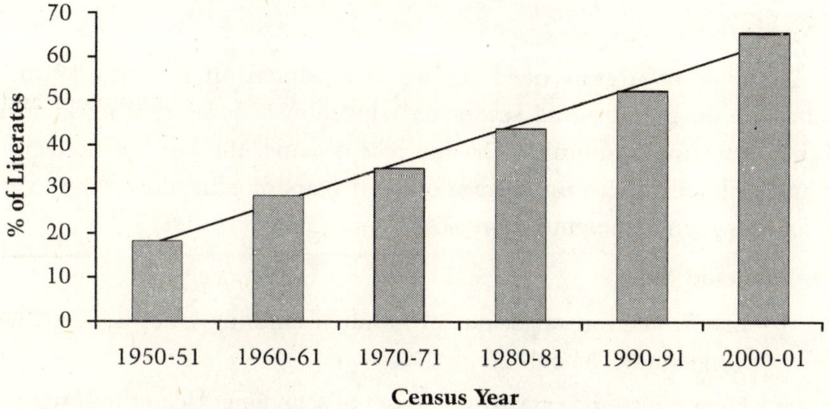

Source: Census of India (2001).

Review of Some of the Past Programmes and Schemes in India

Operation Blackboard (1987-88): this scheme was aimed at improving the classroom environment by providing infrastructural facilities, additional teachers and teacher-learning material to primary schools.

18. However, a person who can merely read, but cannot write, is not recorded as literate in census.

Mahila Samakhya (1989): programme with special aim to promote women's education and empowerment of women in socially and economically marginalised groups.

Mid-Day Meal Scheme (1995): it aims to give a boost to universalisation of primary education by increasing enrolment, retention, attendance and simultaneously improving the nutritional status of students in primary class. Under this scheme, cooked meals are served with calorie value equivalent to 100gm of wheat/rice per student per school day.

Sarva Shiksha Abhiyan (2003-2007): it aims to provide elementary education to all children in the 6-14 age groups by 2010. This programme also aims at improving the performance of the school system and provides community-owned quality elementary education, bridging gender and social disparities at the elementary level. The scheme is expected to absorb most of the existing programmes, within its overall framework with the district as the unit of programme implementation.

Key Challenges

There is an urgent need to improve education in India. Public expenditure on primary and secondary education is somewhat lower than in other emerging economies. Despite recent gains, the level of literacy is low and children receive on average only 10 years of education, three years less than in many emerging countries.

- **Demand Side:**
  - Low transition rates: out of hundred entering grade 1, less than 50 graduate school.
  - High direct and opportunity costs of schooling, lack of information on the benefits of education and value of girls' education.
  - Poor quality and low student achievement at the elementary levels.
  - Not much emphasis on quality of education.
  - Many sectors are facing supply constraint when it comes to skilled, qualified manpower.
- **Supply Side:**
  - Poor distribution of schools in villages (e.g. over 1/3rd of villages have schools beyond 5kms).

Figure 5.6

High School Graduation Ratios

Source: UNESCO (2007).

- There is no regular system of benchmarking students comparatively with other countries or even across states.
- Too much emphasis on rote learning: insufficient development of conceptual understanding.
- Insufficient quality assurance and accountability by schools.
- Little incentives for teachers to improve attendance and work.
- Low capacity in institutions for teacher pre-service and in-service training.
- More private sector involvement in the education sector needed.
- Need for more vocational training institutions[19] to tackle unemployment.

19. In India, hardly 2 per cent of the population receive formal vocational education and training (VET). So far, formal VET training exists in only 71 trades against the globally identified 2,500 trades. India has 11,000 VET training institutes against China's 500,000, Japan's 1,000,000 and South Korea's 750,000.

The Vision

- Easy access
- Education for all
- Retention of students
- Revamp and revitalise the education system
- Equity: Bridge all gender and social gaps

The Model

To achieve the vision, I suggest a two stage model:

Stage I: Improving the Skill Acquisition of Those Already Enrolled in Schools

Professional Development of Teachers

Teachers are a critical factor in the quality of education imparted to students. To that extent, I suggest the following:

- Ensure pre-service training to all elementary school teachers so that all untrained teachers can be trained, including through distance learning mode.
- Enhance pre-service training facilities in selected districts where the present capacity is not adequate and strengthen existing training institutions.
- Develop specialised correspondence courses for teachers in collaboration with open universities, higher education institutions and NGOs.
- Develop courses for in-service education of teachers that will carry credits and linking these to promotions and benefits.
- Teacher performance assessment system.

Strategy for Dropouts

The NHS-II[20] conducted in 1998-99 observed that the main reasons for students dropping out include their not being interested in studies, high

20. National Health Survey-II.

private cost of education and the need for them to work, whether in own farms, business/households or outside. The reason held true for 75 per cent of dropouts.

The main challenges for education authorities at the Central, state and district levels are:

- Introduce innovative methods of providing education to students to suit their timing and interest. This can be done through building a positive environment that would include more attractive classroom designs, local contextual curriculum and more friendly evaluation techniques.
- Where the children are dropping out because of the need to work, the emphasis should be on involving the community in motivating the parents to bring their children back to school.
- For those children who have already dropped out, suitable alternative education systems such as bridge-courses, back-to-school camps should be provided.

Suggestions for Quality Improvement

- Curriculum reform: alignment of national needs with syllabus and textbook.
- Participate in international studies for capacity building and benchmarking of students.
- Promote competition: so that parental demand will create strong incentives to individual schools.
- Autonomy in local decision-making: so that individual schools will take actions to promote student achievement.
- An accountability system that identifies good school performance and leads to rewards based on this.
- Better incentives: that will lead to management keyed to student performance and that will promote strong schools with high quality teachers.

- Giving the poor parents cash grants[21] to that are linked the continued education of their children, hence helping to reduce poverty through accumulation of human capital.
- Control over schools and teachers should be transferred to local bodies, which have a direct interest in teacher performance.

Stage II: Gradual Expansion of Good Quality Schools to the Entire Population

Expansion of good quality schools to the entire population requires the following.

Community Participation

Decentralisation provides a clear correlation between the needs of people and the steps taken by government to meet these demands.

Planning from below and contextualised resource allocation for schools would be cost effective, ensure that the quality of the services is directly proportional to the degree of community control and supervision, and also leads to efficient distribution of schools especially in rural areas.

Planning, supervision and management of education would have to be through local bodies at the district, block and village levels. Efforts should be made for the social mobilisation of local communities for adult literacy campaigns and for promotion of primary education.

States should be encouraged to transfer the management of primary schools to *panchayat*/local bodies with special emphasis on:

- Encouraging community participation in promoting enrolment, retention and other aspects of education;
- Evolve a community-based monitoring system with full transparency;
- Community mobilisation through intensive micro-planning and school-mapping;
- Satellite-mapping of rural areas to provide basis for planning and resource allocation of schools.

21. A concept from Brazil and Mexico, though it requires a strong local administration to implement the programme.

Synergetic Partnership with the Private Sector

The task of providing basic education in a country with diverse conditions is so stupendous that it is difficult to expect the government sector alone to do this effectively. The private sector can contribute not only in monetary and material terms, but also in the form of expertise for improving quality through effective management of the system and the development of locally relevant teaching-learning materials. Some efforts in this direction have already been made by many states including Karnataka, which has a school adoption scheme. More collaborative efforts at the institutional level as well as in programme implementation should be designed to expand the private initiatives in elementary education.

Specifically, the following measures should be encouraged:

- Collaborative efforts between the government and the private sector to expand schools in rural areas.[22]
- Improve functioning of government schools in partnership with the private sector.
- Provide support to initiatives introduced by private schools.
- Encourage opening of private schools, without compromising on quality. Private schools are more cost effective. The unit cost per student is lower than public schools as a result of more market based teacher salaries. It would also lead to better attendance of teachers.
- Provide computer education to children, utilising the expertise and resources of the private sector.

Conclusion

This paper started with the search for the rationale that supports public and private investments in education. We have seen that education can improve agricultural productivity, enhance the status of women, reduce population growth rates, enhance environmental protection, and generally raise the standard of living through increased human productivity, which in turn, contributes to economic growth. The positive externalities arising

22. Approximately, 16.64 per cent villages of the country do not have facilities of primary schooling [*Source:* UNICEF (India)].

from education would require some significant degree of public investment. The social and political rationales, combined with the economic argument focused on poverty reduction and equity impacts of education, appear to tip the scales in favour of support for investments in education.

The paper then moved on to study South Korea's economic success and how education played a driving force behind the economic miracle. The paper also finds that systemic factors: lack of teachers, teacher absenteeism, irregular classes, overcrowded classrooms, and traditional methods of rote learning have diminished the quality of teaching/learning in India.

As part of a growing move toward greater accountability and transparency, political leaders and administrators have begun to raise the issues of motivation and commitment among teachers and local administrators. While the literacy rate of India has reported a sharp increase from 18.39 per cent in 1950-51 to 65.38 per cent in 2000-01, one-third of the population, or nearly 300 million people are still illiterate.[23] There are also problems related to high dropout rates, low participation of children from disadvantaged sections of society, inadequate school infrastructure, non-availability of teachers in remote rural, hilly and tribal areas, and inadequate allocation of resources on education to meet the expenditure. Teacher absence is more correlated with daily incentives to attend work: teachers are less likely to be absent at schools that are inspected regularly, that have better infrastructure, and that are closer to a paved road. To overcome the problem of teacher shortage and teacher absenteeism, the para-teacher scheme has been introduced in India.[24] Para-educators are generally members of the same community in which they teach, and therefore, share many of the experiences and cultural practices of their students, including their primary languages.

In Section 4, I have suggested a two-stage strategy for revamping the education system in India. With increased involvement of the private sector and the community in management and running of schools, it is expected that the drawbacks in the education system in India will be addressed soon.

---

23. Compared to other developing countries like Cameroon (68%), China (91%), Turkey (87%), Malaysia (89%) and Thailand (93%) [*Source:* UNESCO (2007)].

24. In India, the state of Rajasthan has successfully overcome the problem of both teacher shortage and teacher absenteeism through these para-teachers under the 'Shiksha Karmi Project'.

Annexures

Annex A-5.1

According to the giants of the IT industry,[25] India's predominant position in software outsourcing industry is because of the fact that a number of Indians can use English language much better than people from any other non-English speaking country.

India offers a good control over the quality of the software engineering and support to the companies that outsource to India. India-based outsourcing work drives many banking systems, airlines and insurance companies, thus creating a mutually beneficial association.

India has innovatively turned the challenge of excess population into the strength of human capital edge by utilising such manpower in the outsourcing industry to its advantage. To sustain this sort of momentum in the outsourcing industry, the top IT giants in India are making heavy investments in education, giving scholarships to the deserving students, sponsoring special projects and contributing huge R&D grants. They are also helping in updating curriculum in the colleges and universities to suit the fast paced developments in the outsourcing industry.

Annex A-5.2

Schultz (1961) claims that the improvement in the capabilities of the labour force will generally have a positive income effect. Workers not investing in education (UU) will have the same earnings throughout their career as higher paid employment requires education. Workers investing in education (TT) will receive higher wages in the long run. The line T″T″ adjusts the life income to take into account the loss of earning during education and the cost of education. It still exceeds the income of the uneducated worker (UU). A well-educated labour force will attract highly paid employment.

25. Tata Consultancy Services (TCS), Infosys, Wipro among others.

This means that a highly skilled labour force will receive higher wages in the long run than had they not invested in education as illustrated in Figure A-1. These higher earnings will increase the consumption possibilities of the labour force.

Figure A-1

Positive Relationship between Education and Earnings

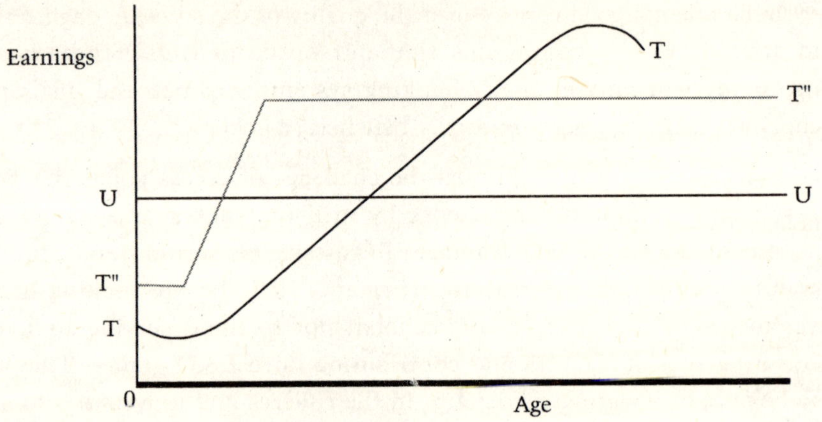

References

Books

Birdsall, Nancy, David Ross and Richard Sabot (1995). "Inequality and Growth Reconsidered: Lessons from East Asia", *World Bank Economic Review* 9(3): 477-508, September.

Brown, C.V. and Peter Jackson (1991). *Public Sector Economics*. 4th Edition. Wiley-Blackwell. pp.40,41.

Clawson, Patrick (1995). *The East Asian Miracle: Economic Growth and Public Policy.*

Coulombe, Serge (2004). "Intranational Trade Diversion, the Canada-United States Free Trade Agreement, and the L Curve", *The B.E. Journal of Economic Analysis & Policy* 1. Berkeley Electronic Press.

CSO (various years). *National Accounts Statistics*. New Delhi.

Dyson, Tim, Robert Cassen and Leela Visaria (eds.) (2004). "Chapter 7: Education and Literacy" in *Twenty-first Century India: Population, Economy, Human Development and the Environment.* UK: OUP. pp.130,132-135,138-157.

Friedman, Milton (1955). "The Role of Government in Education", in Robert A. Solo (ed.), *Economics and the Public Interest*. New Jersey: Rutgers University Press.

Fuente, Angel de la (n.d.). *Education and Economic Growth: A Quick Review of the Evidence and Some Policy Guidelines.* Universitat Autonòma de Barcelona.

Government of India (n.d.) *Census of India (2001) Statistics.*

Hanushek, Eric A. and D.D. Kimko (2000). "Schooling, Labor Force Quality, and the Growth of Nations", *American Economic Review* 90(5): 1184-1208.

Hanushek, Eric A. and Ludger Wobmann (2007). *Role of Education in Economic Growth.* World Bank/Washington/Etats-Unis. 2007/02.

Knight, John B. and Richard H. Sabot (1990). *Education, Production and Inequality: The East African Natural Experiment*. World Bank Research Publications.

Kuznets, Simon (1955). "Economic Growth and Income Inequality", *American Economic Review* 45:1-28.

O'Dubhslaine, Aibhistin (2006). "The White Paper on Education: A Failure to Invest" in *Student Economic Review* 20.

Planning Commission (1997). *Ninth Five Year Plan: 1997-2002.* New Delhi.

Pradhan, Basanta K. (2002). "Role of Education in Wage Inequality Change in India: 1988-97", Paper was presented at the Workshop on *Globalization and Income Distribution* organised by Center for Study of Globalization and Rationalization, University of Warwick, U.K., March 15-17.

Psacharopoulos, George (1981). "Education, Employment and Inequality in LDCs", *World Development* 9(1): 37-54, January. Elsevier.

———. (1994). "Returns to Investment in Education: A Global Update", *World Development* 22(9): 1325-43.

Ray, Debraj (1998). "Chapter 2: Per Capita Income and Human Development", in *Development Economics.* Princeton University Press. p.29.

———. (1998). "Chapter 2: Income Distribution in Developing Countries", in *Development Economics.* Princeton University Press. pp.21-25.

———. (1998). "Chapter 4: New Growth Theories: Total Factor Productivity and the East Asian Miracle", in *Development Economics*. Princeton University Press. pp.119-123.

———. (1998). "Chapter 7: Inequality and Development: Interconnections", in *Development Economics*. Princeton University Press. pp. 199-211.

———. (1998). "Chapter 9: From Economic Development to Population Growth", in *Development Economics*. Princeton University Press. pp.314-318.

———. (1998). "Chapter 14: Rural Credit Markets", in *Development Economics*. Princeton University Press.

Roy, Jayanta (n.d.) "Special acknowledgement", *India: A Nation on the Move... Still Some Catching Up To Do*.

Sen, Amartya (1973). "Chapter 4: Work Needs and Inequality", *in On Economic Inequality*. New York: Norton. (Expanded edition with a substantial annexe by James E. Foster and A. Sen, 1997). pp. 90-91, 99-100, 103.

———. (2000). "Asian Values and Economic Growth", *World Culture Report. http://www.unesco.org/culture/worldreport/html_eng/wcrb12.htm*. December 3.

Wu, Kin Bing and Amit Dhar (n.d.). *Secondary Education in India- Investing in the Future*. World Bank.

Websites

http://www.ibef.org/artdisplay.aspx?cat_id=391&art_id=5898

http://www.unicef.org/india/education_1551.htm

http://www.ungei.org/infobycountry/india_704.html

http://www.india-today.com/itoday/13101997/agenda2.html

http://www.education.nic.in/cd50years/g/Z/7A/0Z7A0201.htm

http://finance.indiamart.com/india_business_information/education.html

http://www.indiastat.com/India/ShowData.asp?secid=6370&ptid=0&level=1

http://www.thehindu.com/2005/04/12/stories/2005041204141000.htm

http://www.efytimes.com/efytimes/fullnews.asp?edid=17110

http://news.bbc.co.uk/1/hi/world/south_asia/4994590.stm

6 The Impact of Education Expenditure on Economic Growth of Bangladesh

An Error Correction and Causality Approach

Mezbah Uddin

Introduction

The education sector remains key priority sector for Bangladesh since its Independence. Bangladesh's public policy and expenditures have consistently been directed towards education and sharp increase in education spending that mainly occurred in mid 90s have been sustained. And education by far, has been the largest recipient of budgetary funds in combined annual development programme (ADP) and recurrent budgets (IMF, 2004). Giving consideration to Bangladesh's intensity of poverty and vulnerability to calamities of all sources, its education outcomes are highly impressive, particularly in ensuring wide coverage and access to primary, and to some degree, secondary education (IMF/World Bank, 2003). The achievement of gender parity and urban-rural parity in shortest period of time is notable. In addition, gross enrolment rate for primary education stood at 94.3 per cent for females and 94.1 per cent for males in the year 2006. Though increase in government expenditures led to increase in enrolment, however it has not been matched by improvements in the quality of education. Quality remains unsatisfactory because of the poor quality of education inputs and learning processes, weak accountability and incentive mechanism, and inadequate check and balances for teachers and administrators. In this paper, a time-series analysis has been conducted by using the augmented Solow growth model to analyse the effect of increase in government expenditure per head on real GDP both in the long and short run, and the policy implications in relation to the result, that is needed to be taken for improvement in the quality of education.

Literature Review

The linkages between investment in human capital and economic growth, in the indirect way, have been measured by many researches including Appaih and McMahon, 2002; Barro, 1997; Carnoy, 1975; Lall, 1990; Schultz, 1961 etc. The traditional Solow (1956) growth model did not directly measure the role of human capital, however, he concluded that, among the residual 87.5 per cent, much of it was contributed to human capital. And, as a result many researchers developed augmented Solow models, which contained human capital as a regressor in explaining economic growth.

Few versions of the augmented models where direct effect of human capital on economic growth are being estimated can be found in Romer (1990), Barro and Sala-I-Martin (1995), Knight *et al.* (1993), Benhabib and Spiegel (1994) and Lucas (2002) in the existing literature. Using different estimation technique and inferences, this author did not find human capital to be statistically significant. Mankiw *et al.* (1992) after conducting a study in the context of the developing countries stated that, "particularly for the developing countries, investment in human capital also becomes more quantitatively important when a more open trading environment and a better public infrastructure in place." In relation to this, Judson (1998) used cross-country growth decomposition and showed that the correlation of human capital with capital accumulation and GDP growth is not significant in countries with poor allocations but is significant and positive in countries with better allocations. Moreover, in the context of Mankiw-Romer hypothesis, as many developing countries now-a-days are opening their markets to global competition and focusing on building knowledge infrastructure, many studies like Bassanini *et al.* (2000), and Bassanini and Scarpetta (2002), by using OECD country data showed that human capital is statistically significant to growth.

In search of linkage between human capital and growth recently, many studies have been conducted. Among them, Temple (1999) in his cross country study found mix correlation between human capital investment and growth. In the study for some country, educational attainment seemed to be positively related to growth, and for some country no relations have been determined. In addition, Oketch (2006) in his study on

African nations, identifies two way links between human resource development produced by formal schooling and economic growth and between investment in physical capital and growth. The study concluded that sources of labour productivity growth are high investment in physical capital and human capital. This converges with the hypothesis that both human and physical investments are necessary for growth in Africa. Keller (2006) in his research on analysing the effects of primary, secondary and higher education on per capita growth, by using world wide panel since 1960s recommended that raising enrolment rates and prioritising public expenditures toward lower education stages while ensuring that expenditure per student keep up with increases in student cohorts. Moreover, Vinod and Kaushik (2007) used human capital in the form of education to explain GDP growth in the augmented Solow models. The study used time series and panel regressions for data on a group of 18 large developing countries for the period 1982-2001. Research result showed that in all country cases, human capital was statistically a significant factor to explain GDP growth.

Furthermore, with regard to directly estimating the impact of public expenditure on education and economic growth, Musila and Belassi (2004) carried out a study using time-series technique to estimate relationship between government education expenditure per worker and economic growth in Uganda during period 1965-1999. The empirical result showed that education expenditure per worker has a positive and significant impact on economic growth both in the long run and in the short run. The cointegration estimate showed that a 1 per cent increase in average education expenditure per worker will increase output by 0.6 per cent in the long run.

Government Expenditure Pattern on the Education Sector of Bangladesh

Most government expenditure on education is directed to basic education—primary and mass education and secondary education (see Table A-6.8). However, during the past decade there has been a significant shift within basic education from the primary to secondary level. For example, primary education's share of the recurrent education budget decreased from 48.5 per cent to 39.5 per cent over the course of the 90s while secondary education's share increased from 36.8 per cent to 48.4 per cent. While pressure to accommodate the increasing demand for continuing education from the cohort that finished primary school contributed to this trend, it also reflected a policy shift to widen the provision of secondary education, particularly to the girls. The expansion of primary education took place both within and outside the public sector, while the rapid expansion of secondary education occurred mainly through partnerships with private providers. There was a large expansion in primary schools in Bangladesh in the early 1990s, and by 1996 there were 37,710 government primary schools (GPS) and 19,683 registered non-govermment primary schools (RNGPS) operating in the country. The large expansion in primary enrolment eventually resulted in increased demand for continuing into the secondary level. To achieve rapid expansion of secondary enrolment, the Government opted for even wider partnership with the private sector, which allowed lower per-pupil costs. As a result, today more than 95 per cent of secondary schools are non-government, with a unit cost per pupil of $16, compared with $68 in government secondary schools. This difference in unit cost is due to lower teacher-student ratios as well as lower teacher salaries (in non-government secondary schools, the government pays 90 per cent of the base teacher salary; see World Bank, 2000c).

In assessing the equity in public sector spending on education, *Bangladesh Public Expenditure Review* (2003) concluded that public spending on education has achieved equity in terms of gender. Moreover, public primary education expenditures are strongly pro-poor. The key factor driving the pro-poor distribution of primary education spending is the age composition, which more than offsets the lower enrolment rates among the poor. In addition, there is considerable scope to improve the pro-poor focus of government expenditures, even at the primary level. This is especially important given the high dependence on households for education financing and the inability of poor households to match the contributions of the wealthier households. And in the recent *Mid-term Budgetary Framework* (MTBF) for the financial year 2008-2010, in primary and secondary education, allocations will be directed towards improving the quality of education. This will require increased spending on teacher training, on the preparation and supply of pedagogical materials, and on improving the educational infrastructure. Priority will continue to be given to improving access to education at all levels, particularly for female students and students from poor families, with further improvements being made by the successful programmes for student stipends, education allowances and targeted grants. Provision for expanding of merit based scholarships both at the primary and secondary levels will be included in this budget. Reducing dropout, particularly at the higher secondary level and particularly among female students still remains a priority objective.

Econometric Analysis

The Model

The model used in this paper is based on the following aggregate production function

$$Y_t = AK^{\alpha t} L^{\beta t} H^{\gamma t} \quad (1)$$

Where Y_t is real income (i.e., real GDP), K^t is physical capital, L^t is the number of workers, H^t is the total amount of human capital, A is the technology parameter, t is the observation subscript, and α, β and γ are parameters to be estimated from the model.

Human capital is defined as follows:

$$H_t = E_t L_t \quad (2)$$

Where E_t is the average level of education per worker. In this study, it is assumed that the average level of education per worker is directly proportional to the average expenditure on education per head. By substituting equations (2) into (1) obtains

$$Y_t = AK^{\alpha t} L^{\beta t} E^{\gamma t} \quad (3)$$

From equation (3), the econometric model will be developed to assess the impact of government education per head on economic growth. Theoretically from the literature, positive signs are expected for the coefficients α, β and γ.

The Empirical Model

The aim of this paper is to estimate the effect of changes in government education expenditure on output. The model in equation (3) enables us to relate output to education expenditures. Using logarithmic transformation, the growth of output is a function of growth in capital stock, employment and average education expenditure per head. In this study, no restrictions is being imposed with regard to the returns to scale (i.e., increasing or constant or decreasing returns to scale) on the parameters of the production function. Rather, we leave it to the data to determine the nature of returns-to-scale. The econometric model used in the empirical analysis in logarithmic transformation becomes the following:

$$LOGRGDP_t = \beta_0 + \alpha\, LOGK_t + \beta\, LOGL_t + \gamma\, LOGE_t + e_t \qquad (4)$$

where

LOGRGDP = log(Y) is the logarithm of output (i.e., real GDP), LOGK = log(K) is the logarithm of gross fixed capital formation, LOGL = log(L) is the logarithm of employment, LOGE = log(E) is the logarithm of government education expenditures per head; α, β, γ and y are the parameters to be estimated. And e is the error term.

Regression model in equation (4) is estimated using annual data from the period 1980 to 2005. The data of real GDP, gross fixed capital formation and employment are collected from World Development Indicator CD-ROM and education expenditure per head data are collected from *Bangladesh Statistical Yearbooks* published by Bangladesh Bureau of Statistics.

Cointegration Test

As the estimation of the regression model will be time series data, it becomes a primary concern whether the variables are stationary. Therefore, the study needs to test for integration and cointegration of the variables in the model in order to determine the appropriate estimation approach. Technically, the components of an n-dimensional vector of time series jct, (xlt, x2t, ..., xnt) are said to be integrated of order d (denoted Xt~I(d)) if after differencing d times have stationary invertible non-deterministic ARMA representation. Using this definition, we can classify a stationary time series as being an 1(0) process while a non-stationary time series will be an I(k) where k is a positive integer which depends on the order of integration (Musila and Belassi, 2004).

Two series, say, yt and xt, are cointegrated of order (d, b) denoted CI(d, b), if they are both 1(1); and there is a linear combination of them which is l(d-b) where b>0. The definition applies to several series (Engle and Granger, 1987).

In this study, the nature of stationarity and the order of integration are being obtained by applying the augmented Dickey-Fuller (ADF) unit root test and the order of cointegration of a vector or a time series by applying Johansen's Cointegration Tests.

Stationary Test and Cointegration Test Results

Table A-6.3 reports the ADF test results—from there it can be seen that all the variables are I(1) and residuals are I(0). It is to be noted that, econometrics literature suggests that if the variables are non-stationary, and if their residuals are found to be stationary, linear combinations of these variables can be found to be stationary and cointegrated in the long run. In order to do the cointegration test, in this study, Johansen's cointegration test is being applied and results of the test are reported in Table A-6.4. From the table, it can be seen that under all the criteria of no deterministic trend, no deterministic trend (restricted constant), linear deterministic trend and linear deterministic trend (restricted constant), at least one cointegrating equation was found in all cases. So, the above tests indicate that there exists a long term cointegrating relationship between the variables log(Y), log(K), log(L) and log(E).

Regression result:

OLS estimation result of equation 4 shows that

$$LOGRGDP_t = 8.25 + .3639\ LOGK_t + .6120\ LOGL_t + .1104\ LOGE_t + e$$

The estimated long run equilibrium equation indicates that all the coefficients except log(L) are found to be statistically significant at 5 and 10 per cent significance level. Moreover, the coefficients are positively signed, as expected from the theoretical perspective. From the long run analysis, it is seen that 1 per cent increase in education expenditure per head raises output by 0.11 per cent, 1 per cent increase in investment raises output by 0.36 per cent, 1 per cent increase in employment raises output by 0.61 per cent (See Table A-6.2).

Causality between Education and Growth

Though the endogenous growth theory suggests that increase in human capital leads to growth, arguments have been put up by economists as whether increase in education expenditure causes growth or growth causes increase in education expenditure. And as a result of that, many researchers like Hicks and Kubisch (1984), Looney (1987), Brempong (1998) and Blis and Klenow (2000) tried to find out the causality between education and growth. So, to test the causality in the case of Bangladesh, Granger Causality test is being conducted, and the results are reported in Table A-6.4. From the table, it can be seen that education does not cause growth; null hypothesis is being rejected at 5 per cent significance level. So, from the test it is found that in the case of Bangladesh, it is education expenditure which causes economic growth.

The Error Correction Model

In this part of the paper, an error correction model, which is also known as short term model will be estimated, to see whether the model has the tendency to converge to its long run cointegrating position. To find that, the following model will be estimated:

$$\Delta(LOGRGDP)_{t-1} = \beta_0 + \alpha\Delta(LOGK_{t-3}) + \beta\Delta LOGL_{t-3} + \Pi\Delta LOGE_{t-4} + \Omega EC_{t-1} + e$$

In the above, EC_{t-1} is one period lag of the residual of the cointegrating equation, which will capture the deviation of the observed value of the natural logarithm of real GDP from its long run equilibrium path. If Ω is found to be statistically significant, then it tells us what proportion of disequilibrium in real GDP is corrected in the next period.

After estimating the model, results showed that:

$$\Delta(LOGRGDP)_{t-1} = \underset{(3.573)}{9.38} + \underset{(.312)}{.489}\Delta(LOGK_{t-3}) + \underset{(1.831)}{.251}\Delta LOGL_{t-3} + \underset{(1.782)}{.047}\Delta LOGE_{t-4} - \underset{(-1.549)}{.057}EC_{t-1} + e$$

The estimated long run equilibrium equation indicates that all the coefficients are found to be statistically significant at 5 and 10 per cent significance level. Moreover, it shows that the Ω, which is negatively signed, shows that change in the value of the natural log of the real GDP depends inversely on the past error, and the coefficient value is significant. As Π captures the short term position of the log(E), the estimate also shows that 1 per cent increase in the average education expenditure per worker will lead to about 0.047 per cent increase in the output in the short run. In addition, it is also seen from the above model that log(K), log(L) and log(E) is 3, 3 and 4 period lag model consecutively. These optimum lags have been chosen by using Akaike Info Criterion (AIC) (See Table A-6.6).

Policy Recommendations

From the econometric analysis, we see that increase in the education expenditure per head leads to increase in the economic growth. As we have seen from the public expenditure review and from the MTBF that education sector is still among the key priority of the government budget, given the country is a developing country. However, quality remains unsatisfactory because of the poor quality of education inputs and learning processes, weak accountability and incentive mechanism, and inadequate check and balances for teachers and administrators. So, key policy implications that can be prescribed is not only to increase expenditure but also take steps to increase quality of education. Many of the strategies in National Education Policy (2000) are technically fine. But, among them policy like improving the quality of primary education should be given more priority than extending primary education from five to eight. Thus, policy priority and sequencing in this regard in imperative. And, rebalancing expenditures on labour and non-labour teaching inputs, increasing allocation for teaching and learning material might help to raise the quality of education. In addition, government should extend the programme of cooperation with the NGOs and private sector. Furthermore, management of primary and secondary education should be decentralised to the district and thana levels, while the Central government's role in basic education should be confined to the provision of technical services, including transparently allocating resources among districts, setting standards, setting sector policy and curricula, conducting national assessments at regular intervals, conducting research, and disseminating research results and other education-related information to local governments and to the general public.

Conclusion

In this paper, relations between education expenditure per head and economic growth have been estimated with the augmented Solow growth model. And from the econometric analysis, it is observed that increase in education expenditure per head lead to increased output both in the short run and long run. But, increase in the education expenditure alone will not increase output; for rapid increase in the growth of the country, quality of the education must be improved, so that the country can gain from the government expenditure even more and it can quickly transform to a country where human resources are skillful.

References

Appaih, E.N. and W.W. McMahon (2002). "The Social Outcomes of Education and Feedbacks on Growth in Africa", *Journal of Development Studies* 38: 27-68.

Barro, R.J. and Xavier Sala-I-Martin (1995). *Economic Growth*. New York: McGraw Hill.

Barro, R.T. (1997). "The Determinants of Economic Growth: A Cross Country Empirical Study", Lionel Robbins Memorial Lectures. Cambridge MA: The MIT Press.

Bassanini, A. and S. Scarpetta (2002). "Does Human Capital Matter for Growth in OECD Countries? A Pooled Mean Group Approach", *Economics Letters* 74: 399-405.

———. (2001). "The Driving Forces of Economic Growth Panel Data: Evidence for the OECD Countries", *OECD Economic Studies* 33: 9-56.

Bassinini A., S. Scarpetta and I. Visco (2000). "Knowledge, Technology and Growth: Recent Evidence from OECD Countries", *National Bank of Belgium Working Paper* No. 6.

BBS (various years). *Bangladesh Statistical Yearbook*. Bangladesh Bureau of Statistics.

Benhabib, J. and M. Spiegel (1994). "The Role of Human Capital in Economic Development: Evidence from Aggregate Cross-Country Data", *Journal of Monetary Economics* 34(2): 143-74.

Blis, M. and P. Klenow (2000). "Does Schooling Cause Growth?", *American Economic Review* 90: 1160-83.

Carnoy, M. (1975). "The Role of Education in Strategy for Social Change", *Comparative Education Review* 19: 393-402.

Hicks, N.L. and A. Kubisch (1984). "Cutting Government Expenditures in LDCs", *Finance and Development* 21(3): 37-39.

IMF (International Monetary Fund) (2004). *Public-Private Partnerships*. Fiscal Affairs Department (In consultation with other departments the World Bank and the Inter American Development Bank).

IMF/World Bank (2003). *Joint Staff Assessment of Bangladesh*. IPRSP. June 26.

Judson, R. (1998). "Economic Growth and Investment in Education: How Allocation Matters", *Journal of Economic Growth* 3: 337-359.

Keller, Katarina R. (2006). "Investment in Primary, Secondary, and Higher Education and the Effects on Economic Growth", *Contemporary Economic Policy* 24: 18-34.

Knight, M., N. Loayza and D. Villanueva (1993). "Testing the Neoclassical Theory of Economic Growth", *IMF Staff Papers* 40: 512-41.

Lall, S. (1990). "Human Resource Development and Industrialization", *Human Development and International Strategies for the 90's*. pp.129-57.

Looney, R.E. (1987). "The Impact of Political Change, Debt Servicing and Fiscal Deficits on Argentinian Budgetary Priorities", *Journal of Economic Studies* 14(3): 23-40.

Lucas, R. (2002). "On the Mechanics of Economic Development", *Journal of Monetary Economics* 22: 3-42.

Mankiw, G.N., D. Romer, and.D.N. Weil (1992). "A Contribution to the Empirics of Economic Growth", *Quarterly Journal of Economics* 107: 407-437.

Musila, Jacob Wanjila and Walid Belassi (2004). "The Impact of Education Expenditures on Economic Growth in Uganda: Evidence From The Time Series Data", *The Journal of Developing Areas* 18: 31-40.

Oketch, Moses O. (2006). "Determinants of Human Capital Formation and Economic Growth of African Countries", *Economics of Education Review* 25: 554-564.

Romer, P.M. (1990). "Endogeneous Technological Change", *Journal of Political Economy* 98: 71-102.

Temple, Jonathan R.W. (1999). "A Positive Effect of Human Capital on Growth", *Economics Letters* 65(1): 131-34, October.

Theodore W. Schultz (1960). "Capital Formation by Education", *Journal of Political Economy* 68: 571. University of Chicago Press.

Vinod, D., Hrishikesh and Surendra K. Kaushik (2007). "Human Capital and Economic Growth: Evidence From The Developing Countries", *The American Economist* 51: 29-39.

Annexures

Table A-6.1

Dependent Variable: LNRGDP

Variable	*Coefficient*	*Std. Error*	*t-Statistic*	*Prob.*
C	8.250295	9.10623	0.906006	0.3747
LNK	0.363919	0.138799	2.621916	0.0156
LNL	0.612012	0.703611	0.869816	0.3938
LNEDU	0.110405	0.046671	-2.365584	0.0272
R-squared	0.988267		Mean dependent var	28.01423
Adjusted R-squared	0.986667		S.D. dependent var	0.334591

Table A-6.2

Method: Least Squares

Variable	*Coefficient*	*Std. Error*	*t-Statistic*	*Prob.*
S.E. of regression	0.038635	Akaike info criterion		-3.52868
Sum squared resid	0.032839	Schwarz criterion		-3.335127
Log likelihood	49.87285	F-statistic		617.6741
Durbin-Watson stat	0.478557	Prob(F-statistic)		0

Table A-6.3

ADF Test of Stationarity

(P Values are being Quoted)

Variable	*Level (intercept)*	*Level (intercept & trend)*	*Difference (intercept)*	*Difference (intercept & trend)*	*Order of Integration*
LNK	0.2688	0.4965	0**	0**	I(1)
LNL	0.8174	0.1017	0.02**	0**	I(1)
LNEDU	0.2631	0.9921	0.0072**	0.0048**	I(1)
E	0.011	0.004	NA	NA	I(0)

Note: ** indicates that the variable is significant at 5 and 10% significance level.

Table A-6.4

Johansen's Cointegration Test

	Hypothesised No. of CE(s)	*Prob.*	*Decision*
No Deterministic Trend	None	0.0147	At least one cointegrating equation
	At most 1	0.0449	
	At most 2	0.1261	
	At most 3	0.0354	
No Deterministic Trend (restricted constant)	None	0.0004	At least one cointegrating equation
	At most 1	0.0342	
	At most 2	0.0875	
	At most 3	0.2934	
Linear Deterministic Trend	None	0.0063	1 cointegrating equation
	At most 1	0.2666	
	At most 2	0.7755	
	At most 3	0.9644	
Linear Deterministic Trend (restricted)	None	0.0135	1 cointegrating equation
	At most 1	0.2275	
	At most 2	0.5554	
	At most 3	0.7073	

Table A-6.5

Pairwise Granger Causality Tests

	P Value
lnGDP does not Granger causes lnEDU	0.61979
lnEDU does not Granger causes lnGDP	0.0355

Table A-6.6

Regression Result

Dependent Variable LNRGDP *Variables*	*Coefficients*
C	9.38
DLNKt-3	0.48919**
DLNLt-3	0.251**
DLNEDUt-4	0.047**
Ect-1	-0.05734

Table A-6.7

Education Expenditures by the Govt. of Bangladesh (Revenue Budget and ADP) in TK

Year	*Education Expenditures*
1980	2984963014
1981	3255876915
1982	3595643837
1983	4431779612
1984	5312404438
1985	6812836576
1986	7836556356
1987	9500574009
1988	10440876075
1989	12611985192
1990	12381546947
1991	15010013859
1992	21348543832
1993	25739842359
1994	33955868664
1995	33538930272
1996	36754373946
1997	42306000000
1998	47070000000
1999	53208000000
2000	54457000000
2001	58134000000
2002	64192000000
2003	66361000000
2004	70896000000
2005	72329360760

Table A-6.8

Bangladesh—Public Education Expenditure by Level of Education

Fiscal Year	As a Percentage of GDP	Percentage Distribution					
		Primary	Non-formal	Technical Education	Secondary and Higher	University	Other Higher
Revenue Expenditure							
1991-92	1.14	48.5	36.8	2.4	8.5		37
1992-93	1.34	455	40.6	2.3	7.9		3.7
1993-94	1.30	47.0	41 1	22	79		1.8
1995-96	1.30	44.2	42.5	2.1	8.0		3.3
1996-97	1.30	43.5	42.9	2.1	7.9		3.6
1997-98	1.39	42.6	46.0	1.5	7.3		2.7
1998-99	135	40.4	47.6	1.4	7.0		3.7
1999-2000	1.37	39.5	48.4	1.4	8.0		2.7
Development Expenditure							
1991-92	0.21	62.1	1.5	10.7	3.3	10.1	0.84
1992-93	0.47	66.7	1.2	20.4	2.1	7.1	49.2
1993-94	1.06	56.5	2.3	34.1	0.4	0.7	5.9
1995-96	0.83	57.6	2.3	34.9	0.4	3.0	33.4
1997-98	0.73	46.0	6.9	33.7	1.6	9.9	5.1
1998-99	0.80	46.7	9.2	29.5	3.1	1.7	5.9
1999-2000	0.84	49.2	5.9	33.4	5.1	5.9	0.4

7

Investment in the Social Sectors: Necessities and Outcomes

In the Context of SAARC and Nepal

Nabaraj Gautam

General Background

Economic growth with social equity has become the main theme of development with the beginning of the 21st century. The world is now concentrating on the poverty reduction agenda by widening its dimension. Today, poverty not only incorporates income, consumption and human development—education, health and sanitation—but also empowerment and social security against vulnerability.

Poverty in rural areas is widespread and more persistent, which accounts nearly four-fifths of the world's poor (IFAD, 2002). In the developing countries, about 69 per cent of the rural population subsists below nationally defined minimum levels of income and consumption. Asia holds about one-third commonality of the rural area in a state of poverty. Nearly half of the world's poor live in South Asia, a region that accounts for roughly 30 per cent of the world's population. South Asia's poverty is not just feminised, but caste and identity based as well. Amongst the poor, it is women, so called low castes and minority communities that constitute the majority. This has profound implications for the people of this region and indicators show that while the gross domestic product may have grown, inequality has grown alongside it. This has resulted in "opening up" of all these economies through privatisation of services that were earlier under the state control in conjunction with the general withdrawal of the state from social and public sectors. Even in a country like India, which is stated to be an economic powerhouse, in spite of food self-sufficiency at the national level, food security cannot be ensured to vast number of people.

Introduction

South Asian states remain focused on the state security rather than people's security. They emphasise on territorial integrity and sovereignty that they historically inherited from colonial rule. Now, it is time to concentrate on state activities, investing in social sectors which uplift the life of poor and backward.

Table 7.1

Status of South Asian Countries

HDI Rank	*Country*	*HDI Index*	*Life Expectancy at Birth*	*GDP Per Capita*	*Life Expectancy Index*	*Education Index*
99	Sri Lanka	0.743	71.6	4595	0.776	0.814
100	Maldives	0.741	64.0	5061	0.701	0.862
128	India	0.619	63.7	3452	0.645	0.620
133	Bhutan	0.579	64.7	-	0.662	0.485
136	Pakistan	0.551	64.6	2370	0.659	0.466
140	Bangladesh	0.547	63.1	2053	0.635	0.503
142	Nepal	0.534	62.6	1550	0.626	0.518

Source: HDR 2007/08, UNDP.

The SAARC countries' social sector indicators are very poor. Among the South Asian countries, Nepal's position is very alarming. Investment in social sectors and its outcome is very low due to different constraints.

Status of Nepalese Economy

As per Census 2001, the population of Nepal was 23.2 million and the average annual growth rate of population was estimated to be 2.24 per cent. The literacy rate went up to 53.7 per cent as per the Census. According to the *Nepal Living Standards Survey, 2003/04*, absolute poverty has decreased by 11 per cent from 42 to 31 in the last 10 years. The reasons for such decrease in poverty are: wage increases in the agricultural and non-agricultural sectors, increasing urbanisation, increasing investment in social services, the rise in the economically active population sector, and large amount of remittances entering the country. However, during the same period, the Gini Coefficient has increased from 0.34 to 0.41, in other words, the difference between the rich and poor is seen to

Table 7.2

The Current Macroeconomic Indicators of Nepalese Economy

Sector	*Year*		
	2000	*2005*	*2006*
Population, Total	24.4 million	27.1 million	27.7 million
Population Growth (annual %)	2.3	2.0	1.9
Life Expectancy at Birth, Total (years)	60.5	62.7	..
Fertility Rate, Total (births per woman)	4.0	3.5	..
Mortality Rate, Infant (per 1,000 live births)	69.0	56.0	..
Mortality Rate, Under-5 (per 1,000)	95.0	74.0	..
Births attended by Skilled Health Staff (% of total)	11.9	..	18.7
Malnutrition Prevalence, Weight for Age (% of children under 5)	..	..	45.0
Immunisation, Measles (% of children ages 12-23 months)	71.0	74.0	..
Prevalence of HIV, Total (% of population ages 15-49)	..	0.5	..
Primary Completion Rate, Total (% of relevant age group)	65.6	74.7	76.0
School Enrolment, Primary (% gross)	116.5	113.3	126.0
School Enrolment, Secondary (% gross)	35.3	45.7	43.1
Ratio of Girls to Boys in Primary and Secondary Education (%)	77.1	89.5	93.3
GNI, Atlas Method (current US$)	5.6 billion	7.4 billion	8.1 billion
GNI Per Capita, Atlas Method (current US$)	230.0	270.0	290.0
GDP (current US$)	5.5 billion	7.4 billion	8.1 billion
GDP Growth (annual %)	6.1	2.7	1.9
Inflation, GDP Deflator (annual %)	4.6	4.6	7.2
Agriculture, Value Added (% of GDP)	39.6	38.2	39.5
Industry, Value Added (% of GDP)	21.5	21.0	21.1
Services, etc., Value Added (% of GDP)	38.9	40.8	39.5
Exports of Goods and Services (% of GDP)	23.3	16.1	18.6
Imports of Goods and Services (% of GDP)	32.4	32.6	37.7
Gross Capital Formation (% of GDP)	24.3	28.9	30.3
Revenue, Excluding Grants (% of GDP)	10.6	12.8	12.4
Cash Surplus/Deficit (% of GDP)	..	-1.2	-1.9
Time Required to Start a Business (days)	..	31.0	31.0
Workers' Remittances and Compensation of Employees, Received (US$)	111.0 million	1.2 billion	1.2 billion

Source: *www.worldbank.org*, November 2007.

have increased. Similarly, according to the Human Development Index, 2007, although Nepal's human development has grown to 0.534 from the previous year's 0.527, Nepal still remains as the country with least human development in South Asia. Nepal remains on the 142th position in the global human development.

Nepal's economic growth rate remained below 5.0 per cent in the last six years because of the country's precarious economic circumstances. In FY 2005/06, Nepal's GDP growth rate stood at a meagre 3.3 per cent of which the agricultural sector's growth was 1.1 per cent and the non-agricultural sector's 4.6 per cent. The growth rate further decelerated in FY 2006/07 to 2.5 per cent (*Economic Survey, 2007*). Low economic growth rate, growing unemployment and intensifying poverty culminating in a vicious circle of low income, low savings and low investment have led the country to a low level equilibrium trap.

The prevailing macroeconomic indicators of Nepal show that there is no consistent growth in population and GDP as well. There is a mismatch between the growth in population and growth in per capita income. The increase in population is higher than the per capita income which is the major cause of increase in inequality, lower living standards and high rate of hunger and deprivation.

Social Sector Investment Pattern in South Asia

The government spending in the public sector to promote and foster the social services around South Asia is increasing. Development and extension of every sector of social services is a prerequisite for overall development of any country. Entire objective of social development can be achieved through the production of efficient, disciplined, educated and healthy citizens. It has become imperative to take firm steps for ensuring easy access to education, health services, housing, decontamination and free drinking water to all classes of people and individuals of the country. Therefore, for social development, there is need for improvement in management of economic and human resources of all governmental (public) and non-governmental (private) machinery involved in this sector to ensure and sustain easy access to education, health, housing, pure drinking water by people of all classes and regions. And also for fulfilling commitments made in international forums regarding rights of children and senior citizens of the country.

Table 7.3

Priorities in Public Spending in South Asia

Country	*Public Expenditure on Health (% of GDP)*	*Public Expenditure in Education (% of GDP)*		*Military Expenditure (% of GDP)*	
	2004	1991	2002-2005	1990	2005
Sri Lanka	2.0	3.2	-	2.1	2.6
India	0.9	3.7	3.8	3.2	2.8
Bhutan	3.0	-	5.6	-	-
Pakistan	0.4	2.6	2.3	5.8	3.5
Bangladesh	0.9	1.5	2.5	1.0	1.0
Nepal	1.5	2.0	3..4	0.9	2.1

Source: HDR 2007/08, UNDP.

A Brief History of Social Sector Investment in Nepal

Investment in social services is categorised as public investment and private investment. Public investment plays the key role in advancing the social sector services. The formal investment from government to social services started from the beginning of systematic planning. Till now, Nepal has passed through 10 formal planning periods under different political stages. In the First and Second plan period, the social sector services were not formally recognised, rather the plan objective was to build up the physical infrastructure such as roads, telecommunications, industry etc.

The formal introduction of private investment in social sector was identified during the Eighth Plan period (1993-1997). During the Eighth Plan period, efforts were made to transform Nepalese economy from a regulated economy to open market-oriented economy. It helped to achieve 7.5 per cent annual growth in non-agricultural sector; its share rose from 51 per cent to 59 per cent of overall GDP during the period. Unfortunately, the efforts of the private sector were confined to the urban areas only. As a result, poverty in Kathmandu declined to 4 per cent; however, these early reforms did not help in reducing rural poverty. During the Ninth Plan (1997-2002), various efforts were made to increase the participation of the private sector in the economy. Private sector development and investment has been an important part of the Ninth Plan strategy. Although some areas such as hydropower, airlines, health, education and tourism initially attracted substantial private investment, the overall investment climate was affected by weak domestic demand, political instability, poor security situation created by violence, and bad governance created by administrative hurdles.

During the Tenth Plan (2002-2007), economic growth rate was estimated to be 6.2 per cent per annum under normal scenario and 4.3 per cent under constrained environment. During this period, participation and development of the private sector toward social services was accorded a top priority. The private sector was developed as a focal point for all the economic activities and the role of the government was limited to a facilitator, policy formulating body with strong monitoring, supervision and follow up. Various policies were devised in order to promote the active participation of the private sector in almost all the economic areas like infrastructure, road, transport and communication, industry, tourism, supply, trade, education, health, sanitation and finance.

Social Sector Indicators and its Analysis in SAARC

The social sector comprises different aspects and dimensions of the whole economy. Broadly speaking, the social sector includes education, health services, water and sanitation, social security and targeted areas. The status and dimension of social sector is briefly discussed below.

Education

South Asia has achieved greater success in improvement of education system and literacy rates. Having the greater endowment on the productive resources, these days most of the South Asian countries export high level skilled and unskilled manpower to the foreign countries. Specially, in the sector of information technology, India, a power house of South Asia is leading the way. A recent data shows that the rate of youth literacy is increasing satisfactorily.

Table 7.4

Literacy Rate and Enrolment Rate in South Asia

Adult Literacy Rate (% aged 15 and older)		Youth Literacy Rate		Net Primary Enrolment Rate	
1985-1994	1995-2005	1985-1994	1995-2005	1991	2005
47.6	59.7	60.7	74.7	-	87

Source: HDR 2007/08, UNDP.

What is Investment in Education?

Education has both investment and consumption components. Economists have increasingly recognised that education is predominantly an investment, which provides future satisfaction or enhances the future earnings of a person as a productive agent. Investment is defined as an economic activity that forgoes consumption today with an eye to increasing output or income in the future. Alternative approaches to educational investment may broadly be classified as follows:

- *The social demand approach*, which seeks to maximise the social welfare and social demand in determining public expenditure on education.
- *The manpower requirement approach*, in which educational investment in different types and levels is guided by human capital requirements of an economy. A common feature of this approach is the projection of manpower and trainings needs, usually between five years (medium-term) and 20 years (long-term) into the future.
- *The rate of return approach,* which stems from an essential concern with the scarcity of resources and their efficient allocation among investment alternatives. This approach relies on labour market signals and cost-benefit assessments to identify the priorities, and seeks to push educational expenditure in different types and levels to the point where marginal rates of return on investment in all types and levels of education are equalised. The estimates of private and social rates of return guide the policy makers to decide upon public subsidies by level of education and a corresponding expectation of cost-saving by households.

The public spending on education sector of South Asian region shows the trends of growing investment in education sector.

Table 7.5

Public Spending on Education

HDI Rank	*Country*	*Public Expenditure on Education*			
		As a % of GDP		*As a % of Total Government Expenditure*	
		1991	*2002-2005*	*1991*	*2002-2005*
99	Sri Lanka	3.2	-	8.4	-
100	Maldives	7.0	7.1	16.0	15.0
128	India	3.7	3.8	12.2	10.7
133	Bhutan	-	5.6	-	12.9
136	Pakistan	2.6	2.3	7.4	10.9
140	Bangladesh	1.5	2.5	10.3	14.2
142	Nepal	2.0	3.4	8.5	14.9

Source: HDR 2007/08, UNDP.

The public spending pattern of South Asian countries in education is increasing to foster economic growth and eradicate rural poverty. Education is one of the major component for measuring the level of economic growth and government role towards the backward and poor class of the society. Economic growth is directly associated with education. These days the South Asian countries are focusing to increase the school enrolment rate and modernise the education system. Developing countries like Nepal, Bhutan, Pakistan and Bangladesh are allocating large portion of budgetary investment on education.

The State of Education in Nepal

Education is one of the major sectors in which Nepal has made remarkable progress over the past 50 years. It has been one of the most rewarding fruits of democracy. Impressive gains have been made on all fronts of formal education, from early childhood development to advanced levels of higher education.

Table 7.6

Expenditure of Government of Nepal on Education

Year	*Total Budget (in billions of Rs)*	*Per cent Allocated to Education*	*Education Budget as % of GDP*
1993/94	33.60	13.58	2.3
1996/97	57.60	13.48	2.8
1999/2000	77.24	13.17	2.7
2000/01	82.40	15.60	3.1
2004/05	111.68	16.05	3.7

Source: MOES, 2000 and 2001, budget for 2004/05.

The participation of both girls and boys is seen to have increased at various levels of education including the primary schools. In the primary schools, the total rate of admission is 87.4 per cent. Of the total children of school-going age, the percentage of girls is 48, the percentage of indigenous groups is 38, the percentage of Dalits is 18, and the percentage of disabled is 1. The total number of schools has reached to 28,026 including government and private schools. At the primary level, the percentage of female teachers is 30.6, Dalits 2.5, Janjatis 17.8. The total literacy rate of the country is 53.7 per cent, of which the literacy rate of women is 42.5 per cent. The general literacy equity index was targeted to reach 0.8 by the end of the Tenth Plan, whereas it has reached only 0.61. Still, some 13 per cent of children are seen to be excluded from primary education. There is a high rate of repetition and dropouts; the graduation rate is also not satisfactory. Although the access of children to every level of education is increasing, the admission rate of poor, Dalit, especially the Dalits and indigenous groups of Madhesh, is very low. In addition, there are only five universities in the country.

Health

Health and economic prosperity go hand in hand. In micro and macro data, there is abundant evidence that a wide array of health indicators are positively associated with different dimensions of economic prosperity. A positive correlation between health and economic prosperity has been widely documented; but the extent to which this reflects a casual effect on health on economic outcomes is very controversial.

Isolating the casual pathways linking health and economic outcomes has been a central issue. It is likely that causality runs in both directions. First higher income individuals invest more in human capital, including health; as their income grows, they invest in better diets, improved sanitation and better health care. Second if a worker is healthier, less susceptible to disease, and more alert and more energetic then he or she will probably be more productive and command higher earnings.

The South Asian countries comprises high rate of infant mortality, under-five mortality rate and low life expectancy at birth. The public and private investment in health sector is increasing which is fostering the availability of the health services to the poor and backward classes. South Asian countries are focusing their attention on education and health to improve the living standard of the people.

Table 7.7

Progress and Setbacks of South Asian Countries in the Health Status

Country	*Life Expectancy at Birth (years)*		*Infant Mortality Rate (per 1000)*		*Under-five Mortality Rate (per 1000 live births)*	
	1970-1975	*2000-2005*	*1970*	*2005*	*1970*	*2005*
Sri Lanka	65.0	70.8	65	12	100	14
Maldives	51.4	65.8	157	33	255	42
India	50.7	62.9	127	56	202	74
Bhutan	41.8	63.5	156	65	267	75
Pakistan	51.9	63.6	120	79	181	99
Bangladesh	45.3	62.0	145	54	239	73
Nepal	44.0	61.3	165	56	250	74

Source: HDR 2007/08, UNDP.

Figure 7.1 shows the decrease in the infant mortality rate of South Asian countries in a very successive way. It seems that the investment in health sector is being very efficiently utilised but still the South Asian countries have a far way to go. Overall life expectancy at birth in South Asia was 50.3 in 1970-1975 which increased to 62.9 in 2000-2005. Likewise, the infant mortality rate per 1000 was 130 in 1970 which decreased to 60 in 2005.

Figure 7.1

Infant Mortality Rate

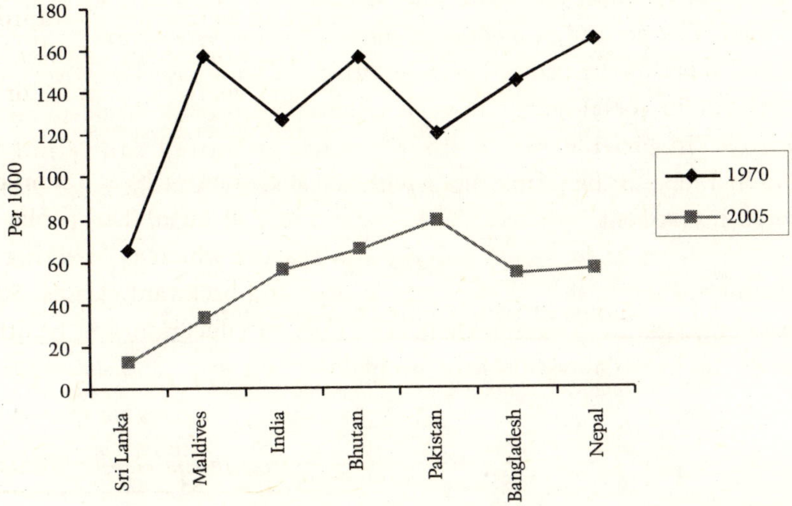

The State of Health in Nepal

By accepting the global principle of health as a fundamental right of the people, the Interim Constitution, 2003 has for the first time in history, established the obligation of the state to the health of Nepali citizens. Due to policy level implementation and institutional reforms in the health sector, the reach of the people to health service is increasing. Health organisations are being operated from the regional, zonal and district hospitals for every Village Development Committee. As a result, according to the Nepal Population and Health Survey, 2007, maternal mortality is 281 per 100,000; child mortality rate is 61 per 1,000; infant mortality rate is 48 per 1000; and neo-natal mortality rate is 34 per 1,000. The average age of Nepalis has reached 62 years and the average age of females is more than that of males. For the improvement of the health sector, National Health Policy and other sub-sectoral policies are operational. There is an expansion of alternative health services including *ayurvedic* health services. As for children's nutrition, the percentage of stunting has decreased from 57 per cent in BS 2058 to 49 per cent in BS 2064. However, the dismal physical condition of health agencies, and lack of health workers, medicine and equipment, has made it difficult for the people to access necessary and quality health service.

Drinking Water, Sanitation and Nutrition

South Asian region being the club of poor countries with poor people, the problem of improved water and sanitation and undernourishment is very high. The per capita income of these countries is very low. Thirty per cent and more of the people earns less then 1$ in a day. The government investment in social sector is very essential to provide basic necessary facilities. To provide safe drinking water, improved sanitation and nutritional food to the people along with social security is the basic purpose of social investment.

Table 7.8

Status of Water, Sanitation and Nutrition

Country	*Population using Improved Sanitation (%)*		*Population using an Improved Water Resource (%)*		*Undernourished Population (% of Total Population)*	
	1990	*2004*	*1990*	*2004*	*1990/1992*	*2002/2004*
Sri Lanka	69	91	68	79	28	22
Maldives	-	59	96	83	17	10
India	14	33	70	86	25	20
Bhutan	-	70	-	62	-	-
Pakistan	37	59	83	91	24	24
Bangladesh	20	39	72	74	35	30
Nepal	11	35	70	90	20	17

Source: HDR 2007/08, UNDP.

The government expenditure in health sector shows government's credibility towards the citizens to maintain the rapid economic growth by reducing the income disparity among poor and rich, and decreasing the level of poverty and deprivation as well.

Table 7.9

Government Expenditure on Health within SAARC Region

Country	*Health Expenditure*		
	Public (% of GDP)	*Private (% of GDP)*	*Per Capita (PPP US $)*
Sri Lanka	2.0	2.3	163
Maldives	6.3	1.4	494
India	0.9	4.1	91
Bhutan	3.0	1.6	93
Pakistan	0.4	1.8	48
Bangladesh	0.9	2.2	64
Nepal	1.5	4.1	71

Source: HDR 2007/08, UNDP.

Public-private partnership (PPP) can be seen in the health sector. Private investment is higher in some countries like Sri Lanka, India, Pakistan, Bangladesh and Nepal whereas the public investment is higher in Maldives and Bhutan. A significant per cent of GDP of private and public sector is being spent in the health sector to foster the economic growth and equity among rural and urban people. Still, the health services are more allotted in urban areas. To remove this disparity and provide the service to the poor and backward class people, increase in public expenditure is necessary.

The State of Drinking Water and Health in Nepal

There has been extensive increase in the participation of consumer groups in the construction, operation and maintenance of drinking water systems. According to the Nepal Population and Health Survey, 2007, around 90 per cent of urban households and 80 per cent of rural households have access to drinking water. Similarly, under sanitation, about 37 per cent of urban households and 20 per cent of rural households are using improved latrines. From the administrative records, it is found that some 77 per cent of the population has access to drinking water, and 46 per cent of the population is using proper latrines. The supervision and coordination of various agencies working in the sector of drinking water and sanitation is found to be weak, and necessary facilities have not been provided in many places.

Policies and Priorities of SAARC in Retrospect to Nepal

The public-private partnership in development has been adopted by the South Asian governments in recent policies. Such education policies should be adopted that make all citizens literate and provide them with quality and job-oriented education gradually. Increasing the people's access to quality health services and decentralising the management of the agencies that provide health care is quite challenging. The health policies adopted must be in the spirit and provision of the Constitution to guarantee citizens' the fundamental right to quality health services without being discriminated based on caste, creed, sex, religion, ethnicity and political beliefs. The principal challenge is to provide and improve the quality of drinking water and sanitation facilities in areas where there are no traditional sources. The water and sanitation policies should be implemented to improve the public health situation by providing drinking water on a sustainable basis.

After a decade of Maoist armed-conflict in Nepal, the peace process is under way and the main priorities of the government lay towards reconstruction and rehabilitation of the physical infrastructure as well as the social security. The government adopted the system of market economy in general and public welfare economic development was adopted through government (public), cooperative and private sectors. The process involves identifying people living under poverty line, and formulating economic and social policies and programmes based on social justice, economic growth and equitable distribution by focusing development efforts on poverty alleviation.

Challenges of SAARC Region in Retrospect to Nepal

The following challenges for rapid development of South Asian region on social services (public and private) have been observed:

- To justify the presence and utility of the state.
- To orient the state towards sustainable peace and prosperity by integrating development process and making the citizens hopeful for the future by providing them with a realisation of change.
- To provide relief to all those affected by the past conflict, to rehabilitate them, and reconstruct damaged and destroyed infrastructures.
- To include regions, communities and groups excluded in the course of development and to ensure fruits of development.
- To establish a relation of mutual trust between the state, citizens and the private sector.
- To promote people's participation in the country's governance system by pushing forward decentralisation and devolution, to make effective the local level service delivery, and to carry out institutional development of democracy from the grassroots level.
- To extensively promote human resource development and employment.

- To develop the practice that reflects non-monetary activities in plans and planned investment, and mobilisation of household savings.
- To give momentum to economic activities and to prepare conducive investment environment for high economic growth rate.
- To promote investment in productive sectors, and to increase the productivity of capital and labour.

Conclusion and Recommendations

At present, the South Asian governments are carrying out some social security programmes for the extremely poor, conflict-affected, Dalit, senior citizens, people with disability, orphans, children and women at risk and individuals and groups affected by natural disasters. New and expanded policies and programmes are needed for guaranteeing human rights of such individuals and groups.

The South Asian region is characterised by the high potential of productive resources and cultural diversity. It is also characterised by the unjust distribution of these resources, resulting in deep rooted inequality, conflict, destitution and systematic marginalisation. This unequal distribution of resources is encountered by various communities within the region. All South Asian countries are steeped in a variety of conflicts. The Pakistan-India dispute has resulted in three wars. In Sri Lanka, conflict with the Tamil Tigers has led to militarisation of the entire system. In Nepal, the Maoists and national political parties continue to wrangle over the nature of the new state.

The increase in social sector investment by public and private sector is necessary these days to foster the rapid economic growth by reducing the regional disparity among nations and nationalities. The investment in social services (public goods) is the only way to eradicate the extreme poverty and deprivation amongst the poor, backward and marginalised classes. The increase in education level and improved health situation can create a skilled and healthier human capital which can be counted as assets of the country.

8 Non-Communicable Diseases and the Urban Poor

The Role of the Private Sector

Dulanii Liyanahetti and
M.S. Shanaz Banu

Introduction

Non-communicable diseases (NCDs) are diseases of long duration and slow degeneration. Currently NCDs such as heart disease, cancer, stroke, diabetes, hypertension etc., are the leading causes of mortality in the world and Sri Lanka is no exception. Deaths caused by such diseases account for about 60 per cent of all deaths around the globe.[1] In the recent past, international organisations such as the World Health Organization (WHO), the United Nation's Development Programme (UNDP) and the World Bank have increasingly focused their attention on NCD interventions, noting not only premature mortality but their high economic burden as well, resulting from high direct costs of treatment and massive indirect costs due to lost earnings arising from morbidity and mortality in the productive age range. Restricting the disease burden of a country depends on a two-pronged approach: limiting incidence through primary prevention and reducing the adverse impacts of NCDs through proper disease management. Prevention and treatment of NCDs, involves both the public and private sectors in countries like Sri Lanka, where the private sector share of the health sector is sizeable. This paper seeks to verify whether the services provided by the private sector are better able to limit the burden of NCDs, while accepting that the public sector continues to play the major role in providing services to the masses in Sri Lanka.

Overview of the Health System in Sri Lanka

In Sri Lanka, the overall health system is predominantly government based with the public sector health facilities being supplied free of charge.

1. Retrieved on December 27, 2007, *http://www.pubmedcentral.nih.gov/articlerender.fcgi?artid=5464174*

The public health sector involves the National Hospital of Sri Lanka, teaching hospitals, provincial hospitals, base hospitals, district hospitals, rural hospitals, peripheral units, maternity homes and central dispensaries, with a few other institutions such as the armed forces and the prisons having their own health facilities. The private health sector in Sri Lanka, which is expanding rapidly, consists of private hospitals, private nursing homes, channel consultation centres, dispensaries and pharmacies. The role of the private sector can be two-fold: it can either be seen as an alternative to public heath sector services or as a complementary service for those who can pay for such services. The National Health Policy states that the government will facilitate the development and regulation of the private health care sector and promote better coordination with this sector.[2] In 2007, the Private Hospitals Bill was passed, giving the state the right to monitor private sector health care institutions; however, to date there has been little intervention and no real control by the state of private sector activities.[3] Concerns exist regarding the fees charged, the quality of services and the facilities in the private sector. Another feature of the health system in Sri Lanka is the absence of a proper health insurance scheme. Insurance currently amounts to only about 1 per cent of total per capita health expenditure in 2002 (Samarage, 2002). Two issues however are important, specifically in the context of NCDs: can the government sector alone adequately address the issue of NCDs and if not, how can the state ensure that the private sector services are provided in a safe, efficient and equitable manner.

Interestingly, the sector-wise expenditure scenario paints a picture of insufficient government involvement despite the fact of free health services in Sri Lanka. For example in 2002, the total health expenditure in Sri Lanka was Rs. 59.6 billion. The government health sector expenditure amounted to Rs. 25.8 billion, which was 43 per cent of total health expenditure, while the private sector financed Rs. 33.8 billion, equivalent to 57 per cent of total health expenditure. In 1997, the respective shares of the government and private sectors were about 50 per cent each. In five years, the government's share of the total financing has dropped from 50 to 43 per cent (Perera *et al.*, 2007).

---

2. Read more on health policy of Sri Lanka at *http://www.health.gov.lk/HealthPolicy.htm*
3. Read more on the bill at *http://www.lankanewspapers.com/news/2006/6/7242.html*

In contrast, coverage by the public sector is far greater than that by the private sector. Government hospitals such as teaching, provincial and base hospitals are spread throughout the country, equipped to provide tertiary in-patient care facilities. In the private sector, the major hospitals are situated mainly in Colombo, with a few others in the larger towns. In the case of NCD prevention, however, the major role is played by out-patient care and clinics. Most large government hospitals have NCD clinics. Patients also tend to access general practitioners and consultants (including public sector employees) in their private capacity. At present, many people seek private out-patient care due to limitations in the public sector such as inaccessibility of specialist services and lack of laboratory facilities in lower level state hospitals. In addition, recently the private sector has also started disease-specific prevention centres for diseases such as diabetes and cancer. Therefore, the contribution by the private sector towards controlling NCDs in Sri Lanka is noteworthy.

Research Methodology

This paper will follow an analytical approach in drawing on published literature and data relating to the central theme. A comparative analysis of the role of the private sector in NCD treatment in India will also be undertaken.

Assumptions and Limitations

A topical issue like the role of the private sector in non-communicable disease treatment needs to be analysed from many aspects and involve the opinions of many experts. However, the scope of this paper is restricted to the urban poor, more specifically to those living in the Western Province. The lack of private sector health documentation in Sri Lanka is another grave limitation encountered in this study. It stands as a major obstacle, needing urgent attention, given the importance of the issues being explored. The manner in which the private sector deals with NCDs and the importance of addressing the issue of NCDs will be discussed in Sections 2 and 3 of this paper. In Section 4, a comparison will be performed with the Indian situation followed by the presentation of conclusions in the final section.

Non-Communicable Diseases (NCDs) in Sri Lanka

Unlike many other developing countries, Sri Lanka has achieved high health standards that are similar to a developed country. For instance, by

2004, the life expectancy at birth in Sri Lanka had reached 74, the highest in South Asia, and child mortality was only 14 per 1000 live births despite a gross national income per capita of only 1010 USD (Perera *et al.*, 2007). For instance, the deaths caused by diseases such as malaria, TB, influenza, typhoid etc., are now a rare phenomenon. The main reason behind this success is the free public health system operating since 1951. Yet with regard to NCDs, the situation is not satisfactory. Nowadays most deaths are caused by heart diseases, cancer and diabetes mellitus etc., which are NCDs. Sri Lanka has been able to control communicable diseases but not NCDs. Therefore, a discussion on NCDs and the contribution made by both public and private health sectors in controlling their spread and their impact seems a timely requirement in the context of Sri Lanka.

The reasons for focusing on the urban poor in relation to NCDs are, firstly the fact that private sector health care facilities are mainly centralised in urban areas with the urban poor having access to a wide variety of health care providers, including for-profit modern hospitals, private practitioners, pharmacies, NGOs, public sector health facilities and traditional healers. Secondly, the causes of NCD tend to be urban-biased. Many researchers point to environmental and lifestyle conditions as the root cause for NCDs. Four of the most common NCDs—cardiovascular disease, cancer, chronic obstructive pulmonary disease and diabetes mellitus—are linked by common preventable risk factors related to lifestyle. For example, pollution, highly competitive lifestyles, struggle for survival, tobacco use, unhealthy diet and physical inactivity are more visible in metropolitan areas than in rural areas.[4] As studies reveals, such risk factors tend to be concentrated in urban areas of low-middle income countries and so, NCD prevalence is increasing as a result of rapid urbanisation and the increasing globalisation of the food, tobacco and alcohol industries.[5] Thirdly, the income factor and NCDs go parallel (for example, as in the Barker Hypothesis) and thus, the effects of such diseases are felt more by

4. For more information, read *http://www.pubmedcentral.nih.gov/picrender.fcgi?artid=383378&blobtype=pdf*

5. A survey conducted by some scholars on "Are urban poor vulnerable to NCDs?" in urban slums of Faridabad, India concludes that the high prevalence of risk factors for non-communicable diseases across all age groups in this urban slum community indicates the likelihood of a high future burden of illness. Thus, urban poor are more vulnerable to NCDs. Source: *http://lib.bioinfo.pl/pmid:17867614*

the poor.[6] As mentioned before, NCDs differ from communicable diseases (CDs) in two significant ways: firstly, there is no public health argument for spending on NCD treatment; and secondly, NCDs affect individuals over long periods, and are more complex to treat, hence involve higher expenditure. Both these factors result in the burden of NCD treatment being borne mainly by the patient and his/her family (de Silva, 2007). Hence, concentrating on the urban poor and NCDs is vital, particularly if the country's objective is investing in health for development.

Private and Public Sector Involvement in Addressing NCDs

In assessing private and public sector interventions on NCDs, it is essential to examine how the two sectors handle the care of NCDs. Firstly, unlike the public health sector out-patient departments (OPD) that are limited to day time hours, with clinics on specific days (and time), the private sector provides consultancy services early in the mornings and during the evening up to late at night, in addition to its 24 hour OPD care. Since most urban poor are daily paid workers, they find it more economically rational to go to a private nursing home or dispensary to obtain treatment. As public hospitals function only during day time, the poor have to sacrifice their day's wage in order to get medicine. At the state OPD clinics, patients have to wait in a long queue to meet the doctor, then in another queue to obtain their medicine, and often they have to return numerous times to get laboratory tests done. This is extremely detrimental to a daily earner. Delays are rare in the private sector so treatment time is minimal and the time spent is often after working hours. Therefore, even though the services provided by the public sector are highly beneficial, the poor are forced to seek private services involving high costs.

Secondly, choice is an issue. In the case of NCDs, patients desire access to specialists. They are also keen on meeting the same doctor on a regular basis. However, a person taking treatment for diabetes from the public sector for example may have to consult a new doctor each time he/she visits the OPD and the doctor might not have sufficient time to spend

6. The Barker Hypothesis explains that many chronic disorders that occur later in life are related to poverty and prosperity. Read more *http://www.medscape.com/viewarticle/453242_2*

on each individual due to the large crowds seeking free health care. The patient too may tire of narrating his story to each and every doctor he consults and there may even be privacy issues involved (with public sector consultancy sometimes occurring in the hearing of many, as patients throng for care). This results in imperfect information on the part of the doctor providing care, which is particularly detrimental to controlling the disease and its complications (secondary and tertiary prevention). In the private sector, the patient can select the specialist or general practitioner, which will ensure systematic and continuous prevention and treatment.

Thirdly, since public sector health is free there can be a low commitment by the health sector personnel involved. In contrast, in the private sector, payment generally ensures a better doctor-patient relationship from the chosen doctor, in a bid to expand and maintain his/her clientele, which is beneficial in the context of NCD management.

Fourthly, non-communicable diseases require sustained, long-term or recurrent care and specialist facilities for diagnosis and treatment (Perera *et al.*, 2007). Such facilities are sometimes lacking or not in working condition in certain public sector hospitals due primarily to budgetary problems. Large private hospitals have state-of-the-art equipment due to large scale investments and foreign tie-ups. Even public sector patients are then forced to access the private sector for specialised tests and scans, creating an economic burden even for those seeking 'free health care'.

Fifthly, a factor driving even the urban poor towards the private sector, are the long delays for surgery in the public sector. This results both from scarcity of trained manpower and surgery facilities. Such major surgeries cannot be delayed so the large financial burden is borne by the poor, through selling of assets, pawning, loans, gaining assistance from family, friends and benefactors through appeals in the press and grants from the President's Fund in the case of former or present government employees.

Sixthly, much research involving NCDs are carried out by the private sector as there are specialised institutes and units established for treating various NCDs, for example the Centre for Diabetes and the Ceylinco Cancer Detection Centre. Such units use state-of-the-art technology and involve renowned professionals in the field, including foreign experts.

While many individuals in the public health care system are involved in NCD research, the funding and technology available is limited.

Finally, the private sector often also has the advantage of pleasanter physical surroundings: clean environment, landscaping, clean linen, good furniture, better lighting and sanitation, that contribute to an environment more conducive to regular seeking of treatment and recuperating over long periods, as demanded by NCDs.

Taking all these factors into account, it can be argued, that in Sri Lanka at present, the private sector has a better capacity to tackle NCDs than the public sector. In summary, it is the triple "A" concept: accessibility, affordability and availability. The public health facilities are more easily accessible and affordable than the private sector. But with regard to NCDs, it may not be readily available as in the case of a patient needing urgent heart surgery. On the other hand, private health care is easily accessible and available but it is not affordable to the poor. Despite the unaffordability, the urban poor are compelled to seek private health care facilities for NCD treatment, in the case of surgery due to the danger of delays and for OPD care due to the opportunity costs of accessing the public sector often being greater than the private sector charges.

Comparison with Neighbouring India

This section will focus on NCDs in India, through giving an overview of its health system and the sectoral contribution to NCD care in India. The final sub-section will involve a comparative analysis with the situation in Sri Lanka. The reasons for choosing India for this study are firstly because it is the largest country in the region and thus, much affected by NCDs. Secondly, the similarities between the countries' socio-cultural backgrounds and their colonial past, make it interesting to compare how their respective health systems are gearing to combat NCDs.

NCD Background in India

According to statistics, India has a higher number of people with diabetes than any other country in the world. In addition, in India 52 per cent of cardiovascular deaths occur below the age of 70, compared with 23 per cent in countries with established market economies.

Recent studies suggest that the metabolic syndrome[7] is indeed very common among urban Indians. As a result, there has been a big shift in the health burden of the country from communicable to non-communicable diseases. It is useful to examine the various measures taken in the context of this epidemiological transition, to reduce the level of NCDs among the Indian population, by the relevant authorities, be they private or public sector.

Overview of the Health System in India

The health sector is one of the fastest growing segments in India.[8] It is primarily constituted of the public and private sectors. The public health sector consists of sub-centres, primary health centres, community health centres and district hospitals. The private health care sector in India is believed to be one of the largest sectors in the world. It comprises of private hospitals, nursing homes, pharmacies and dispensaries.

The National Health Policy of India encourages the participation of the private sector in providing health care in all areas of health activities primary, secondary and tertiary.[9] A larger proportion of the out-patient and hospital services are provided by the private sector creating a virtual monopoly. The public sector exists mainly to cater to the poor; however, since the 1990s, the public health system of India has been collapsing due to low funding and investment, further assisting the private sector to flourish.[10] When it comes to health insurance, the situation is similar to that of a developing country since there is no strong health insurance mechanism.[11]

A significant aspect of the public health sector is the decline of the expenditure ratio since the 1990s. This has adversely affected the poor and

---

7. Metabolic syndrome is a combination of medical disorders that increase one's risk for cardiovascular disease and diabetes. Source: *http://en.wikipedia.org/wiki/Metabolic_syndrome*
8. Retrieved on December 28, 2007, *http://www.slideshare.net/vaatsalya/healthcare-in-india*
9. Read more on the National Health Policy of India, *http://mohfw.nic.in/np2002.htm*
10. Read more on *http://www.slideshare.net/vaatsalya/healthcare-in-india*
11. Only a small fraction of India's population is covered by insurance schemes of any sort, whether private or employees' schemes. The vast majority of Indians must either make out-of-pocket payments for health services in the growing private sector or go to the public sector which is both small and increasingly demanding compensation. Source *http://www.infochangeindia.org/Healthlbp.jsp*

other vulnerable sections of society. For instance, the government expenditure on health out of total health expenditure (THE) in 1997 was 23.5 per cent and this has gradually decreased to 17.6 per cent in 2005. In contrast, the private sector spending on health which was 76.5 per cent in 1997 has increased rapidly to 82.4 per cent in 2005.

With regard to coverage, the corporate health care services are mainly concentrated in urban areas of India. The infrastructure is primarily with the private sector but it is centralised in the urban areas where the middle and upper-middle classes live. In other areas where the private sector operates, the necessary facilities are lacking.[12] The National Health Policy of India has committed towards providing health services to all by 2000. Yet findings reveal that government hospitals in India are unevenly distributed. Therefore, in the absence of proper public health care facilities, the private health sector is not only the privilege of the rich but also the only option for the poor. Since a large portion of out-patient health care is taken over by the private sector, and most NCD patients seek out-patient care, the role of the private sector with regard to NCDs cannot be disregarded in the context of the urban poor.

Private and Public Sector Involvement in Addressing NCDs in India

As noted in the previous sub-section, the private sector plays a dominating role in providing out-patient services (OPD) and so could be pivotal in NCD control in India. Some of the possible reasons for large numbers accessing private out-patient services in India are listed below.

Firstly, the sector-wise contribution towards research with regard to NCDs can be examined. Most of the research on NCDs, for instance studies on pathological patterns, is conducted by the private sector. The data available does not illustrate sufficient public involvement in this area. This may be due to lack of funds, low commitment or lack of qualified personnel. Secondly, quality of care in the health sector of India is said to be variable. Findings reveal the fact that corporate hospitals possess latest equipment, qualified doctors, skilled medical personnel and patient-friendly environment which are essential for NCD patients. However, in the public

12. Retrieved on December 28, 2007, *http://en.wikipedia.org/wiki/Healthcare_in_India*

sector there is a question of availability and technical support. At times, it goes to the extent of lacking even basic equipment or a continuous supply of water and electricity. Thirdly, affordability of health care becomes a crucial issue. For instance, critics point out that when it comes to NCDs, public health care, which is not free in India, can be equally costly as private care because such diseases require long term treatment[13] and outcomes are extremely dependent on the quality of care. The rapid development of the private health sector has led to the emergence of a new concept where private health care is chiefly profit-oriented. For instance, many private hospitals over-charge and deny their patient information about diagnosis and treatment.[14]

In conclusion, it is possible to say that other factors such as rapid population growth, poor participatory involvement at the local level, lack of resources, non-availability of infrastructure and bureaucracy can also contribute to the disparity between the two sectors. It should be noted that pricing for example in the private sector is market determined, and that though the state may seek to regulate this market, it is extremely complex to do so given the differences in treatment protocols, sophistication of technology and even patient and doctor idiosyncrasies. Policy relating to the private health sector is an extremely important means of guiding patient welfare.

Comparing India and Sri Lanka

As observed in the previous sub-sections, the health systems in both countries are more or less analogous owing to the fact that even in Sri Lanka, the private sector dominates in treating NCDs and the public sector is lagging behind. The lack of a proper insurance scheme for health care in both countries is also noteworthy. This fact can be seen in many developing countries and as a result, the government has to play the role of the insurer, a role it is finding increasingly hard to manage given budgetary constraints and rapidly rising NCD treatment expenditure.

---

13. Fifty per cent of the patients in Mumbai's public hospitals spend more every day than the daily income of their entire household. In private hospitals, average costs for medicines, doctors' and hospital fees can amount to twice a family's monthly income. Source: *http://vaatsalya.com/front/?q=node*

14. Retrieved on December 28, 2007, *http://vaatsalya.com/front/?q=node*

Comparing the epidemiological patterns in the two countries, we note that the three main NCD killers are cancer, heart diseases and diabetes mellitus. However, while India has much larger numbers of deaths for each of these conditions in line with its much larger population, when death rates per 100,000 population are considered, Sri Lanka has significantly higher figures for both diabetes mellitus and cancer. This results from Sri Lanka being far ahead in its epidemiological transition (note that in the category communicable, maternal, prenatal and nutritional deficiencies, the death rate per 100,000 for India and Sri Lanka are 401.9 and 103.2 respectively) and in its demographic transition as well. In comparison to developed countries, the number of deaths due to cardiovascular disease, particularly at lower ages is high in India and Sri Lanka, and the level of diabetes mellitus in Sri Lanka is extremely high. The need for state policy action to be adopted with regard to prevention and treatment of NCDs, both in India and Sri Lanka, as they face health transition is crucial in safeguarding patient welfare and in investing in human development.

Conclusion and Policy Recommendations

The above discussions show that the private sector can play a complementary role to the public sector in controlling and treating NCDs. In conclusion, it can be stated that in the case of NCD treatment it is clear from the arguments above that the private sector in Sri Lanka currently has a better capacity to handle NCDs than the public sector. The major problem encountered by the urban poor in this context is the cost factor. While the urban population, particularly the poor are facing graver risks of NCDs, with a need for greater prevention activities addressing this group, those currently afflicted need to be focused on as well in assisting them to access appropriate care including secondary and tertiary prevention. On the one hand, the private sector could be better regulated by the state to keep their fees affordable and/or encouraged through selective fiscal policies to provide concessionary rates for a quota of poor patients. On the other hand, the public sector could step in to provide equivalent services (such as clinics after working hours, mobile/rotating specialist services). In the long run, it would be more beneficial to the urban poor if the public sector could be upgraded to the level of the private sector so that their 'forced demand for private sector services' could revert to the public sector, and the cost burden be taken off them.

Policy Recommendations

When suggesting policy recommendations, it is important to identify how the public and private sectors operate. The private heath sector is based on the market mechanism involving profit maximisation. Hence, it is not practical, nor advisable from a growth perspective, to attempt to control supply or price setting in this sector too closely. Thus, it is better to provide guidelines, recommendations and incentives to encourage the private sector to provide affordable services to the poor.

The public sector is capable of changing. It can either choose to compete with the private sector or provide complementary services. This paper encourages the latter since competing given the current budgetary constraints would involve either rationing or user charges, both of which would adversely affect the urban poor. Based on the analysis, the following policy recommendations are made to upgrade the health system.

- Promoting collaboration between public and private sectors. This may include a private-public partnership in planning, management and information system development and basic in-service training of health workers and sharing information and experiences.
- Supporting innovations. The private sector can be used for research and to test new ideas and concepts that can subsequently be adapted to the public sector.
- Enhancing management capacity. High managerial skills are required in both sectors so it is important to strengthen such skills.
- Conducting a private health sector assessment. The role played by the private sector is hardly acknowledged specially in the case of NCDs. It would be useful to assess the role of the private sector.
- Benchmark private and public sector prevention, treatment and care protocols so that similar good practices can be encouraged in both sectors.
- Give a wider definition to the corporate social responsibility (CSR) concept. Encourage the private health sector to concentrate on providing more NCD services to the poor at a lesser cost.

References

Abayawickrama, R. (2006). "Financing of Health Care in Sri Lanka: An Overview of Public Financing", *Economic Review* 32: 6-7.

Anand, K., B. Shah, K. Yadav, R. Singh, P. Mathur, E. Paul, *et al.* (2004). "Are the Urban Poor Vulnerable to Non-Communicable Diseases?", A survey of risk factors for non-communicable diseases in urban slums of Faridabad. Abstract retrieved December 27, 2007, from *http://lib.bioinfo.pl/pmid:17867614*

Attanayake, N. (2002). "Household Costs of Long-term Illness: Diabetes, Heart Ailments and Mental Illness", (Paper presented to JICA as a background paper for the master plan study for strengthening Health System in Sri Lanka).

———. (1997). "The Sri Lankan Health Sector: Policy Perspectives and Reforms", *Economic Review* 23: 2-6.

Balankulame, I. (2003). *Conceptualisation of the role of the Private Health sector in Sri Lanka in the period 2000-2010*. Health Research and Development Programme: Socio-economic Group, University of Colombo.

Balasubramaniam, K. (2007). "Restoration of National Health Services", *Daily Mirror*. Retrieved from *http://www.dailymirror.lk/2007/09/12/edit.asp,* September 7.

de Silva, Amala (2007). "Financing NCD Treatment: Burden of Out of Pocket Expenditure", Report of the Working Group on Financing of the National Committee on Macroeconomics and Health.

de Silva, S.T.G.R. (1997). "The Hospital System in Sri Lanka: Shortcomings and Remedies", *Economic Review* 23: 7-12.

Duggal, R. (2007). "The Private Health Sector in India: Nature, Trends and a Critique", Abstract retrieved on December 28, from *http://www.cehat.org/publications/ra01r6.html*

Gangolli, L.V., R. Duggal and A. Shukla (2007). "Review of Health Care in India", Abstract retrieved on December 28, from *http://www.cehat.org/rthc/rhci.html*

Ghaffar, A., K.S. Reddy and M. Singhi (2004). "Burden of Non-Communicable Diseases in South Asia", *Clinical Review*. Retrieved on December 18, 2007 from *http://www.pubmedcentral.nih.gov/picrender.fcgi?artid=383378&blobtype=pdf*

Health Transition (2007). Retrieved on December 18, from *http://www.searo.who.int/LinkFiles/NCD_InforBase_introduction.pdf*

India National Expenditure on Health. Retrieved on December 28, 2007, from *http://www.who.int/nha/country/IND.pdf*

Major Trends in the Health Sector: The Epidemiological Transition. (2007). Retrieved on December 27, 2007, from *http://www.adb.org/Documents/Policies/Health/health302.asp*

Ministry of Health and Family Welfare India. National Health Policy India. Retrieved from *http://mohfw.nic.in/np2002.htm*

Ministry of Health and Nutrition Sri Lanka. National Health Policy Sri Lanka. Retrieved from *http://www.health.gov.lk/HealthPolicy.htm*

Mortality Country Fact Sheet (2006). Retrieved on December 26, 2007, from *http://www.who.int/whosis/mort/profiles/mort_searo_lka_srilanka.pdf*

National Commission on Macro-Economics and Health Sri Lanka (2006). *Economy and Health: Taking Sri Lanka Towards the Global Best*. Colombo: D. Varatharajan.

Newbrander, W. and D. Parker (1992). "The Public and Private Sectors in Health: Economic Issues", *International Journal of Health Planning and Management* 7: 38-49.

Perera, M., G. Gunatilleke and P. Bird (2007). "Falling into the Medical Poverty Trap in Sri Lanka: What can be Done?", *International Journal of Health Services* 37: 379-398.

Preventing Chronic Disease: A Vital Investment", Abstract Retrieved on December 18, 2007 from *http://www.searo.who.int/en/Section1174/Section1459_10496.htm*

Profile of Selected NCDs-Regional Estimates. Retrieved on December 18, 2007, from *http://www.searo.who.int/LinkFiles/NCD_InforBase_selected-ncd.pdf*

Rabel, A. (2007). "Role of the Private Sector in Delivery of Health Care", Retrieved on December 18, 2007 from *http://203.94.76.60/AHF/pdf/Abstract19RoleofPrivate sectorinHealthcaredelivery.pdf*

Rodrigo, L. (2006). "Private Medical Bill before House Today", *Lanka News Papers*. Retrieved on June 8 from *http://www.lankanewspapers.com/news/2006/6/7242.html*

Shah, B. and P. Mathur (2005). Risk Factor Surveillance for Non-Communicable Diseases (NCDs): The Multi-site ICMR-WHO Collaborative Initiative", Retrieved on December 18, 2007, from *http://www.globalforumhealth.org/filesupld/forum9/CD%20Forum%209/pape rs/Shah%20B.pdf*

Siwagami, A. (n.d.). "The Role of the Public and Private Sectors in Health Care: Emerging Ethical Dilemmas in India", Retrieved on December 18, 2007, from *www.stc.arts.chula.ac.th/ABC2007/abc2007pptfiles/220307updated/Session%2021/Dr.%20Aruna%20 Sivagami.ppt*

Sri Lanka National Expenditure on Health. Retrieved on December 26, 2007, from *http://www.who.int/nha/country/LKA.pdf*

Srinivasan, S. (n.d.). "Health Indicators/The Burden of Disease/Health Infrastructure/Issues and Debates in Health Care/Future Strategies and Possible Solutions", Retrieved on December 28, 2007 from *http://www.infochangeindia.org/HealthIbp.jsp*

Vaatsalya Health Care, Health Care in India [Power point slides]. Retrieved from *http://vaatsalya.com/front/?q=node/11*

World Health Organization (2002). Poverty Transition and Health: A Rapid Health System Analysis. Colombo.

————. (2001). "Report of the Commission on Macro-economics and Health", *Macro-Economics and Health: Investing in Health for Economic Development* (2nd ed.). Geneva. Jeffrey D. Sachs.

————. (2007). "Measurement and Health Information", Retrieved on December 28 from *http://www.who.int/research/en/causes_of_death.xls*

9 Role of Social Sector in Efforts to Eradicate Poverty

Abdul Rafeh Iqbal

Introduction

In the poorest regions of the world, areas where mass poverty is geographically concentrated, poverty by any reasonable measurement is so pervasive that policies of poverty alleviation encompass practically the whole range of development policies. Poverty is basically associated with three things—education, health and institutions. Social and economic exclusion of some people characterises them as poor. In a broader sense, justice, rights, participation and equality, all of these concepts can also be incorporated in this definition. Efforts to link poverty to specific manifestations—starvation, severe malnutrition, illiteracy, standard clothing and housing—are inconclusive. In social terms, the poor are those who must live below what most people in a particular time and place regard as the minimum acceptable standard. The general poverty trends seen in Pakistan are also very interesting—rural poverty in the country is much higher than urban, rural NWFP has the highest headcount measure of about 45 per cent population living below poverty line, Sindh generally is more poverty stricken than Punjab and the gender structure in the country has more influence on poverty than dependency ratio or family size. Households with the least number of earners, female-headed households or households that are reliant on their incomes are usually characterised as very poor. Ownership and access to land is a huge component of rural poverty.

The poverty line used by Pakistan is an arbitrarily chosen one based on minimum calorie intake or basic needs basket. For rural areas, it is 2450 calories and for urban it is 2150, these are higher than the intake requirements of both India and Bangladesh. To see why poor people remain poor in Pakistan is a mystery. However, two issues shed some light on this matter. The first is rent seeking behaviour, which people are making money without doing anything. The other is the poverty culture, which is even worse than poverty itself when the poor start taking refuge in protests and strikes. As long as these practices are prevalent in Pakistan, poverty is impossible to eradicate.

Deprivation of Resources: Education

Education can be defined broadly as all forms of human learning or more narrowly as the process that occurs in specialised institutions called "schools". For poor people, education can serve as a bulwark against volatility: even the fundamental skills learned in primary school can make a critical difference for the survival of families when government services fall short, or during times of economic crisis. The widening of educational access thus can help to eradicate poverty even before it begins to yield returns in the labour market (Stern, 2001).

Education is one of the most important forms of human resource development; the reason for this is the high correlation that it has with income on both the individual and societal level. The correlation between national incomes and educational attainment is also very strong. Mass education is still relatively a recent phenomenon in the poorer countries, but it is seen to have a huge influence on the per capita incomes of the country.

Pakistan, like many developing countries, has a low educational status and this is characterised by high fragmentation and segmentation. Under the given labour market conditions, these two issues have created many unavoidable problems in the optimal utilisation of human resources. Pakistan failed to capitalise on the large rates of return of female schooling on economic productivity and the country has forgone a great opportunity and this is evident by the huge gender gap in education.

Pakistan thus missed economic opportunities that have been exploited by many developing countries by increasing educational levels for most of its labour force, failed to provide technical expertise and thus, enhancing their household incomes and reducing poverty.

In some positive developments, education has been made compulsory and free up to secondary school levels in Punjab and Sindh provinces. The Punjab Education Sector Reform Program (PESRP) in collaboration with the

World Bank has set up a workable model which focuses on expanding access, and improving governance and quality of education. Some of the salient features are:

- Provision of free textbooks to primary school students.
- Monthly stipends to girls enrolled at the middle schools.
- Appointment of better qualified teachers and improvement in physical infrastructure have led to an overall 13 per cent increase in enrolments in primary schools and 20 per cent increase in enrolments of girls at middle level in 15 low literacy districts of Punjab.

Because of the wider participation of civil society organisations, department staff, parents and the teachers, this model has proved to be very successful. An overarching objective of this programme is to reduce gender inequalities in the province. If the objectives and role of this model are successfully replicated to other provinces, it is quite likely that the unsatisfactory performance of the past several decades could be reversed and the country be saved from the burden of poverty. Higher education for women, who were in the past just dependent on men for their needs, shows that females can earn almost as high as men now that they are educated and female-headed households especially need not be in such bad conditions as before.

Deprivation of Resources: Health

The World Health Organization (WHO), the United Nations agency responsible for programmes to improve health standards, defines the concept of health as, "a state of complete physical, mental and social well being", although normally what is meant by health goes far beyond this very general definition.

The goal of improving health conditions in developing countries has often been accorded one of the lowest priority, both by the developing country governments and the development specialists. In nearly every country, the ministry of health receives one of the smallest budget allocations. The past 25 years has surprisingly seen a reverse scenario. Interest in health and development was boosted in the 1970s, and thereafter expenditures on health, like those on education have increasingly been regarded as investments in human capital, which was a great move towards a healthy workforce and thus, higher incomes in the future.

The health-development relation is a reciprocal one. Economic development tends to improve health status, while better health contributes to economic development. But proponents of health sector programmes frequently warn that development alone cannot be relied on to cut morbidity and mortality; they emphasise that special programmes in nutrition, health care and environmental sanitation are also needed.

Nutrition: Infants and children face the greatest nutritional problem in the developing countries. Infants are usually adequately fed through the breastfeeding stage but usually suffer a nutritional decline after weaning. If this is not in any way corrected, this can cause reduction in physical and mental growth, which results in low resistance to diseases and would impair their ability to get proper education in school and earn a good livelihood for themselves to help them get out of poverty. Pregnant and lactating women also require special nutritional care because of their relation to the child's nutrition. But keeping all these people aside, in reality the most immediate and direct effect on economic growth is due to the working adults and nutritional intervention targeted towards them is in some ways justifiable.

Health services: In developing countries, health services are usually significantly underfinanced. The World Bank has observed that prices have generally played a minor role in generating ample financial resources for health services or in determining who in the economy should have access to them. If the emphasis of health services is on primary health and preventive services are generally aimed at the masses of people, only then should free medication be allowed to prevail; if on the contrary the services are enjoyed by the elite, high prices should be charged. Low medical expenditures have led to the inadequate stocks of health facilities and personnel in most developing countries and particularly in the poorest ones. Medical training in many of the poorest countries might not benefit society because doctors are highly mobile and once trained, many emigrate to seek higher income elsewhere. In many cases, increasing the supply of nurses and other health auxiliaries may be a better way to improve services. Thus, in order to help the poor that suffer from various health issues, efficient and cheap services should be provided by the government, so that they can expect to see a healthy workforce who thus can support their families by earning a good livelihood.

Poverty Alleviation Strategy: Policy Measures

Over the last 25 years, there has been a running debate on the relative importance in poverty alleviation policies of market-driven growth as it trickles down to the poor as opposed to a programme of direct massive intervention to help the poor. The governments of developing countries and the development analysts work on both these lines. Some economies use the first approach while others emphasise on the second, but as is evident by the experiences of some developing countries, direct help to the poor has far better results than the trickle-down effect.

The main components of the poverty reduction strategy and human development are:

- There should be substantial economic growth at a fast pace resulting in an increase in per capita income. This is to take place through the infrastructural development, taxation reforms, financial sector development, restructuring of manufacturing sector and an overhauling of the agrarian system. Growth has to be labour-intensive and people-friendly because if the growth is capital-intensive it would drive out the labour and exacerbate poverty, and restructuring of the manufacturing sector has grave effects on the country. Tax reforms should be designed to attract investment that requires mass manpower. This would cause the per capita income to rise. But the taxation system in Pakistan does not favour such a manufacturing sector. Very high taxes on raw material imports as opposed to finished products have caused many manufacturing units to close down which has resulted in poor workers becoming unemployed.
- Another policy that needs to be undertaken is to provide employment opportunities to counter the recessionary trends and to provide employment for poverty reduction. As explained earlier, the recognition lag has taken rather a long time to be countered and

appropriate steps must be taken to create a path out of the black hole for the poor.

- The quality of social services should be both expanded and improved. Foundations like Edhi and Shaukat Khanum Memorial and Research Centre are effective and they provide the best available services at their disposable, increasing the share of their responsibility in the country. Governments of developing countries should support these private groups and promote other such activities to take place that help the poor in ways that though cannot get them out of poverty directly can in some ways help them from the grave adverse situations that poverty puts them into.
- Mobilisation of support organisations, NGOs and partnerships with the private sector should also be considered in order to adapt to the changes and systematic working of effective NGOs; the government may also collaborate with them on some level.
- Community-based participatory development programmes should be promoted.
- System of social safety nets should be introduced; this helps the poor in many ways.
- Microcredit programmes for the poor should be started. The NRSP (National Rural Support Programme) is the only programme working nationwide providing microcredit with the help of the Bill & Melinda Gates Foundation. It is still analysed that more of such microcredit programmes are required at such levels.
- Development of human resources and basic skills: Teaching Teachers is a private agency working for the improvement of government hired teachers so that they can help the public institutes to become more focused and effective. This is the only one of its kind agency and its operations have just started, but this can prove to indirectly help alleviate poverty in a very non-obvious way. Better qualified teachers mean better delegation of knowledge, as well as better trained and intellectual students who can thus prove to be better workers and who can earn better wages to support their families and get them out of poverty.

- Empowerment of women needs to be done so that female-headed households which are usually in the worst conditions among the poor are able to have a say in the country and hold a standing in the workplace.
- Governance issues should be solved. Although corruption cannot be eradicated in a matter of days or months, the emphasis should be upon the implementation of programmes which are being co-ventured by the government as well as private investors. In addition, it should highlight the focus upon the poor and deprived.
- Schemes to eradicate child labour should be started. Although the under-18 child labour law exists in Pakistan, no real national level efforts are being made to follow it. Zindagi Trust, an NGO started by a renowned singer Shehzad Roy has, by now, 34 informal schools in which students are paid to learn. This is to attract poor families who force their children to work, to get educated up to the primary level and earn Rs.10 as a stipend every day. Such programmes by the government or through joint ventures can be successful in keeping the current income of the poor families stable while educating their kids for potentially higher wages in the future.
- Increase employment generating capacity by developing the access and capability of the world wide web.
- The government should provide greater focus on technical, vocational and professional education at subsidised costs.
- Restructuring of the labour laws, and regulations should be made that discourage employment in the formal sector.

The conventional programmes in Pakistan in the shape of Zakat Fund, Ushr and Baitul Maal, all of which require effective targeting and increased direct involvement of government, have not been providing a springboard for the poor out of poverty. The institutional failure and issues of governance have been the key feature resulting in the poor quality of focused government. Findings have shown that the Zakat Fund is not working effectively. Many economists are reported to have said that the government support for the poor remains insignificant even today and the state in Pakistan has failed to erect a strong policy to catch the people who fall into the trap of poverty as a result of socio-economic changes. With respect to the private sector, it is widely known that apart from a few NGOs which reach out to the poor, they do not reach the poorest within them. The government of Pakistan has also realised that there are 'very few' NGOs which work at the grassroot level of poverty alleviation, participatory development and capacity building.

Poverty Alleviation Agencies in Pakistan

Pakistan's Poverty Alleviation Fund (PPAF): The PPAF has been established to enhance the accessibility of resources and services to the poor across Pakistan. It started its operation in April 2000. It operates on following two levels:

- The micro credit and micro enterprise operation is designed to facilitate access of poor communities to financial services, capacity building with emphasis on institution building and human resource development for efficient use of financial resources and sustained recurring benefits made available through the programme.
- In community physical infrastructure, it provides communities access to water for drinking and irrigation purposes, building link roads, bridges and culverts as well as sanitation facilities at a smaller scale. Major operation takes place in rural areas.

Both sides of the programme help the poor to improve their financial status in the country.

Agha Khan Rural Support Programme (AKRSP): The AKRSP is involved in community infrastructure development in the northern areas especially in Chitral since 1982. They have initiated more than 2,000 projects to date, for the benefit of 130,000 households. Out of these, 1,980 projects have already been completed. The projects include mainly irrigation schemes, roads, bridges, flood protection bunds and drinking water supply schemes. In addition to these, one micro hydel project has been completed. Most of these projects are productive, especially irrigation schemes (about 53 per cent of the total number of projects) which enhanced the assets of the poor rural households by providing additional land for agricultural production. And as mentioned earlier in the paper, rural poverty is influenced highly by asset ownership of the people.

Health and Nutrition Development Society (HANDS): HANDS aims at providing basic health services, primary education, income generation opportunities and development of institutions to empower the underprivileged communities. It has been pouring its untiring efforts for empowering and strengthening the communities to deal with the issues directed towards poverty alleviation. The vision, mission and objectives of HANDS have motivated and enlightened more than 125 fulltime paid staff, 600 community based staff and thousands of volunteers so that a concrete and effective mind mapping, integrated system and methodologies could be streamlined for every possible viable outcome.

National Rural Support Programme (NRSP): NRSP is the largest integrated services (micro-credit, infrastructure and education) provider working nationwide at the grassroot level. Micro-credit is the single largest component of this integrated and holistic approach to community development.

Edhi Foundation: Edhi Foundation is the largest and most organised social welfare system in Pakistan. The Foundation works round the clock, without any discrimination on the basis of colour, race, language, religion or status. The Foundation modifies the phrase "Live and Let Live" to "Live and Help Live".

Its activities include a 24-hour emergency service across the country through 250 Edhi centres which provides free shrouding and burial of unclaimed dead bodies, shelter for the destitute, orphans and handicapped persons, free hospitals and dispensaries, rehabilitation of drug addicts, free wheelchairs, crutches and other services for the handicapped, family planning counseling and maternity services, national and international relief efforts for the victims of natural calamities.

All donations for Edhi Foundation come from individuals and a few business enterprises with exemplary tenacity. Edhi has pursued its mission for the last five decades and has quietly brought about a remarkable change in the social attitude in Pakistan towards community welfare by instilling in ordinary citizens a consistent desire to participate in public welfare programmes.

Bill & Melinda Gates Foundation: The Bill & Melinda Gates Foundation believes every life has equal value. In 2000, the Foundation was created to help reduce inequalities in the United States and then around the world.

Following are just a few contributions the foundation has made in Pakistan:

Agha Khan Foundation USA—$5,549,000 over five years to create a viable and sustainable model for micro-insurance for the poor and implement in Pakistan, Tanzania and Afghanistan.

Family Planning Association of Pakistan—$1,377,325 over five years to improve access to family planning through an innovative and integrated community-participation approach in Baluchistan, Pakistan.

Summary and Conclusion

Can poverty be completely eradicated from the face of Pakistan? All signs suggest that the answer to this question is an unequivocal 'No'. A general situation which is seen to prevail in the past few years is that growth rates are seen to increase but reach only slightly above the rates that are minimally required to reduce poverty, and are likely to continue to be below such levels for sometime into the future. General government efforts and development expenditure on social sectors has made a noticeable contribution to poverty reduction in the past few years, but shows a declining trend and is now less than one-third of what it was in the early and mid-1980s. Remittances earned by Pakistani nationals living abroad, which have been a key poverty alleviating instrument, and is seen to have a wide decentralised distributional impact, fell to very low levels. With a far greater donor dependence and reliance on funding for structural adjustment and stabilisation from the IMF and the World Bank, all indications suggest that the trends which resulted in an increase in poverty and in the worsening of income in equality are likely to continue and probably be aggravated.

The basic theme that needs to be kept in mind is that poverty alleviation does not simply depend on economic growth, but also that the nature and distributional impact of that growth, and the general pace and the remittance culture in the economy has specific poverty alleviating outcomes. It is also important to emphasise that while a number of researchers feel that the decade long, near 7 per cent growth rates of the 1960s will be sufficient to bring about the conditions for poverty alleviation, the structural nature of the economy now, at the beginning of the twenty-first century, is radically different from that of the three decades ago and hence, there are likely to be different outcomes. For example, the role of government in the provision of basic services has diminished considerably since the 1960s and now, most services and utilities will have to be bought from the market requiring, perhaps, larger incomes. Also, at a macro level, with a far more closed economy then, than now, increases in growth may have been consumed and reinvested in the country; now with a far greater import component in the economy, some gains in incomes may be lost to the domestic economy.

Of the 60 per cent of Pakistan's population that lives in the rural areas, nearly 35 per cent is below the poverty line. This means that around 32 million Pakistanis in the rural areas live in poverty. The incidence of rural poverty is highest amongst those who own no land, and over 40 per cent of the landless households are poor and together constitute 70 per cent of the rural poor. Without extensive land and agrarian reforms, one cannot even think of alleviating, leave alone reducing, poverty in Pakistan; land reforms have to be the prime instrument for reducing poverty.

And finally, even though there are many NGOs and private sector foundations that are working at the national level to help empower women, educate men, provide employment opportunities and give health benefits and food and shelter, more efforts would have to be made to completely erase poverty from the face of the country.

Figure 9.1

Fragmentation and Segmentation of Education System

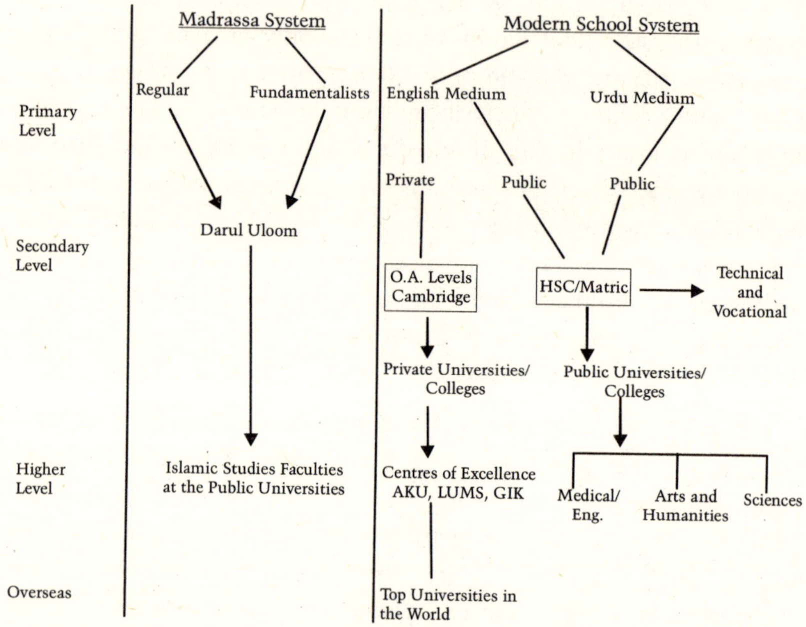

References

Bardhan, P. (1996). "Efficiency, Equity, Poverty Alleviation: Policy Issues in Less Developed Countries", *The Economic Journal* 106(438).

Besley, T. and R. Kanbur (1988). "Food Subsidies and Poverty Alleviation", *The Economic Journal* 98(392).

Husain, Ishrat (n.d.). *Education, Employment and Economic Development in Pakistan*.

———. (1999). *Pakistan: The Economy of an Elitist State*. Karachi: Oxford University Press.

Jalal, Z. (2004). *Pakistan: Public Private Partnership in the Education Sector*. Ministry of Education, Government of Pakistan.

Khan, A. Prof. and S. Naqvi (2001). "Statistics on Higher Education in Pakistan", *Higher Education Commission* (HEC), Government of Pakistan.

Stern, N. (2001). "Reform, Poverty Reduction and the New Agenda in PRC" (*mimeo*), World Bank.

World Bank (2003). "Pakistan Poverty Assessment", World Bank, PREM Sector Unit, *http://links.jstor.org/sici?sici=0013-0133%28199609%29106%3A438%3C1344%3AEEAPAP%3E2.0.CO%3B2-J, http://links.jstor.org/sici?sici=00130133%28198809%2998%3A392%3C701% 3AFSAPA%3E2.0.CO%3B2-8*

III
Improving the Quality of Physical Infrastructure

10 Access to Safe Drinking Water and Sanitation of the Poor in Bangladesh

Mahjuja M. Taznin

Introduction

It is a scientifically established fact that water is the basis of life and the importance of sanitation, through its vital link to hygiene and thus, health, follows in step. This warrants safe water and sanitation as a basic human right. Sadly, the fact is that safe drinking water and sanitation is a rather scarce commodity around the world. In major South Asian cities, even among those fortunate enough to have connections to central utilities, only 1 per cent or less, receive 24 hour water supplies. Alarmingly, one-third of Asians do not have access to safe, sustainable water supplies, even worse, one-half do not have access to adequate sanitation. This indicates the magnitude of the development issue even in developing countries with commendable success in working towards other Millennium Development Goals (MDGs). As the MDGs are a multidimensional endeavour towards understanding and tackling poverty, the urgency of accessing safe drinking water and sanitation can be better comprehended through its relationship with other MDGs and associated targets such as MDG 4—Reduce child mortality and MDG 6—Combat HIV/AIDs, malaria and other diseases.

- 1.8 million people die due to diarrhoeal diseases (including cholera) each year; 90 per cent are children under age of five, mostly in developing countries.
- 88 per cent of diarrhoeal disease is attributed to unsafe water supply, inadequate sanitation and hygiene.
- Improved water supply reduces diarrhoea morbidity by 6-25 per cent, if severe outcomes are included.
- Improved sanitation reduces diarrhoea morbidity by 32 per cent.

- An estimated 160 million people are infected with schistosomiasis which is strongly related to unsanitary excreta disposal and absence of nearby sources of safe water.
- Basic sanitation reduces schistosomiasis by up to 77 per cent.
- 500 million people are at risk from trachoma, 146 million are threatened by blindness and 6 million people are visually impaired by trachoma, which is strongly related to lack of face washing, often due to absence of nearby sources of safe water. Improving access to safe water sources and better hygiene practices can reduce trachoma morbidity by 27 per cent.
- 133 million people suffer from high intensity intestinal helminthes infections, which often lead to severe consequences such as cognitive impairment, massive dysentery or anaemia.
- These diseases cause around 9400 deaths every year.
- There are 1.5 million cases of clinical hepatitis A every year.
- In Bangladesh, the number of cases of skin lesions related to drinking water with elevated levels of arsenic is estimated at 1.5 million.

MDG 2—Achieve universal primary education and MDG 3—Promote gender equality and empower women.

- Improved school attendance due to improved health and reduced water carrying burden, especially for girls.
- Increased earnings and savings by women due to time saved and improved health, by emancipation from water carrying burden.

MDG 7—Ensure environmental sustainability and MDG 8—Develop a global partnership for development.

- Reduced water-borne pollution and wastewater discharge and improved environmental health in slum areas.
- Water problems (e.g., water scarcity, salinity, pollution) are a major constraint on the development of developing countries.

The focus of this paper is to study how development factors such as economic status, education and gender interact with the accessibility of safe drinking water and sanitation in Bangladesh and to try to discern ways in which these factors may be coordinated to achieve better access to safe drinking water and sanitation of the poor in Bangladesh.

After presenting the importance of access to safe drinking water and sanitation in Section 1, I have tried to depict the obstacles in accessing the aforementioned to the poor in Bangladesh in Section 2. In Section 3, an econometric model has been used to see what factors are critical in accessing safe drinking water and sanitation; the data for this model has been obtained from an independent baseline survey, WAB (WaterAid Bangladesh) of both rural and urban water and sanitation situation in Bangladesh. Policy implications are presented in Section 4. Section 5 concludes the paper.

Impediments in Accessing Safe Drinking Water and Sanitation to the Poor in Bangladesh

To begin with, Bangladesh has institutional ailments in the form of corruption, inefficient bureaucracy, weak rule of law, etc., which obstruct growth and development in general. In addition, water and sanitation are essentially hybrid goods[1] as they have some characteristics of public goods, for example, the marginal cost of water is ideally zero, while sanitation systems have free-rider problems. Safe water and sanitation are also merit goods as we can understand from all the positive externalities they generate. So there is a natural tendency for them to be undersupplied. This means government intervention is desirable to ensure adequate supply of these commodities which can be done by direct production by the government or, by subsidisation and regulation. To date, the government of Bangladesh has undertaken the former option so that, provision of safe water and sanitation is fundamentally the monopoly of the government. But coupled with governance problems, rampant poverty and low living standards, access to safe water and sanitation makes for a rather complicated issue. Some of the dire problems consequently obstructing access to safe water and sanitation are thus discussed next.

Lack of Effective Governance

The lack of sufficient and stable finances for water and sanitation infrastructure projects from national allocations and uncoordinated donor-

1. Hybrid goods are those goods which have characteristics of both public and private goods.

assisted infrastructure projects that frequently override local capacity, aggravate the derelict condition of state-run utilities. There is also a lack of trained personnel and managerial leadership for planning and integration of financial, hardware and administrative systems both within and between local and Central government offices. Routine monitoring systems and capacity remains inadequate. This favours supply of safe water and sanitation by the private sector, but this is blighted likewise by the inability of the government to ensure proper regulation and subsidisation which would jeopardise the quality and accessibility of safe water delivery and sanitation services. So, governance problems prove to be a critical factor in accessing safe water and sanitation to the poor. These daunting supply-side deficits are matched by impoverished communities lacking the energy and drive to demand change.

Inadequate Infrastructure

Inadequate infrastructure is a ubiquitous development problem for Bangladesh. This lack of investment in safe water and sanitation, whether on behalf of the government or, in the form of development assistance, is the direct result of mal-governance, given the fact, water and sanitation providing enterprises are state-owned (SOEs) and are afflicted with the mismanagement of a corrupt and inefficient bureaucratic structure. A trend towards 100 per cent funding of urban projects by donors has led to a lack of ownership by the government as well, which in turn has led to delays in initiating projects. Disenchanted with this situation, the Dutch government stopped funding urban water projects in 2002, the ADB pulled out in 2004 and DANIDA is now stopping its support as well.

Inefficient Delivery System

As stated, in major South Asian cities including Dhaka, less than 1 per cent of those with water supply connections enjoy 24 hour service availability. The delivery process in the urban water supply sector falls within two main sections: i) the core areas of towns/cities with established piped water supply system, and ii) the fringe and slum areas of town/cities. WaterAid Bangladesh cites experiences that reveal, fringes and slum areas are mostly neglected by the public sector. The result is that low income areas are faced with costlier alternatives such as, buying water from informal vendors at much higher prices than those charged by the state-run utilities or facing unaffordable prices to use public toilets. Thus, the poor are effectively bypassed.

Box 10.1

Case Study-1

The slum area of NatunBazaar Char is located at No.1 Customs Ghat in Khulna city, with some 250 people living in 16 large, shabby bamboo-built houses. The slum is situated beside a narrow by-road and is enclosed by the river on two other sides. The river banks are lined with 6 *kaccha* latrines. There are no sanitary latrines in the slum area. So, slum residents use these *kaccha* latrines and pollute the river water. The residents usually bathe and wash their clothes, dishes and cooking pots in the very same river, despite the bad odour. Water-borne diseases are common among the residents. Ironically, a public toilet exists adjacent to this slum. The public toilet contains 2 chambers for defecation and 3 chambers for urination. City corporation authorities completed this toilet in 2003. Since then, the toilet remains locked and unavailable for public use because the Mayor has not inaugurated it. Some of the slum residents articulated that the erection of the toilet started in the previous political regime in 2001. The local commissioner had initiated this project through his rapport with that regime. But as soon as the toilet was completed, a new Mayor was elected. The newly elected Mayor and the local commissioner are from rival political parties. So, the Mayor has not inaugurated the public toilet as he believes that it will further increase the popularity of the local commissioner. Obviously, the city corporation authorities deny this allegation.

Slum residents also complained about the probable high charge of the public toilet: one taka for urination and two taka for defecation. Interestingly, this planned charge rate is the same as the charge applied in Dhaka city public toilets. So, it will be hard for them to pay and use the toilet. Slum residents expressed the view that they will not use the toilet if such high charges are applied. But, the city corporation authorities are reluctant to revise the user charge rate. So, there is a high possibility that most slum residents will keep using *kaccha* latrines even after the opening of the public toilet.

Source: Unnayan Shamannay (2007). *A Baseline Survey on Water and Sanitation for New Programme Areas of WaterAid Bangladesh.*

Lack of Stable Housing of the Poor

Access to safe water and sanitation is part of a larger problem faced by the poor, which is one of proper housing. The poor in urban areas, who live in illegal shanty slums, and also the poor in rural areas, are vulnerable to instability in housing due to reasons ranging from natural calamity to land-grabbing. Although National Policy for WSS[2] 1998 and the National Sector Development Programme 2005 set WSS coverage for all, no legal acts or by-

2. Water Supply and Sanitation (WSS).

laws deal with houses without holding numbers, effectively excluding all slums and squatters from WSS services. Recently, Dhaka WASA[3] has developed guidelines which state the rights to WSS services for urban poor irrespective of their land tenureship or holding numbers in Dhaka. However, these guidelines have yet to be implemented. This also impedes the poor from self-financing safe water and sanitation.

Box 10.1

Case Study-2

Abu Naser is 36 years old and has been living in a slum of ward no. 22 of Khulna City Corporation for about 6 years. This ward includes a large number of shrimp processing factories situated on the banks of the Rupsha river. These factories employ a large number of low paid workers. Therefore, a huge but dispersed slum has developed in this area, mostly on government owned land, for the accommodation of these workers. Like other slum residents, Abu Naser works in one of the shrimp processing factories. He usually gets Tk.40/less than $1 per day. As it is hard to live on this income, his wife and elder son, who is only 14 years old, also work there.

The part where Abu Naser lives with his family is known as Mizaner Goli. About 12 more families live in this Mizaner Goli. The Rupsha river is very close to this part. Abu Naser, his family members and all other slum residents bathe and wash their clothes, dishes, etc., in this river. However, slum residents usually obtain their drinking water from deep tube wells. The closest tube well is more than 1 km and it takes almost 1 hour to fetch water, not unusual for such slums.

But Abu Naser narrates a horrific account of their defecation practice. Previously, they used *kaccha* latrines on the riverbanks of the Rupsha river. This polluted the water. But about 4 years earlier, the nearest shrimp processing factory destroyed those *kaccha* latrines without building any alternate latrines to ensure bad odour-free river water to wash shrimps. The factory owner not only threatened the slum residents against defecating beside the river, but also erected a fence so that residents are not able to visit that part of the riverbank. So, for the last 4 years, the practice of Abu Naser and other slum residents for defecation was to dig a hole in one corner of their slum and, defecate in polythene bags in their homes and then throw those polythene bags in the hole.

Last year, Abu Naser and other slum residents tried, unsuccessfully, to build a sanitary latrine by collecting money from each family in the area. A politically influential local, who is trying to acquire this government owned land, asked them not to erect latrines on the land. Abu Naser recounts that they had visited the local commissioner and described their miserable condition, but to no avail. The whole situation can be summarised in the desperate words of Abu Naser, "Our situation is horrific. There is no one who works for our development. We have lost hope."

Source: Unnayan Shamannay (2007). *A Baseline Survey on Water and Sanitation for New Programme Areas of WaterAid Bangladesh.*

3. Water Supply and Sewerage Authority (WASA).

Depleting Water Tables and Arsenic Contamination

Bangladesh is almost wholly dependent on groundwater. However, demand pressures of a rapidly expanding population have caused water tables to deplete. Also, arsenic contamination is making groundwater unusable, constraining safe water supplies in large areas. But again, this takes us back to the basic problem of service delivery, emphasising the need for revamping the utility services.

Natural Calamities

Bangladesh is highly prone to both hurricanes and floods. These two natural calamities destroy or damage to a great extent, safe water sources and sanitation facilities especially of the poor, in both rural and urban areas since both areas are flood-prone. This increases the costs and risks of investing in safe water and sanitation by the poor.

An Econometric Model: How Do Development Factors Interact with Access to Safe Water and Sanitation?

Data Background

An econometric analysis has been conducted using the multinomial logistic regression model to see how development factors like economic status, education, gender and location interact with the accessibility of safe drinking water and sanitation. The data used is household data obtained from an independent baseline survey used to collect basic information on both the rural and urban water and sanitation situation in Bangladesh. This study was designed and commissioned by ASEH (Advancing Sustainable Environmental Health), a core programme of WAB (WaterAid Bangladesh) and undertaken by Unnayan Shamannay, a research organisation in Bangladesh, in the year 2006.

Econometric Model

Here 'safe access' is a dummy variable for access to safe drinking water with four categories. A value of 1 refers to access to safe water source (or 'safe use'), defined as households collecting their drinking water from tube well with green mark or, from deep tube well or applying proper purification method if collected from any other unsafe source. A value of 2 refers to 'safe storage' of drinking water indicating that households keep the water pot covered while storing and keep at a high place. A value of 3 refers to 'safe transportation' of drinking water reflecting that households clean their water carrying device properly and cover while carrying. And finally, a zero value indicates that access is 'not safe' for any of the above cases. The general form of the regression equation estimated for determining the factors influencing probability of access to safe drinking water in the four categories is:

$$\text{Safe access} = \beta_0 + \beta_1 \text{ pme} + \beta_2 \text{ Poor} + \beta_3 \text{ Sex} + \beta_4 \text{ Education} + \beta_5 \text{ Location}$$

Table 10.1

Variable Descriptions

Safe Access	0 = not safe, 1 = safe use, 2 = safe storage, 3 = safe transportation
pme	Per capita monthly expenditure (in taka)
Poor	Dummy variable for CBN[4] poverty (0= non-poor, 1= poor)
Sex	Dummy variable for sex of household head (0=female, 1=male)
Education	Education of household head (number of years)
Location	Dummy variable for location (0= urban, 1= rural)

The estimated regression results are given in the Annexure. Results suggest that poverty negatively influences certain categories of safe water accessibility of a household. Of all the explanatory variables of the logit regression explaining access to safe water, only location is found to be strongly significant in all categories while education and sex of household head are significant for certain categories too.

Per capita monthly expenditure (proxy for per capita income) is only weakly significant (level of significance $\geq$ 15 per cent) for all categories. This is not surprising since access to safe water[5] seems to depend more on location rather than poverty level as indicated by survey statistics. It should also be kept in mind that safe water is an inelastic good which does not therefore, show much increase in consumption due to increase in income.

4. Here poverty is defined in terms of cost of basic needs (CBN) method.
5. Water was considered 'safe' if it was free from iron, saline, bad smell or discolour and have arsenic (PPB<10) and bacteria (FC<=10).

Figure 10.1

Regional Distribution of Safe Water among Surveyed Households

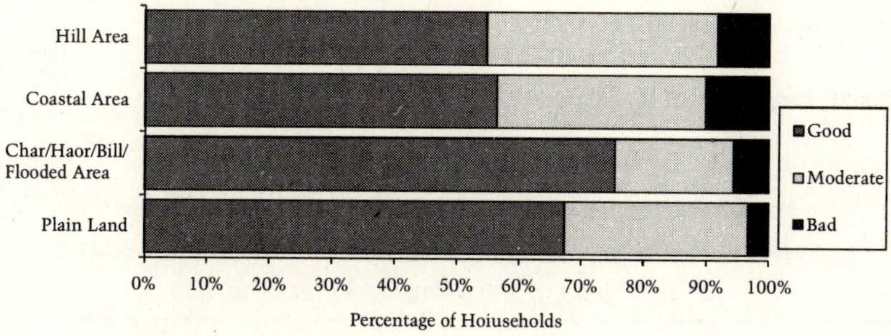

Source: Unnayan Shamannay (2007). *A Baseline Survey on Water and Sanitation for New Programme Areas of WaterAid Bangladesh.*

Policy Implications

Impact of Location on Access to Safe Water and Sanitation

The regression results show that location is the major factor determining safe water access.

Table 10.2

Probability of a Household Having Access to Safe Water in Different Categories according to the Location of Household from Urban to Rural

Category	*Probability*	*Level of Significance*
Not Safe	44 per cent more likely	<1%
Safe Use	14.32 per cent less likely	<1%
Safe Storage	6.59 per cent less likely	<1%
Safe Transportation	23.1 per cent less likely	<1%

Note: For discrete change of dummy variable from 0 to 1; i.e., from urban to rural.

This is a clear manifestation of the arsenic problem; national statistics show that present access to safe water for urban areas is 99 per cent and rural areas is 69 per cent down from 95 per cent in 1999 after discovery of widespread arsenic contamination. Again, present access to basic sanitation is 60 per cent for urban areas and 29 per cent for rural areas. However, around 50 per cent of the available finance in the last five years has gone to urban areas. This reflects how inefficient governance breeds inequality in water supply and sanitation for the poor, the majority of whom reside in rural areas. Thus, a major initiative in improving water supply and sanitation for the poor requires educating and facilitating citizens in demanding that their political representatives deliver their rights to water supply and sanitation services.

Prioritising Hygiene Education

Table 10.3

Probability of a Household Having Safe Water Access in Different Categories due to an Increase in the Education of the Head of the Household by One Year

Category	*Probability*	*Level of Significance*
Not Safe	1.07 per cent less likely	<1%
Safe Use	0.21 per cent less likely	40.9%
Safe Storage	0.24 per cent more likely	11.6%
Safe Transportation	1.04 per cent more likely	<1%

Results indicate that education increases safe water access but is insignificant for safe use. This shows that simply basic education does not give rise to demand for safe water or sanitation. There is a need for widespread hygiene education which should be introduced into the education system for a cost effective means of improving awareness. The impact results for poverty also show that awareness is important because, safe water use is higher for poor households.

Table 10.4

Probability of a Household Having Safe Water Access in Different Categories according to Household Poverty Status

Category	*Probability*	*Level of Significance*
Not Safe	1.38 per cent more likely	59.5%
Safe Use	8.26 per cent more likely	<1%
Safe Storage	7.69 per cent less likely	<1%
Safe Transportation	1.96 per cent less likely	33.7%

Note: For discrete change of dummy variable from 0 to 1; i.e., from non-poor to poor.

Harnessing Established Socio-Economic Structures

Table 10.5

Probability of a Household having Safe Water Access in Different Categories according to the Sex of Household Head

Category	*Probability*	*Level of Significance*
Not Safe	2.94 per cent more likely	31.3%
Safe Use	2.03 per cent more likely	45.8%
Safe Storage	3.55 per cent less likely	7.4%
Safe Transportation	2.64 per cent less likely	28%

Note: For discrete change of dummy variable from 0 to 1; i.e., from female to male.

Although not very significant, results indicate that women tend to have better water usage and storage. This reveals the underlying point that women are bigger stakeholders in safe water supply and sanitation. Since poor or underprivileged women already have a socio-economic network through microfinance institutions, any initiatives for improving safe water supply and sanitation could be through this structure. This would enhance effectiveness and sustainability of the initiatives and improve efficiency. Women have clearer interests in continued functioning of water supply and sanitation systems considering the gender burden of safe water supply and sanitation and, the implications it has for women in terms of earnings, health, time, dignity, mobility, etc.

Conclusion

Findings suggest that poverty status is not a major influence on access to safe water and sanitation. Indeed accessing safe water and sanitation is not a costly goal; the Bangladesh government's debt service payments are 16 times greater than the extra money needed to meet the water and sanitation MDGs. In essence, the critical factor for determining whether water supply and sanitation services successfully reach or work for the poor is governance. This is indicated by the regression results which show location and then education to be the most significant factor in accessing safe water. Conversely, accessing safe water and sanitation is not just urgent and imperative for achieving the MDGs and thus, enjoying the fruits of development. As a developing nation, we not only lag behind developed nations in terms of living standards, but also in preparedness against challenges poised by the new era that is to dawn. We are on the verge of a new reality—the reality of environment and ecological change. It is a frequently cited proposition that any future world war will be for water, this comes from the looming fresh water scarcity that threatens the world as the environment and ecology changes with global warming. Thus, failing to access safe drinking water and sanitation has repercussions that reach far beyond standards of living to the point of our mere survival.

References

ADB (2006). *Asia Water Watch 2015; Are Countries in Asia on Track to Meet Target 10 of the Millennium Development Goals?* A joint publication of the ADB, UNDP, UNESCAP and WHO.

Allen, C.S. (2003). "The WaterAid Bangladesh/VERC 100% Sanitation Approach: Cost, Motivation and Sustainability", Research Paper for London School of Hygiene and Tropical Medicine.

Browning, E.K. and J.M. Browning (1994). *Public Finance and the Price System, Fourth Edition*. India: Pearson Education (Singapore) Pte. Ltd.

Kapoor, K. and Z. Hussain (2006). "Delivery of Basic Services: Citizens' Feedback", in S. Ahmed and W. Mahmud, eds., *Growth and Poverty; The Development Experience of Bangladesh*. Dhaka: The University Press Limited.

Kaufmann, Kraay and Mastruzzi (2006). *Governance Matters V: Aggregate and Individual Governance Indicators for 1996-2005*. The World Bank.

Khan, A.R. and M. Hossain (1989). *The Strategy of Development in Bangladesh*. London: The Macmillan Press Ltd.

Kjær, A.M. (2004). *Governance*. Cambridge: Polity.

Lawrence, Meigh and Sullivan (2003). "The Water Poverty Index: An International Comparison", *Keele Economics Research Papers*.

Mahmud, W. (2006). "Resource Mobilisation and Management of Economic Growth in South Asia", Theme Paper for the SAFA Conference, Dhaka, 15 July.

Rahman, A.A. and P. Ravenscroft, eds. (2003). *Groundwater Resources and Development in Bangladesh; Background to the Arsenic Crisis, Agricultural Potential and the Environment*. Dhaka: The University Press Limited.

Sen, Amartya (1999). *Development as Freedom*. Knopf and Oxford, New York: Oxford University Press.

Unnayan Shamannay (2007). "A Baseline Survey on Water and Sanitation for New Programme Areas of WaterAid Bangladesh", Dhaka.

WaterAid (2006). "WaterAid Bangladesh's contribution to the IDSC submission on Urbanization and Water", *http://www.wateraid.org/Document search WaterAid.htm*

———. (2006). "Water and Sanitation Service Delivery", *http://www.wateraid.org/ Document search WaterAid.htm*

———. (2006). "Water for All? A Study on the Effectiveness of Asian Development Bank Funded Water and Sanitation Projects in Ensuring Sustainable Services for the Poor".

———. (2005). "WaterAid-national water sector assessment; Bangladesh", *http:// www.wateraid.org/Document search WaterAid.htm*

WaterAid Synthesis Report, www.*wateraid.org*

Zohir, S. (2006). "Participation of Non-Government Organisations in the Delivery of Social Services", in S. Ahmed and W. Mahmud, eds., *Growth and Poverty; The Development Experience of Bangladesh*. Dhaka: The University Press Limited.

Annexure Table A-10.1

Results of the Multinomial Logistic Regression

Number of observations = 3377

LR chi2(15) = 718.69

Prob > chi2 = 0.0000

Log likelihood = -3933.833 Pseudo R2 = 0.0837

safe_access	*Coef.*	*Std. Err.*	*z*	*P>|z|*	*[95% Conf.*	*Interval]*
safe use						
pme	.000186	.0001502	1.24	0.216	-.0001084	.0004804
dum_poor	.2545796	.1317482	1.93	0.053	-.0036422	.5128013
sex_head	-.1449421	.144118	-1.01	0.315	-.4274081	.1375239
eduyr_head	.020774	.0130404	1.59	0.111	-.0047847	.0463326
dum_location	-2.085496	.1202348	-17.35	0.000	-2.321151	-1.84984
_cons	.9701689	.2540835	3.82	0.000	.4721743	1.468163
safe storage						
pme	-.000108	.000221	-0.49	0.625	-.0005411	.0003252
dum_poor	-.7619449	.1801112	-4.23	0.000	-1.114956	-.4089334
sex_head	-.4107717	.2028732	-2.02	0.043	-.808396	-.0131475
eduyr_head	.052981	.0186	2.85	0.004	.0165256	.0894364
dum_location	-2.278954	.1575888	-14.46	0.000	-2.587822	-1.970086
_cons	.9806005	.3432582	2.86	0.004	.3078267	1.653374
safe trans~n						
pme	.0002152	.0001495	1.44	0.150	-.0000778	.0005083
dum_poor	-.1243355	.1363112	-0.91	0.362	-.3915005	.1428295
sex_head	.0457884	.1712354	0.27	0.789	-.2898269	.3814037
eduyr_head	.0747437	.0136679	5.47	0.000	.0479551	.1015323
dum_location	-2.532028	.1264103	-20.03	0.000	-2.779787	-2.284268
_cons	.8810508	.2683562	3.28	0.001	.3550824	1.407019

Note: safe_access==not safe is the base outcome.

Source: Study conducted by Unnayan Shamannay for WaterAid Bangladesh.

Annexure Table A-10.2

Marginal Effects after Mlogit

y = Pr(safe_access==0) (predict, outcome (0))
= .38542205

variable	*dy/dx*	*Std. Err.*	*z*	*P>|z|*	*[95% C.I.]*		*X*
pme	-.000036	.00003	-1.16	0.245	-.000097	.000025	778.584
dum_poor*	.0138724	.02609	0.53	0.595	-.03727	.065015	.655611
sex_head*	.0294245	.02916	1.01	0.313	-.027737	.086586	.894581
eduyr_~d	-.0107058	.00247	-4.33	0.000	-.015557	-.005855	3.02576
dum_lo~n*	.4398268	.01449	30.36	0.000	.411429	.468224	.704768

Note: (*) dy/dx is for discrete change of dummy variable from 0 to 1.

Source: Study conducted by Unnayan Shamannay for WaterAid Bangladesh.

Annexure Table A-10.3

Marginal Effects after Mlogit

y = Pr(safe_access==1) (predict, outcome (1))
= .29876166

variable	*dy/dx*	*Std. Err.*	*z*	*P>|z|*	*[95% C.I.]*		*X*
pme	.0000277	.00003	1.07	0.284	-.000023	.000078	778.584
dum_poor*	.0826615	.02228	3.71	0.000	.038984	.126339	.655611
sex_head*	-.0202688	.0273	-0.74	0.458	-.073779	.033242	.894581
eduyr_~d	-.0020922	.00253	-0.83	0.409	-.007054	.00287	3.02576
dum_lo~n*	-.1432302	.01812	-7.90	0.000	-.178754	-.107707	.704768

Note: (*) dy/dx is for discrete change of dummy variable from 0 to 1.

Source: Study conducted by Unnayan Shamannay for WaterAid Bangladesh.

Annexure Table A-10.4

Marginal Effects after Mlogit

y = Pr(safe_access==2) (predict, outcome (2))
= .09350885

variable	*dy/dx*	*Std. Err.*	*z*	*P>|z|*	*[95% C.I.]*		*X*
pme	-.0000188	.00002	-1.09	0.274	-.000053	.000015	778.584
dum_poor*	-.0769163	.01722	-4.47	0.000	-.110672	-.043161	.655611
sex_head*	-.0355187	.01988	-1.79	0.074	-.074485	.003448	.894581
eduyr_~d	.0023568	.0015	1.57	0.116	-.000579	.005292	3.02576
dum_lo~n*	-.0659304	.01254	-5.26	0.000	-.090504	-.041357	.704768

Note: (*) dy/dx is for discrete change of dummy variable from 0 to 1.

Source: Study conducted by Unnayan Shamannay for WaterAid Bangladesh.

Annexure Table A-10.5

Marginal Effects after Mlogit

y = Pr(safe_access==3) (predict, outcome (3))
= .22230745

variable	*dy/dx*	*Std. Err.*	*z*	*P>|z|*	*[95% C.I.]*		*X*
pme	.0000271	.00002	1.31	0.191	-.000014	.000068	778.584
dum_poor*	-.0196176	.02043	-0.96	0.337	-.059665	.02043	.655611
sex_head*	.026363	.0244	1.08	0.280	-.021452	.074178	.894581
eduyr_~d	.0104411	.00217	4.82	0.000	.006192	.01469	3.02576
dum_lo~n*	-.2306662	.0179	-12.88	0.000	-.265758	-.195574	.704768

Note: (*) dy/dx is for discrete change of dummy variable from 0 to 1.

Source: Study conducted by Unnayan Shamannay for WaterAid Bangladesh.

11 Infrastructural Constraints on Agricultural Productivity

Saher Asad

Methodology

The paper first provides a literature review of the existing research already done on the relationship between infrastructure and agricultural productivity. The second part presents an empirical model using 2000-2001 data for 29 districts of Punjab. Based on the analysis, the third part presents certain policy recommendations which could help solve the problem. The last part concludes the paper.

Literature Review

Agricultural productivity has been defined as a function of more than one factor. Some of the factors quoted in the literature include modern technology, resource endowments and human capital. The idea of comparing agricultural productivities was initiated by Hayami and Ruttan who said that most of the variation in agricultural productivity can be explained by the three factors cited above. However, they wanted to compare across countries and not within a country across different regions. A problem with their study was that they could not study a separate production function for agricultural productivity within the developing countries as the sample was too small (Hayami and Ruttan, 1970). Another important study has been carried out by Antle who pursued the model of inter-country comparison and went on to include variables like education, research and infrastructure of a particular country as explanatory variables. The study utilised the 1965 aggregate agricultural production data and the concept of the aggregate production function to study the effects of transportation and communication infrastructure on aggregate agricultural productivity. This study was able to use a much larger sample and was able to estimate a separate production function for developing countries and then tested the Hayami and Ruttan hypothesis. One of the problems with the study was however, the measuring of output considering the fact that relative prices keep on changing. The changing relative prices cause a downward bias in the output of LDCs and hence created a problem. The study however indicates a positive and significant relationship between infrastructure and agricultural productivity (Antle, 1983).

Infrastructure can impact agricultural productivity in more than one way. These include direct as well as indirect ways. The direct mechanism is termed as specialisation effect in which access to market through roads leads to the farmer specialising in a particular product. The other impact is the indirect one which is also called intensification. In this case, productivity is defined as a function of irrigation, fertiliser and specialised seeds etc. The access to market through roads hence, leads to intensification and hence, increased productivity. Studies from different countries have tried to separate out this effect and hence, have supported the hypothesis that direct effect is far stronger than the indirect effect. (Khachatryan *et al.*, 2004) The first study is from India. The data allows testing several hypotheses on market access affecting productivity. In this paper, the data are tested with a model for South India estimating a set of equations separately using panel (longitudinal) analysis approach. Total productivity is expressed as a function of market access, inputs and resources; and also inputs as a function of market, access, productivity and resources. The model tries to separate out the two effects by adding independent variables which include irrigated area, area under fertilisers and the area under HYV seeds. Therefore, by adding the above given variables as controls while having farm to market roads as independent variables, the author has calculated the elasticities and hence, separated out the direct and indirect effects. The elasticity for direct is around 0.8 and that for indirect is around 0.5. The emerging policy recommendation is to allocate resources in a more efficient way rather than stressing on the use of inputs etc. (Khachatryan *et al.*, 2004).

Another important case study is from Nigeria. The study has shown that the process of intensification here has resulted in increase in productivity and the farmer's welfare. They have defined intensification in two ways which includes population-driven and market-driven. Population-driven intensification requires that an increase in population density leads to an increased demand for land, which induces a reduction in fallow periods once the land frontier is reached. As a result, land becomes more valuable relative to other inputs, and increases in land productivity become desirable. In market-driven intensification, Binswanger and McIntire point out that improved access to markets can also induce intensification. Market access can be increased by improving infrastructure, such as the road network, which reduces marketing costs and therefore increases farm gate prices. As market access improves, farmers have an incentive to increase the area under cultivation for cash crop production. Animal traction may be adopted to facilitate this. Improved access to market hence allows for increased incentives to apply more inputs. The paper shows that the essential preconditions for this growth were, first, a good road system that made it viable for farmers to market a cash crop and intensify the production system, and second, a technological breakthrough that provided farmers with a highly profitable cash crop. This again shows the importance of the infrastructure for bringing about increased productivity (Smith *et al.*, 1994).

Another study looking at the direct *versus* indirect effect was targeted at Thailand. Farmers in many mountainous regions like Doi Inthanon of Northern Thailand had to give up their traditional farming systems because of opium prohibition and forest protection. This has added vulnerability to their income and self-sufficiency. Since these changes in the mid to end 1970s, the importance of cash income to secure farmers' livelihood has increased. During the same time, Thailand's rapidly growing economy accelerated the demand for horticultural products opening the doors to new markets such as temperate cash crops in which the farmers of Doi Inthanon have a comparative advantage (Hau, 1999).

In order for farmers to participate in this economic development, adequate incentives in the form of favourable price cost ratio, to insure profitability are needed. Markets must be accessible to farmers because access to and participation in agricultural markets positively influences productivity. In addition, an increase in agricultural productivity can only be achieved through specialisation and intensification because of the high population growth and limited availability of agricultural land in the research area. Therefore, many farmers are dependent on a source of income as their degree of self-subsistent farming is non-existent or diminishing (Hau, 1999).

Study analyses the effects of specialisation *versus* intensification. Productivity is taken as a function of inputs, resources and market access. Inputs are defined as function of resources, market access and total productivity. Results have shown that irrigation and market access have a very significant impact on aggregate productivity. The case study of villages in Doi Inthanon clearly shows that market access affects aggregate productivity of farms in more than one way. Firstly, an improved market access of 10 per cent aggregate productivity increases by 11.1 per cent. Specialisation effects contribute 9.4 per cent and intensification effects contribute 1.7 per cent towards increases in aggregate productivity. In this case study, specialisation effects have been found to be stronger than intensification effects. This leads to the conclusion that again it is not the fact that access to inputs is an issue, just the infrastructure is sufficient in bringing about a change (Hau, 1999). Going further, Easter in his model tries to measure, by use of production functions, the contribution to total output of not only the quantity of traditional inputs (land, labour, fertiliser, etc.), but also the quality of certain inputs like infrastructure which includes markets as well as roads. He says that factors such as the quantity and quality of irrigation or infrastructural investments have varying elasticities of supply. The possibility and cost of expanding the supply of such inputs may vary considerably among regions. Strategies for increasing agricultural output and productivity should incorporate the different factor supply responses among regions. Similar approach has been used for India and hence, similar results are obtained (Easter *et al.*, 1977).

Agricultural Productivity in Pakistan

The literature has identified a few factors which have influenced agricultural productivity in Pakistan. These include, technology, increased usage of HYV seeds, literacy of farmers, fertilisers etc. The model as shown does provide significant results but still there is a lack of the infrastructure element which has been carried out for other countries. As a part of this paper, now I will present my own study of the 29 districts of Punjab and then sum up conclusions about how and what factors are stronger here and then accordingly what policy recommendations should be required. The key motivation is again the lack of literature related to Pakistan, studying the impact of infrastructure on agricultural productivity and its ramifications.

Literature related to Pakistan revolves around finding the links between poverty alleviation and agricultural productivity. Rauf Azhar in his paper takes up the productivity as a function of labour units, irrigation, fertilisers and years of schooling of the farmer (Azhar, 1995). Another paper takes up productivity as a function of cropped area, labour force, fertiliser, area irrigated by all source, tractor supply and credit disbursed (Hussain and Ishfaq, 1997). Therefore, farms to market roads have generally been ignored in the production function. Another motivation is the fact that without infrastructure, it would be mundane studying the impact of education and HYV seeds. The reason is that access to all these facilities comes with roads which are an important aspect of the infrastructure.

In order to test my hypothesis, I have studied 29 districts of Punjab. The data has been obtained from multiple sources which include the Mouza census, Agricultural census and the provincial government department data. The model uses the wheat yield as the dependent variable and tries studying the impact of market roads and irrigation as infrastructure on agricultural productivity in this cross-section of these 29 districts. Controls include education, irrigation, population density etc. The quadratic form has been used to test for any form of quadratic relationship. The model structure and functional form are an amalgam of those used in the papers and case studies discussed above. The key summary for the variables are provided in Table 11.1.

Table 11.1

Summary Statistics

Variable	*Observations*	*Mean*	*Std. Deviation*	*Min.*	*Max.*
Wheat Yield	29	2.215137	.7201552	.6806723	3.256757
Farm to Market Roads	29	758.9445	223.3921	338.49	1479.04
Region	29	2.586207	1.052794	1	4
Population Density	29	526.2828	641.1829	89.6	3565.9
Percentage of Formal Credit for Fertilisers	29	34.45707	17.18095	5.861665	74.54147
Agricultural HH having Education Above Matric	29	9.758621	3.214423	2	16
Wheat Irrigated	29	81.58621	32.04184	2	99

Note: The equation for the model is:

Wheat_yield = b0 + b1 (farm_to_mktroads) + b3 (farm to market roads qr) + b2 (per_formal_cred) + b3 (fertiliser per unit of area) + b4 (wheatirrigated) + b5 (pop_density) + b6 (farms_abv_matric)

Table 11.2

Regression using Wheat Yield as Dependent Variable

Variable	*OLS, robust*	*(t-stat)*
Farm to Market Roads	-.0012103	(-0.98)
Farm to Market Road Sqr	1.02e-06	(1.82)
Farms with Matric and Above	.0082263	(0.62)
Irrigated Area	.0173196	(7.15)
Percentage Institutional Credit	.0039901	(1.75)
Fertiliser	3.097894	(1.74)
Population Density	.0001537	(1.52)
Constant	.3147523	(0.45)
R-Square	0.8470	
F-Statistic	82.89	

The regression results using OLS robust standard errors are in Table 11.2. The results show that as access to market increases at very low level of infrastructure there is an insignificant relationship. However, when roads keep on increasing and the level of infrastructure reaches a certain point, there is a significant positive impact on the wheat yield. This can be explained by the fact that initially at the low level of farm to market road, the road might be far from the village and might have a significant impact. Irrigation which is another measure of infrastructure also has very significant and positive impact on wheat yield. The intensification impact can also be seen here by the fact that the coefficient on fertiliser is statistically significant. This means that as fertiliser used per unit of area increases, the wheat yield also increases. Institutionalised credit mechanism also has a positive significant impact on wheat yield. The R-square for the model is 0.8470 which means that the model explains 84.87 per cent variation into account. The F-statistic is also significant which shows that all the variables are jointly significant. Regional dummy also has a significant negative impact when added to the model. The regional dummy divides Punjab into four parts which are north, central, west and south and hence, assigns a value in the range 1 to 4 to each of the districts. How this division has been done. The linear form of the equation with regional dummy is presented in Table 11.3.

Table 11.3

Regression using Wheat Yield as Dependent Variable

Variable	*OLS, robust*	*(t-stat)*
Farm to Market Roads	.0004722	(1.74)
Region	-.1543531	(-1.80)
Farms with Matric and Above	-.0250569	(-1.18)
Irrigated Area	.020244	(7.03)
Percentage Institutional Credit	-.0250569	(-1.18)
Fertiliser	1.858112	(0.91)
Population Density	.000141	(1.89)
Constant	.3350753	(0.65)
R-Square	0.8517	
F-Statistic	55.59	

This means that moving from north to central to west to south, the wheat yield in Punjab decreases. This means that holding other things constant there are regional differences in productivity of wheat which could be attributed to natural differences. The above model explains the fact that productivity is a function of infrastructure and other inputs like fertiliser and institutional credit. It is also important to study as to what these inputs are a function of. In order to study that, we run the following equation:

fertiliser = b0 + b1 (farm_to_mktroads) + b2 (region) + b3 (pop_density) + b4 (per_formal_cred) + b5 (farms_abv_ matric)

Table 11.4

Regression using Fertiliser as Dependent Variable

Variable	*OLS, robust*	*(t-stat)*
Farm to Market Roads	.0000487	(3.03)
Farms with Matric and Above	.0009409	(0.36)
Irrigated Area	.0001131	(2.33)
Region	.0122586	(1.70)
Constant	.0698883	(1.63)
F-Statistic	3.02	

The results show that fertiliser use is a function of farm to market roads. This means that as farm to market roads increase, the fertiliser use increase. This means that infrastructure has a direct impact on the use of inputs. Therefore, the intensification effect also persists in Pakistan along with the direct effect of specialisation. Regional differences in use of fertiliser are marginally significant at 10 per cent level of significance. These differences could be due to farm size or the wealth of the person. The percentage of institutional credit for fertiliser use is also significant showing that as access to credit increases, so does the use of fertiliser.

Table 11.5

Elasticity Looking at Direct and Indirect Impact of Infrastructure

Variable	*Elasticity for 1.2*	*Elasticity for 1.4*
Farm to Market Roads	0.28	0.24

Estimating the elasticity, we see that the direct impact has an elasticity of 0.28. The indirect impact here has an elasticity of about 0.24. This means that in our case as well, there is going to be higher elasticity for the direct impact than the indirect impact. This means that improvement infrastructure would lead to increased wheat yield. Therefore, investment infrastructure emerges as a key policy recommendation. Unfortunately in Pakistan, emphasis has been placed on increasing irrigation as a sole mechanism for increasing productivity and little emphasis has been placed on improvement of roads.

Also, the green revolution talked about the introduction of high yielding variety seeds and irrigation but very little emphasis was placed on development of markets and roads as infrastructure.

The model is however not free of limitations. Firstly, we have assumed that most of the wheat is procured by the government and hence, there are no district level changes in price. Another problem that what we have is a macro picture which looks at how wheat yield gets impacted at a macro level and not how the wheat yield of an individual farm household gets impacted and what micro level factors determine that e.g. migration.

Policy Recommendations

In our country, Government has emphasised on increasing the availability of inputs which they feel would lead to a change in wheat yield. The importance of inputs cannot be ignored but what needs to be realised is that infrastructure like roads are the key to development. Without the infrastructure, there would be very little use of making input markets as without roads there would be no access to market and farmers would firstly not specialise and also, would have very low yields as they do not have access to the market. Roads provide access to market and hence, specialisation as well as intensification effects on wheat yield. This leads to the conclusion that again it is not the fact that access to inputs is an issue, just the infrastructure is sufficient in bringing about a change (Hau, 1999). It has been shown that the essential preconditions for this growth were, first, a good road system that made it viable for farmers to market a cash crop and intensify the production system, and second, a technological breakthrough that provided farmers with a highly profitable cash crop. (Smith *et al.*, 1994). In order to solve this problem, we suggest some policy recommendation that emerge out of this analysis as provided above.

Firstly, infrastructure is a good that has externalities. The first way to account for this externality is that let the government invest in the infrastructure. The second way which is the nuanced way is that let the people own the infrastructure. The example has been provided by Prof. Muhammad Yunus who said that private ownership could be held by the poor collectively. He gave the example of the upcoming port in Chittagong and said that it could be owned by the poor people of Bangladesh in the form of a port authority. Similar things could be done in Pakistan for building roads by building up a road authority which would be owned by the small farmers.

Another important recommendation is of investment in complementarities which is extremely important. In order to promote investment in the infrastructure by the foreign investors, the government needs to provide incentives to the foreign investors in the form of tax rebates as well as complementary infrastructure that they would require.

Development of clusters of markets in all districts is also required in order to promote infrastructure. Therefore, as large markets will develop, this would eventually lead to the development of roads around it and hence, provide access to markets. These large markets would also attract the foreign investors and hence, would lead to foreign investment being directed to the development of infrastructure.

Other complementarities with the infrastructure also would be needed to increase the wheat yield like education. Investment in public service by the government also needs to increase and this would lead to improvement in wheat yield. The reason is that if any person from the farm household acquires education, he would be able to suggest that certain inputs are needed to increase productivity. Therefore, the farmer would then use these inputs and hence, increase yield. Investment in research is another important determinant of agricultural productivity. Also, tying up agricultural research institutes to universities and policy makers is extremely important.

Conclusion

Many factors have been responsible in effecting the agricultural productivity. The literature highlights education, research, technology, advanced inputs and infrastructure. The literature also shows that there is a significant positive relationship between infrastructure which I have used as roads and agricultural productivity. The relationship is however two-way i.e., direct and indirect. Direct relationship measures specialisation and the indirect measures intensification. Both combine in increasing the wheat yield, hence agricultural productivity. Case studies from different parts of the world have shown that direct impact is stronger than indirect by looking at the elasticity. The empirical evidence from Pakistan also shows that the direct and indirect relationship exists. Again in case of Pakistan as well, the direct relationship is much stronger than the indirect relationship as shown by the elasticities. As an outcome of the analysis, we see that direct impact of infrastructure which is of specialisation is very important for agricultural productivity. Therefore, we need to take relevant policy measures to increase investment in the infrastructure which would eventually lead to an increase in productivity.

References

Agricultural Census of Pakistan (2000). Government of Pakistan.

Antle, John M. (1983). "Infrastructure and Aggregate Agricultural Productivity: International Evidence", *Economic Development and Cultural Change* 31(3): 609-619. April.

Azhar, Rauf A.(1994-95). "Education and Technical Efficiency during the Green Revolution in Pakistan", *Economic Development and Cultural Change* 43.

Easter, William K., Martin E. Abel and George Norton (1977). "Regional Differences in Agricultural Productivity in Selected Areas of India", *American Journal of Agricultural Economics* 59(2): 257-265. May.

Hau, A. (1999). *Rural Market Structures and the Impact of Market Access on Agricultural Productivity - A Case Study in Doi Inthanon of Northern Thailand*. Diplomarbeit der Universität Hohenheim, Germany.

Hayami, Yujiro and V.W. Ruttan (1970). "Agricultural Productivity Differences among Countries", *The American Economic Review* 60(5): 895-911. December.

Hussain, Turab S.M. and Mohammad Ishfaq (1997). "Dynamics of Agricultural Productivity and Poverty in Pakistan", *Working Paper* No. 97-14. CMER Working Paper Series. October.

Khachatryan, N., M. von Oppen, A. Khachatryan (2004). "Market Access and Plant Productivity in Indian Agriculture", *Quarterly Journal of Armenian Agricultural Academy*.

Mouza census of Pakistan (1998). Government of Pakistan.

Smith, Joyotee, Anthony D. Barau, Abraham Goldman, James H. Mareck (1994). "The Role of Technology in Agricultural Intensification: The Evolution of Maize Production in the Northern Guinea Savanna of Nigeria", *Economic Development and Cultural Change* 42(3): 537-554. April.

12 The Case of Traffic Congestion in Mumbai

Manka Bajaj

Introduction

Economic development and urbanisation are two sides of the same coin. As a nation progresses along the path of prosperity, its cities must cope with a growing population and ever-increasing human activity. This human activity manifests itself as trade and commerce and creates opportunities for further growth. Consequently, there is immense pressure on physical infrastructure in these cities. It is this pressure that motivated Shanghai to spring up a 30 km Dong Hai to allow driving across the sea and Mumbai to expand its 'walls' to squeeze in 300,000 employees in a tiny pocket of reclaimed land, the Nariman Point. This paper develops on the transport related infrastructural bottlenecks impeding growth. Using the example of Mumbai, one of the fastest growing cities of South Asia, this paper suggests practical solutions to address a key urban infrastructure challenge—traffic congestion.

Mumbai, once a small fishing village, is now the commercial capital of India. Even though it is one of the most populous cities of the world, scores of migrants continue to pour in. The need to decongest the island city was felt in the early 1970s and was expressed in a proposal by the Bombay Metropolitan Regional Planning Board. Thesc plans were formalised to create a 'twin-city' out of the neighbouring land on the east, now called Navi Mumbai.

However, efforts to decentralise and decongest Mumbai have not been entirely successful. Traffic in the city is on the rise. To address this, there are ambitious plans to upgrade the transport infrastructure. For example, Rs. 2,356 crore to launch the first link of the metro from Versova to Ghatkopar. Hundred and fifty seven new German-designed, high-speed trains costing Rs. 20 crore each. An airport makeover worth Rs. 7,500 crore. Rs. 6,288 crore to revamp roads and build flyovers. And yet it does not seem enough. The exploding demand for commuting has forced Mumbai to look beyond the existing limits of land, and even 'fish' for space in the sea.

This paper presents a detailed analysis of Mumbai's transport infrastructure. Section 2 outlines key concepts in urban transport planning. Minimising use of private transport is established as the prime policy objective for decongesting Mumbai. Section 3 uses economic theory to suggest a solution to achieve this policy objective—road pricing. The author uses "The Tragedy of the Commons" to examine the "fairness" of levying a congestion charge. The paper also draws on other cases of road pricing around the world, in order to understand the best practices for service delivery. Section 4 suggests "progressive" alternatives to manage the urban transport issue. Special emphasis is given to alternatives that ensure inclusive growth, where access is not limited by a person's ability to pay.

Towards Sustainable Urban Transport

A study by the Union Ministry of Urban Development suggests that above 75 per cent of commutation takes place for purposes of employment and education. In a developing economy like ours, a rising per capita trip rate is a sign of economic growth as it implies spread of education and increase in employment levels. Therefore, instead of targeting reduction in per capita trips, it is better to reduce the travel demand by minimising the average trip length.[1] This is done through decentralisation of economic activity in a city and discouraging the traditional pattern of growth every city seems to fall into—a concentrated business centre surrounded by sprawling residential suburbs. This leads us to related issues of urban planning that are beyond the scope of this paper. However, it would be of practical use to policy makers to keep in mind that planning to meet the transport needs of a city need not necessarily be about matching the ever increasing travel demand of commuters; it is wise to also explore solutions that contain the travel demand without compromising on economic development.

The key to transport planning however, is how the travel demand is addressed. Traffic congestion results from surplus demand for road space. A 9 per cent GDP growth rate for India means that the purchasing power is

1. *India Infrastructure Report 2006*.

increasing and so is the number of vehicles on road. This is a strong incentive for the government to increase infrastructure supply by building new roads. This increase in road capacity has a direct impact of reducing traffic congestion and increasing vehicle speeds. A second-level impact however, is that free flowing traffic attracts additional travel from other routes and facilitates a shift from public transport and non-motorised travel to the more convenient (and increasingly affordable) use of private vehicles. In the long run, a third-level impact from increasing road supply results in congestion once again.[2] Only this time, the limited capacity of land to be expanded further is under greater pressure. Thus, expansion of transport infrastructure must be planned in order to make optimum use of the limited capacity of land.[3]

> Years back, when the authorities were developing Bangkok's transport network, they decided to build roads as they are cheaper and faster to construct. But the more roads you build, the more cars people are tempted to buy. We then (after constructing 200 km of expressways) decided to build the rapid transit system.

—Prapat Chongsanguan

[Governor, Mass Rapid Transit Authority, Thailand]

Meeting the growing travel demand and addressing the growth of vehicles in a sustainable manner requires that limited resources like land and fuel be put to optimum use. Compared to other motorised modes of travel, public transport occupies less road space, consumes less fuel and emits fewer pollutants per passenger-km. It is because of these positive externalities that the importance of public transport is gaining recognition the world over. The best way to make a transport system sustainable is to reduce the demand for private commuting and increase the supply of public transport. This approach should guide investment decisions in urban transport infrastructure.

Road Pricing

This part of the paper develops a practical solution to address the supply-demand mismatch outlined in the section above. To reduce the

---

2. "Urban Transportation", Available from: *http://people.hofstra.edu/geotrans/eng/ch6en/ch6menu.html*
3. "Urban Transportation", Available from: *http://people.hofstra.edu/geotrans/eng/ch6en/ch6menu.html*

demand for private transport, a congestion charge or some other form of road pricing can be imposed. Road pricing realigns economic incentives in such a way that traffic flow is reduced. The subsequent paragraphs examine this in greater detail.

Relative to public transport, the social cost generated by private transport is significantly higher. There are two kinds of externalities associated with private transport, user-on-user externality and the impact on the environment. This paper is primarily concerned with the first kind, the cost of congestion. When a person decides to drive, he is only concerned with his marginal private cost (MPC) and not with the congestion he adds to the existing flow of traffic. Congestion leads to an increase in the vehicle operating costs per mile and also lengthens the journey time (for all). By definition, social cost incorporates all the costs associated with an economic activity, including the private cost borne by the user and all other costs borne by society. Thus, the marginal social cost (MSC) is the sum of the MPC of the driver and the cost of congestion he imposes on other road users. People will continue to join a stream of traffic so long as the additional private benefit from their journeys exceeds their MPC.

A simple algebraic example gives an expression for the cost of congestion that is not compensated by the driver. If the average social cost (ASC) of a journey on a congested road with n vehicles is c, then the $n + 1_{th}$ vehicle increases this to $c + \Delta c$. The MSC of the $n + 1_{th}$ vehicle is given by $(n + 1)(c + \Delta c) - nc = c + \Delta c + n\Delta c = ASC + n\Delta c$. Assuming that the costs for all vehicles are the same, a person's perceived cost of his journey is the same as all the other drivers; $MPC = ASC = c + \Delta c$. Thus, the MSC exceeds the MPC by $n\Delta c$. Since this component of the MSC is not borne by the driver, he does not account for it when deciding to make the trip.

In Figure 12.1 the traditional demand curve DD (demand varying inversely with price) cuts the MSC curve at a lower traffic flow than its intersection with the ASC curve. Q_f is the threshold value, beyond which problems of congestion arise because MSC then exceeds MPC. Beyond this point, additional road users are imposing a cost on the other users that they are not paying for. On the same demand curve, the socially optimum level of traffic flow is Q_o. To bring the traffic flow down from Q_a to Q_o, the price structure needs to be altered by introducing a 'tax' equivalent to T_1 T_2

on each motorist contributing to congestion (Button, 1976). Using this economic theory, the paper puts forth a case for road pricing in Mumbai.

Figure 12.1

Using Tax Policy to 'Optimise' Congestion

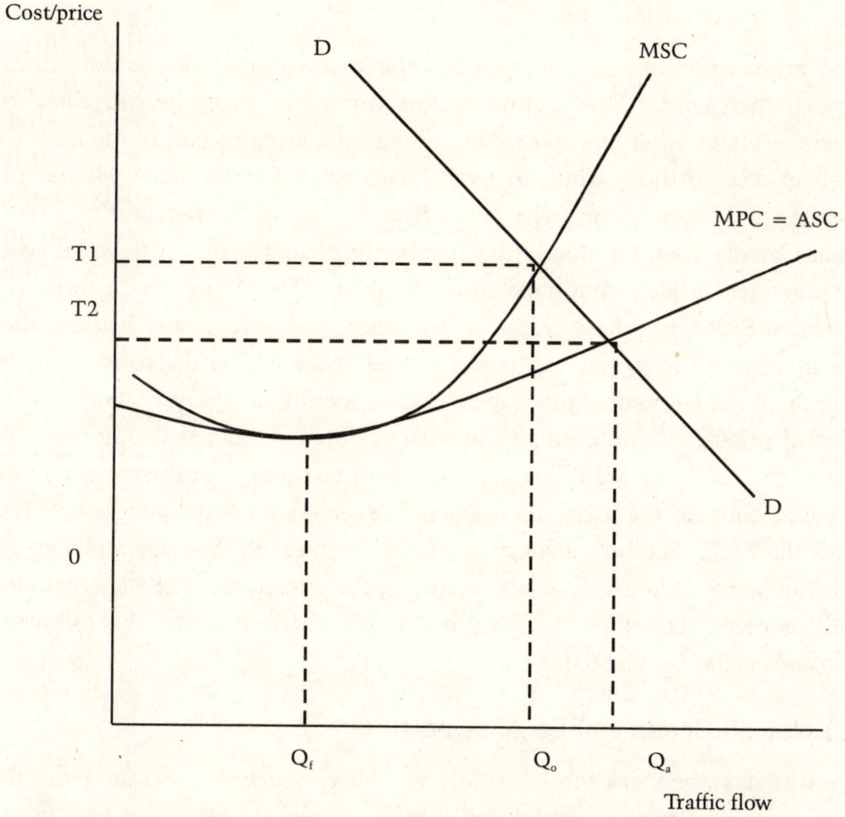

The above figure suggests that if left unregulated, the divergence between the MPC and the MSC curves will continue to grow, leading to increasing social costs. This in economic terminology is referred to "market failure". The use of a public resource without any regard for others is the central theme of Hardin's essay, "The Tragedy of the Commons". To elucidate the population and resource problem, Hardin uses the analogy of a common pasture shared amongst local herders. To maximise profit, every shepherd would like to have as many of his sheep to be able to graze freely. The herder is only concerned with the proceeds that each additional animal can yield. He is oblivious of the negative externality; that the pasture is slightly degraded by each additional animal. The tragedy of the commons is that while the individual herder gains all of the advantage, the disadvantage is shared amongst all herders who can access the pasture. In a similar way that while the user alone enjoys the convenience of a private vehicle, the inconvenience of increased congestion caused by him is distributed amongst potential road users.

From here emerges, a need for the management of the commons. Should each herder have a limit to the number of sheep he can allow for grazing? That's what Singapore does. Should the greenest part of the meadow be restricted to those who can pay? That's what London does. Should the pasture get a new owner who can better ensure its sustainability? That's what Canada does. Or should the shepherd pay in proportion to social costs he generates? That's what most cities are about to introduce, in the form of a modified ERP. Only these cities are not managing pastures and herders, they are managing the surplus demand for road space. Using the concept of the tragedy of the commons, this paper seeks to identify a relatively "fair" system of road pricing. Using examples of road pricing operational in international cities, the following are different methods of charging a Pigouvian tax i.e., a tax that corrects the above mentioned market failure and equates the MPC with the MSC. Hardin's analogy has been extended to these examples to get a better sense of 'fairness' while analysing the effectiveness of these demand management strategies. To sustain the life of the pasture, the following methods could be adopted:

(a) Not all Sheep will be Allowed to Graze

- Every shepherd can have only two sheep grazing at a time. From the point of view of social equity, this is probably the best method to manage the insatiable demand of an individual herder. But if the number of herders who can afford to own a sheep is on a rise, this method may not be very effective. Applying this to the streets of Mumbai, even one car per person is too much demand for available supply of road space. Mumbai officially has 2,045 km of road length.[4] If cars with an average length of 5 metres were to be parked along Mumbai's roads, not even 5 lakh cars would fit in a single

4. Bhayana, Neha (2007). "Parking a Problem, 21 Times Over", *Hindustan Times*, December 09.

lane. The population of Mumbai is over 140 lakh. Given that purchasing power in India is increasing, this method will work only if the 'quota' for a single person is barely a fraction (one car per family, carpools etc).

- The shepherd can buy a sheep that is always allowed to graze. A modified version of the previous point is controlling the number of vehicles on the road through the 'Cap and Trade method'. Singapore's Vehicle Quota System is a classic example. The government issues a limited number of licences periodically and sells them through an open bidding system. Since one does not have the permission to drive without a Certificate of Entitlement (COE), the demand for these licences tends to be inelastic. Thus, although this method is highly effective in controlling the growth rate of vehicles, the economically weaker sections of society are at a disadvantage in this system. But it would be worth considering starting this scheme for new vehicles in a city like Mumbai whose vehicles are increasing by 9-10 per cent every year.

(b) The Shepherd Must Pay for his Sheep to Graze on the Greenest Grass

- This is similar to charging private vehicles for entering or travelling within the central business district (CBD) or other commercial zones in the city that are congestion prone. Usually a cordon (physical or virtual) is placed outside these zones and the tax is either paid manually or deducted automatically from stored-value smart cards at entry points. Cordon charging collected from vehicles crossing through a cordon or a ring is widespread in Norway. Area charging on the other hand is levied on vehicles for both entering and also travelling within a specified area. The London congestion charge implemented in 2003 is a famous example of area charging.
- Mumbai is a north-south stretch with its CBD in the south and a large proportion of the population resides in the northern suburbs. Consequently, a continuous flow of cars is pumped into the city from the north end in the mornings that reverses direction in the evenings. The congestion is exacerbated because there are only two

main routes for north-south commuting. Once the public transport is adequate and efficient, cordons can be used to discourage this direction of traffic flow.

(c) The Shepherd Must Pay in Proportion to the Damage He Causes

- If Shepherd A has a sheep consuming one kilo of grass per visit as opposed to two kilos of grass consumed by Shepherd B's sheep, it is obvious that Shepherd A is causing lesser damage to others and to the life of the pasture. Since Shepherd A generates a lower negative externality, it is only fair that he pay less than Shepherd B. This is the rational used by advocates of the Electronic Road Pricing (ERP) system in the context of traffic congestion. Those who cause more congestion should pay a higher tax than the others.
- A crude form of ERP has been operational in Singapore. Similar to the cordon charging, this system consists of gantries located at different entry points and an in-vehicle unit (IU) installed in each car. As opposed to a fixed charge for entry and exit, the advance technology allows for differentiated charges for peak travel hours. This has encouraged people to cut down unnecessary travel during office hours but on the flip side, also to enter through secondary routes that are not equipped with gantries.
- Different transport authorities of the world are experimenting and conducting research to improvise on this system because this is the most equitable form of taxing. It has been suggested that a sophisticated IU should be equipped with a tracking cookie to trace the degree of congestion. The higher the congestion at that moment, higher should be the charge. It would be very valuable if the new system could also incorporate accurate traffic forecasts so that the driver can be in a position to make a choice in advance between commuting or not and also choose what routes to take.

(d) The Shepherd Must Pay for a Place to Keep his Sheep

- If a shepherd needs to run a personal errand but cannot take his herd of sheep along with him, he might decide to leave his sheep in the pasture, which serves the purpose of not just food but also shelter. Assuming that several shepherds are in the same situation, the demand for free space in the field will overshoot its supply. To solve a similar problem of limited parking space, most cities charge a price for parking. High parking charges in the CBD and other commercial areas of the city has additionally, been a classical method to discourage private vehicles from coming to these congested zones in the first place. A Vancouver study suggests that every $3 increase in parking fee cuts the probability of driving to work alone by 10 per cent.[5]

- A parking charge will have an impact on discouraging the use of private cars, if: (a) The charge is significantly high and (b) the charge is used in conjunction with another charge. While Manhattan and the London CBD have exorbitant parking charges, that for Mumbai's Nariman Point is a meagre Rs. 5 an hour and in some parts even free. This is why cars continue to consume valuable space on the road while the expansive and relatively expensive CR2 car park lies almost vacant. Given that the BMC will soon have created similar spaces including 21 slots underground and a 30-storey car park at Breach Candy, it is imperative to slash road parking which currently has the capacity to take up a third of the island city (65 sq km).[6]

Alternative Demand Management Strategies

The second part of this paper has proposed road pricing as a solution to a major problem of physical infrastructure. If one pays to have a house and if one is already paying to have a car, then there is little logic why one should not pay for road space. By virtue of being limited, road space commands a price. However, this method is regressive because only those who can pay shall have access to roads. This detracts from the broader objective of inclusive growth. Thus, the 'regressiveness' of road pricing remains a key drawback, decreasing its political viability. The final section of this paper puts forth alternative strategies to cut down the demand for

5. "Oikos: Car parking levies – do they reduce congestion?", Available from: *http://greenomics.blogspot.com/2006/02/car-parking-levies-do-they-reduce.html*
6. Bhayana, Neha (2007). "Parking a Problem, 21 Times Over", *Hindustan Times*, December 09.

use of private vehicles. These are devoid of any pricing mechanism and thus not related to an individual's ability to pay.

(a) Non-price Rationing

'Rationing' is defined as "the controlled distribution of (scarce) resources... being distributed on a particular day or at a particular time" (Wikipedia). An example is Greece. Cars are banned from entering central Athens based on a combination of the number on the number plate and the day of the year. A car with an even number plate can be on the road if the date is even. Similarly, an odd number on the number plate means that the car can use the road on an odd number date.

(b) Carpool or High Occupancy Vehicle Lanes (HOV)

This means that vehicles with two or more passengers get preference to use road space and a separate lane is dedicated to such travellers. This is a good way to encourage carpools and ensure that a higher number of people per lane are moving at a faster rate and causing lesser pollution in comparison to those commuting alone. This is a popular practice in parts of the United States and Canada. There are some modifications that the author would like to suggest to the existing practice.

The Transport Research Board of the US reported that in crowded cities like Los Angeles and Washington D.C., adjacent lanes of regular travel are sometimes less congested. If this practice were introduced in Mumbai, it is likely that the experience would be similar. There are two ways to resolve this. Firstly, it should apply to a minimum of three passengers per car. Secondly, new roads that considerably cut travel time should have HOV lanes. This will reduce the number of single passenger vehicles that ply on them. HOV lanes would be radically effective if the Western Expressway (Bandra to Nariman Point) were to be an exclusively HOV lane. This is not recommended as of now for the Eastern Expressways since there is no existing satisfactory route to Navi Mumbai whereas the two north-south arteries are excellent infrastructures—only mercilessly congested.

(c) Taking Responsibility for Congestion: Compensation from Employers

This method would shift the burden of compensating for generated social costs from drivers to the cause of their driving—work (largely). This idea draws inspiration from Dennis Fox who had a fresh take on "The Tragedy of the Commons". According to him, breaking down the commons into smaller segments would facilitate management of the commons. The author of this paper feels that to manage traffic congestion, the management of the commons should be of this group. If the employers were asked to compensate for those of their employees who use private transport, plenty of innovative solutions would be generated to address traffic congestion. This compensation could be in the form of tax or another form of CSR. Companies would thus have incentives to minimise the private transport use of their employees and would have a variety of ways to do so; amongst them being subsidies for public transport, organising carpools for their employees and in the long run, may be even building company flats closer to their offices. To monitor the system, employees could have tickets issued by their companies that could be checked on the road. This system is not yet in practice anywhere in the world and there is considerable scope for refining the idea.

Finally, there are other means to complement the primary approach adopted for reducing the proportion of private transport. Technology to establish a good traffic management system, for example, automated highways, synchronised traffic signals and flexible road dividers that can increase the capacity of the road for inbound traffic in the day and outbound traffic in the evening rush.

Conclusion

Current official forecasts imply that congestion will be substantially worse by the end of this decade. The northern and eastern suburbs of Mumbai continue to swell while a heavy dose of about 600 vehicles is injected into the city's roads every day. Already, the average vehicular speed has fallen from 38 kmph in 1962 to 15 kmph today.[7] Classical methods of

7. "Breaking the gridlock: Can Mumbai learn from the London Congestion Charging project?", Available from: *http://www.mastek.com/content/mastekpapers/18Mar2006_1.asp*

solving the congestion problem have failed to ensure a sustainable transport system. Contrary to popular belief, expanding roads to meet heavy traffic feeds congestion in the long run. This paper suggests that traffic congestion adversely impacts the quality of physical infrastructure.

The first part establishes that a sustainable urban transport policy should encourage a shift from private modes of commuting to public transport. The need for extensive (but selective) pieces of urban road construction is recognised. The paper finds that efforts to address congestion in Mumbai are somewhat scrambled. Infrastructure investments will bear little fruit if measures to curb the growing traffic are not taken.

The subsequent parts of the paper identify ways to address traffic growth. Road pricing is found to be an effective means to cut down usage of private vehicles. In fact, it has already been implemented in some of the more developed Asian economies like Singapore. However, before it can be perceived as a viable policy option in South Asian countries like India, Bangladesh, Pakistan and Nepal, the public transport system needs to be strengthened. One way to counter the regressive nature of road pricing and improve access to public transport is to reinvest the revenue generated from road pricing in infrastructure like metros and buses. In addition, the paper also explores some equitable alternatives to reduce the number of personal vehicles on the road.

Finally, the likelihood of success depends on the level of commitment of policy makers. In every city, the responsibility of planning, building, regulating and managing transport infrastructure lies with multiple civic and state bodies. This has made urban transport a marginal function for all parties in charge. While crime and security take precedence over traffic management within the police force, garbage and water supply tend to be the prime concern of municipal bodies.[8] To solve this dilemma, the state could venture into public-private partnerships to ensure sustained quality of transport infrastructure. Without proper implementation, even the most functional solution is bound to fail. After all, implementation is like concrete for the "road" to success.

8. *India Infrastructure Report 2006.*

References

Books:

3iNetwork (2006). *India Infrastructure Report 2006*. USA: Oxford University Press.

Button, K.J. (1976). *Urban Economics: Theory and Policy*. London: Macmillan Press Ltd.

David, M.D. (1996). *Urban Explosion of Mumbai: Restructuring of Growth*. Mumbai: Himalaya Publishing House.

Mongia, J.N. (1985). *India's Economic Development Strategies*. India: Allied Publishers. Holland: D Reidel, Dordrecht.

Pitfield, R.R. (1987). *Mastering Commerce* (Macmillan Master Series). London: Macmillan Press Ltd.

Sharma, R.N. and K. Sita (2001). *Issues in Urban Development: A Case of Navi Mumbai*. New Delhi: Rawat.

Sinha, R.K. (2004). *India 2025: Social, Economic and Political Stability*. New Delhi: Shipra.

Newspaper/Magazine Articles:

Aklekar, Rajendra (2007). "Mumbai's Slow Road Journey", *Hindustan Times*, November 25.

———. (2007). "One New Train, 6 Million Dreams a Day", *Hindustan Times*, November 23.

———. (2007). "The New Railway Station", *Hindustan Times*, November 28.

Badami, Sudhir (2005). "Case for a Bus Rapid Transit System in Mumbai", *Economic and Political Weekly*, October 8.

Ball, Philip (2000). "Case for a Bus Rapid Transit System in Mumbai", *Science*, January 15.

Bhayana, Neha (2007). "Changing Mumbai's Taxis, Singapore Style", *Hindustan Times*, November 22.

———. (2007). "Parking a Problem, 21 Times Over", *Hindustan Times*, December 05.

Girish, Kubar (2007). "Car Owners in Mumbai to Pay Congestion Tax", *The Economic Times*, August 23.

Hardin, Garrett (1968). "The Tragedy of the Commons", *Science*, December 13.

Nandy, Madhurima (2007). "A Leap Across the Arabian Sea: Mumbai's First Big Dream", *Hindustan Times*, November 20.

———. (2007). "A Metro for a new Metropolis", *Hindustan Times*, November 21.

Soubhik, Mitra (2007). "Mumbai's New Flight Plan", *Hindustan Times*, November 27.

Wadhwa, Kiran (2007). "Glide along the Water", *Hindustan Times*, November 24.

———. (2007). "The Bridge to Tomorrow's Mumbai", *Hindustan Times*, November 19.

Internet Resources:

"A Gigantic Investment Deficit", Available from: *http://www.indiatogether.org/2006/oct/opi-uideficit.htm*

"A Strategic Niche Analysis of Urban Road Pricing in the UK and Norway", Available from: *http://oro.open.ac.uk/7312/01/2007_01_02.pdf*

"Breaking the Gridlock: Can Mumbai learn from the London Congestion Charging Project?", Available from: *http://www.mastek.com/content/mastekpapers/18Mar2006_1.asp*

"Build It And They'll Come", Available from: *http://www.transact.org/Ca/congestion2.htm*

"Durham City Congestion Charge", Available from: *http://en.wikipedia.org/wiki/Durham_City_congestion_charge*

"Electronic Road Charging", Available from: *http://www.parliament.uk/post/pn112.pdf*

"Electronic Road Pricing", Available from: *http://en.wikipedia.org/wiki/Electronic_Road_Pricing*

"High-occupancy Vehicle Lane", Available from: *http://en.wikipedia.org/wiki/HOV_lanes*

"High-occupancy Vehicle Lane", Available from: *http://www.3inetwork.org/*

"Indian Urban Transportation", Available from: *http://members.rediff.com/localtrain/current.html#Urban%20Transportation*

"Infrastructure Commons in Economic Perspective by Frischmann", Available from: *http://www.firstmonday.org/issues/issue12_6/frischmann/index.html*

"Is the Remaking of Mumbai Sustainable", Available from: *http://www.indiatogether.org/2007/aug/env-mumbai.htm*

"London Congestion Charge", Available from: *http://en.wikipedia.org/wiki/London_congestion_charge*

"Looking London Talking Mumbai", Available from: *http://www.hindustantimes.com/news/specials/bombay/Main%20article20.shtml*

"Maharashtra Government to Introduce Congestion Tax", Available from: *http://www.khaleejtimes.com/DisplayArticleNew.asp?xfile=data/subcontinent/2007/August/subcontinent_August976.xml&section=subcontinent&col=*

"Manchester Congestion Charge", Available from: *http://en.wikipedia.org/wiki/Manchester_Congestion_Charge*

"MSRDC Takes its Toll, with a Difference", Available from: *http://www.indianexpress.com/res/web/pIe/ie/daily/19990119/01950425.html*

"New York Congestion Pricing", Available from: *http://en.wikipedia.org/wiki/New_York_congestion_pricing*

"Oikos: Car Parking Levies—Do They Reduce Congestion?", Available from: *http://greenomics.blogspot.com/2006/02/car-parking-levies-do-they-reduce.html*

"Private Highway", Available from: *http://en.wikipedia.org/wiki/Private_highway*

"Progressing Electronic Road Pricing", Available from: *http://www.transportroundtable.com.au/rpa/abstracts.html*

"Road Pricing: Singapore Experience", Available from: *http://www.move-forum.net/documenti/B_06032003170931.pdf*

"Road Pricing", Available from: *http://en.wikipedia.org/wiki/Road_pricing*

"Rome (Italy)", Available from: *http://www.progress-project.org/Progress/rome.html*

"Saviour of the Hasseled Commuter", Available from: *http://www.indiatogether.org/2003/aug/eco-bustrans.htm*

"Stockholm Congestion Tax", Available from: *http://en.wikipedia.org/wiki/Stockholm_congestion_tax*

"Technology can ease Traffic Congestion", Available from: *http://www.mastek.com/content/mastekpapers/30November2006.asp*

"The Economic Costs of Road Traffic Congestion (Abstract)", Available from: *http://eprints.ucl.ac.uk/archive/00001259/*

"The Solution to Traffic Congestion-BECKER" Available from: *http://www.becker-posner-blog.com/archives/2006/02/the_solution_to.html*

"Traffic Congestion", Available from: *http://en.wikipedia.org/wiki/Traffic_congestion*

"Tragedy of the Commons", Available from: *http://en.wikipedia.org/wiki/Tragedy_of_the_commons*

"Trondheim (Norway)", Available from: *http://www.progress-project.org/Progress/tron.html*

"Urban Transportation", Available from: *http://people.hofstra.edu/geotrans/eng/ch6en/ch6menu.html*

"Water: The Privatization Debate", Available from: *http://www.indiatogether.org/2003/nov/env-wtrdebate.htm*

13

Improving the Quality of Transport Infrastructure: The Case of Sri Lankan Railways

Challenges, Opportunities and Suggestions

Pramodha Samarasinghe and
Niranjani Kailayanathan

Introduction

A vibrant network of quality infrastructure is a *sine qua non* for economic growth of any country.

An efficient and cheap mode of transportation can be considered important both from economic and social perspectives. A low cost and efficient transport network will provide dynamism in the country by mobilising people and goods from one place to another. It will also help reduce inequality among regions and create employment opportunities. The population intensity in the metropolitan areas can be reduced if an efficient network of transportation is available.

The fundamental railway and road networks of Sri Lanka are essentially a byproduct of plantation agriculture and colonial administration in the 19th century. Since its inception, the rail transportation of both passenger and freight took a new height linking major cities in the country. Sri Lanka was among the very few Asian countries that had the fortune to get a railway network installed in their countries soon after the introduction of railways in England. Ceylon Railways[1] as it was called then, was a relatively efficient and disciplined mode of transportation with a wide network of railways and high quality infrastructure. Nevertheless, the glory of Ceylon Railways and the

1. See *www.scienceland.lk/railway* and *www.srilankarailways.com* for further details regarding Sri Lanka Railways.

government budgetary allocations to the railways sector has declined considerably in the post-1977 period due to a host of reasons including financial constraints and less priority given to the sector. The quality of railway infrastructure declined due to poor maintenance and lack of attention and services offered by the railways has thus declined significantly. Therefore, the potential of the railways as a low cost mode of transportation has not been tapped fully by the country.

The objectives of this paper are:

- To analyse the current structure and performance of the Sri Lankan railway transportation;
- To identify the inherent weaknesses in the Sri Lankan railway transportation in the perspective of its physical infrastructure; and
- To propose remedies in order to overcome those weaknesses and to improve the quality of the railway infrastructure in enhancing the railway services.

The paper is based on a case study of the Sri Lankan Railways, thus main data and information collected from the department of railways. The annual records and survey reports published by the department and personal interviews with the heads of railway department facilitate the research in deep. The information regarding the road network of Sri Lanka collected through relevant authorities such as Central Transport Board and Road Development Authority of Sri Lanka to conduct a comparative study with the Railways.

The main methodology used in the paper is a case study analysis, where final proposals and recommendations are given through a deep environmental analysis to the given case study. In the second section of the paper, the importance of the railway infrastructure and the related services as a mode of transportation is discussed. In the third section, the current status of the Sri Lankan Railways and its infrastructure will be explored by the environmental analysis and the SWOT (Strengths-Weakness Opportunities-Threats) analysis with the use of SCP (Structure-Conduct-Performance) model of the organisational theory. The weaknesses and challenges faced by the railway infrastructure system are examined in Section 4. The opportunities, remedial measures and suggestion are discussed in Section 5. Section 6 concludes the paper.

The Importance of Railway Infrastructure and Services

The railway is a very beneficial and low cost mode of transportation through which a country can gain many economic advantages in investing in its infrastructure. Transportation investment will boost industry competitiveness of the country. When there is a strong transport network, it will reduce costs of production and distribution. Also, this will lower the barriers of mobility and give opportunities to the manufacturing, retail and service sectors to access varied, specialised and industrious sources of labour, a diverse selection of related inventory and raw materials and a wide customer base, both in the domestic and international markets. Transport investments can also encourage leisure travels in the country, where Sri Lanka can improve the tourism industry, which has much potential in the country. This boost of industries will greatly facilitate Sri Lanka in achieving the targets of economic growth.

The transportation investment can enhance the household welfare too. A wider access to many goods and services due to fewer barriers to mobility and effective public transport will reduce the personal cost of travelling compared to private vehicle travelling. In addition, investing in transportation can strengthen the local, regional and state economies of the country. The benefits of transportation investment are not limited to the microeconomic level, as it will energise city centres; break the isolation of rural areas and enhancing state employment and tax revenues of the government in generating macroeconomic benefits.

Transportation investment can minimise the economic losses associated with transport accidents, time delays and wastage of fuel consumption due to the congestion. Not only these benefits, but also it will create more employment in the transport sector providing a timely solution to the current unemployment issue in the country.

The railway transportation as a service is very vital for a developing country like Sri Lanka because of its in-built economic benefits compared to other modes of transportation. Less cost of construction and maintenance, being environment-friendly, high capacity, high energy savings, low fares and reduced congestion are some main positive features compared to other modes of land transportation and these attributes encourage the worth of investments in railways as an important mode of transportation. Even though the railways can play a vital role in the economy, the performance can be largely affected by the quality of its infrastructure because infrastructure is very important in providing satisfying services. Therefore, the railway infrastructure should be in a good quality to gather benefits of railway as an efficient transport method.

Railway is very important to Sri Lanka because it fulfils a social responsibility of providing mobility services at fare rates to low income earners, which are considered as the majority of Sri Lankan passengers. In addition, railway can be important in meeting the growing need of the public transportation in the country as it can successfully execute a high proportion of the overall needs of transportation.

Table 13.1

The Need of Transportation of Sri Lanka as a Percentage

Public Transportation	73%
Private Transportation	23%
Travel Service Transportation	4%

Source: Department of Census and Statistics, Sri Lanka.

Present Railway Infrastructure Network and Its Performance

Sri Lanka Railways (SLR) operates the country's railway network, which as of end-2005, included 1,559 km of broad-gauge track connecting 151 major stations and 144 substations (Please refer Annexure A-13.1). Colombo is the main node in the network, and train routes connect it with the main cities of all nine provinces.

The current tracks, bridges and railway stations are in poor condition because of a lack of maintenance funds. In addition, the number of locomotives is insufficient for scheduled services. Passenger services have preference for locomotives which causes locomotive shortages for cargo. Furthermore, the locomotives that are available are obsolete and signaling and communication systems are outdated. This causes significant delays in train schedules as well as dangerous derailments. In addition, rail transportation continues to face serious competition from road transportation and has been adversely affected by the country's two-decade civil war. The combination of prolonged conflict and inadequate financial resources for maintenance has rendered the rail system unreliable and unprofitable. Even though SLR has somewhat utilised the potentials in the passenger transport sector, it still has not reached the high potential in the freight transportation sector. Rail now accounts for only 5 per cent of freight transportation in Sri Lanka. This has forced most commercial transporters to use roads.

SLR is administrated by the Railway Authority as a Government Department under the Ministry of Transport, headed by a General Manager, who, being chief executive is responsible to the ministry for all its day-to-day activities. When discussing the tariff system, it is evident that the Railway Ordinance (Chapter 200 of the Legislative Enactment of Ceylon) vests authority for making, revoking, adding or altering the rules regarding charges for the conveyance of passengers and goods by the railway. According to this ordinance, "No rule regarding charges for the conveyance of passengers and goods shall be made without the concurrence of the Minister of Finance." The General Manager however, is empowered to reduce charges for transportation by the railway of any passenger or goods by an amount not exceeding 40 per cent of the rates or with prior approval of the Minister, by any other amount.

Sri Lanka Railway Authority (SLRA) has tried several times to overcome from the current situation and still couldn't be successful due to lack of concentration of the government. One of the remedial measures taken from the SLRA was striding to work with the private sector, at least in a narrow way amidst strict rules and regulations of the government. At present, it allows private sector operations by Holcim on the line linking Holcim's cement plant in Puttalam and the limestone quarry. It also hauls privately owned flour wagons for Prima. In addition, SLRA is planning a major restructuring to allow public-private partnerships in association with the Strategic Enterprise Management Agency (SEMA) at present.

Industry Analysis: Structure-Conduct-Performance (SCP) Methodology

Structure—Railway transport industry has a monopolistic structure because SLR fully owned by the government is the only player in the industry and there are many barriers to entry such as high investment cost and strict railway ordinance etc. As the monopolistic structure has adversely influenced the conduct and performance of the industry, there are ongoing discussions regarding public-private partnerships for the progress of SLR service.

Conduct—Strategic actions are not for the progress of the SLR but for fulfilling other government purposes such as providing subsidiary transport method for low income earners, thus government is considering it as the only "poverty stress taker" than any other mode of transport. For example, the government has not altered the fares since 2005, although the oil price has been increased in 80-100 per cent than the set fares during the period.

Performance—Poor continuous financial performance recorded due to the inefficiencies but increased social benefits as a low cost transportation method.

Table 13.2

Negative Financial Performance of the Sri Lanka Railways

Year	*Revenue (Rs. Mn)*	*Recurrent Exp. (Rs. Mn)*	*Loss (Rs. Mn)*	*Increase of Loss%*
1997	1029.8	1841.5	711.7	
2000	1014.5	2685.7	1671.2	134.8%
2003	1320.5	3383.4	2062.9	23.4%
2006	2491.3	6472.6	3981.3	93.0%

Source: Sri Lanka Railways, Facts and Figures, 1997-2006.

The Issues and Challenges

Passenger transportation: SLR is considerably backward relative to other passenger services in the region. The unsatisfactory status of the infrastructure has led the services provided to the passengers into poor standards. The inadequate railway network to provide an island-wide service and the prevailing isolation of the railways due to lack of linkage with other modes are other general issues. Even though it is difficult to construct new infrastructure, SLR has not tried at least to maintain the existing infrastructure network. However, there should be a sound fund allocation to improve the quality of infrastructure. Thus, it has become a challenge to the railway authority with the continuous financial constraints and less priority given to the sector.

Table 13.3

SWOT Analysis: A Comparative Study with Other Transport Services

Strengths	*Weaknesses*
• High Capacity: Reduced Congestion - 1000 passengers—one train - 1000 passengers—50-60 buses • Effective Fuel Consumption - Train—3 litres per 1 km: 1000 passengers - Bus—3 litres per 1 km: 50 passengers - Van—0.1 litres per 1 km: 20 passengers - Car—0.08 litres per 1 km: 5 passengers • Low Travelling Fares - Train—Rs. 0.60 per 1 km - Bus—Rs. 6 per 1 km • Environmental-friendly • Less Construction Cost - Cost of double track for 1 km is less than the cost of sixth lane road for 1 km • Differentiated Passenger Segments and Services • Increased Traffic Absorption • Improved Freight Transportation • Private-Public Partnerships • Contribution to the Tourism Sector • Link with Harbour and Airport (ICD/ Inter modal and Multi modal systems)	• No Government Fund Allocation for Maintaining the Existing Infrastructure when Compared to Road Network (Self Financing) • Poor Conditions in Infrastructure Network • Inability to Reach Every Destination - Rail network—1450 km - Road network[2]—92700 km • Unsatisfactory Standards of Infrastructure - Derailments and obsolete bridges, canals - Outdated signaling and communication system - Speed restrictions imposed for security: average speed of 40 km per hour in the Colombo sub-urban area • Frequent Train Delays and Increased Passenger Complaints • No Commercial Flexibility of SLR in deciding the Price of the Service to Cover the Cost • No Updates of Fares with the Inflation • Centralised Decision-making • Cost Centres are not available—No Connection between the Cost and Income • High Time Lag in the Procurement System • High Labour and other Overhead Cost • Continuous Financial Loss • Legal Restrictions in Privatisation: Private railway transport services are restricted by the Railway Ordinance of Sri Lanka except the private participation in infrastructure. • Isolated Network from other Modes • High Intervention of the Government • External Shocks: Oil price • Competition from Other Modes of Transportation: Accountability, comfort ability, punctuality, all day services • New Transportation Trends and innovative Technologies in the Industry

Freight transportation: The main issue of freight transportation is that railway has not fully utilised the potential of railways in that sector. SLR is responsible for only 3 per cent of the total freight transportation, which can be considered as a very little contribution compared to other countries in the region. Non-use of container transportation is another mislaid

2. Road Development Authority, Sri Lanka.

opportunity of SLR and many issues have to be faced in improving the freight transport sector like a small fraction of double and triple tracks in the network, no electrified service or advanced signaling system, old locomotive fleet, lack of locomotives to operate trains according to schedule, low availability compared with the fleets of other countries, unexploited rail connection to Colombo port, lack of modern piece of container handling equipment to transfer from rail to road, limitation on the height of containers that can be carried through the entrance of the port by rail and unavailability of proper IT system to control and track passenger and freight trains, wagons or containers.

Public-private partnership in financing infrastructure development:[3] It is argued that private sector participation in infrastructure could lead to delivering both less expensive and reliable services to the people at large. However, these partnerships too face many issues in Sri Lanka. The public sector infrastructure providers have been facing increasing financial stringency, flowing from weak government finances whilst the private sector providers too have been facing some issues. The absence of fundamentals governing the basic legal framework for inviting the private sector for infrastructure development, the presence of political and economic instability for large scale investment and unsatisfactory institutional and regulatory framework to govern the public-private partnership in the country.

The cyclic effect of infrastructure and services: There is a continuous cyclic effect between the infrastructure and services; a poor infrastructure network will always lead to poor services and vice versa (Please refer Annexure A-13.2). The issue is the difficulty in getting rid from this cycle and external support such as positive government contribution, price flexibility, differentiated services and private partnerships are necessary to overcome from the poor situation. Therefore, the infrastructure and services cannot be treated separately and should improve together to yield more.

3. See "Public-Private Sector Partnership In Economic Development: A Case For Sri Lanka", Sri Lanka Economic Association and Chapter 7.

Suggestions and Recommendations

According to our findings, it is important to distinguish between two kinds of techniques to improve the quality of physical railway infrastructure.[4] They are:

- Construction of new physical infrastructure[5] expands capacity, reduces overall congestion and improves access, thus helping speed the flow of people and goods.
- Maintaining and preserving the existing transportation infrastructure. This will not only improve travel speed, capacity and safety, but protect and extend the service life of rail investments. Repairing an ageing railway bridge, for example, may save a government the cost of building a new bridge sometime in the future.

The following suggestions can be recommended to employ the above mentioned techniques in improving the quality of Sri Lankan railway infrastructure.[6]

Effective government priorities: The government should identify the great potential of the railway and should prioritise it in the transportation policy.[7] It should take initiatives to improve the infrastructure with relevant strategies and projects and then convincing other parties the worth of contributing to the railways.

Public-private partnership: Strong private partnerships can be a sensible option to meet the gap of demand for infrastructure, when the government faces a financial stringency. However, at first the related issues should be solved by introducing the basic legal framework for inviting the private sector for infrastructure development, reducing the political and economic instability for large scale investment and developing satisfactory

4. To enhance the general excellence in the standards of physical infrastructure as a distinctive characteristic.
5. The categories of physical railway infrastructure: tracks, signaling and communication systems, railway stations and bridges.
6. All the strengths, weakness, opportunities and threats envisaged in the environmental analysis are considered in developing the suggested strategies.
7. At present, the road network is heavily prioritised in the sector of land transportation and less attention is given to the railways.

institutional and regulatory framework to govern the public-private partnerships.

Projects regarding the new investment or maintenance of existing infrastructure can be submitted to private sector with the effective perusal of the government. For example, work with public-private partnership to develop container handling facilities in key stations. Also, private partnerships can be ideal for possible services such as development of railway stations into commercial centres with integrated bus station facilities, cleaning contracts for carriages and for stations, provision of ticketing machines to reduce SLR's procurement risk and take away the responsibility of maintenance and advertising and marketing communications (publication and sale of printed timetables) etc.

Privatisation is another aspect discussed in this concern and it also can be a good approach in overcoming the current management crisis in SLR. However, there is a doubt that privatisation can leads to the success; it is argued that the private sector will aim to maximise the profits purely by neglecting the social responsibility of the SLR. Whatever investment is put into the rail system as a result of privatisation, will be for the sole purpose of extracting profits. Jobs will be lost and fares will rise, putting further burdens on those who can least afford it. Therefore, a unified campaign needs to be mounted, involving all sections of rail workers and commuters, for an affordable, efficient rail transport system that provides decent pay and conditions for its workers. Such a campaign can only be developed on the basis of a socialist programme.

Intermodal transportation network[8] *(rail-port):* Intermodal transportation is the movement of passengers or freight from one mode of transport to another, commonly taking place at a terminal specifically designed for such a purpose. As every mode of transportation has unique advantages when it is combined, synergistic effort can be gained. Thus, intermodal transportation networks can be introduced to SLR than being isolated to improve current services in enhancing the quality of infrastructure. This network will be a logistically link system using two or more transport modes with a single rate. Modes are having common handling characteristics, permitting freight (or people) to be transferred

8. See Jean-Paul Rodrigue *et al.*, 1998.

between modes during a movement between an origin and a destination.

Intermodal transportation network can be proposed to improve the standards of Sri Lankan Railways linking the rail with the harbour in Colombo city. From this network, the railways can contribute the Colombo harbour to become a world-class logistic hub by encouraging the export and import sectors that lead to economic growth in the country. This can be initiated with the minimum effort because there is a rail connection to the port that is not in use. In developing a rail-based dry port linkage to Colombo port, investments in track and container handling equipment, and setting up a separate operating unit for the dry port connection with its own equipment and creating a state-of-the-art information technology system for planning and management will be essential.

Also, the railway can reduce the container congestion through introducing Internal Container Depots (ICD) in potential areas that link with rails which comes from harbour. This reduces the dwell time of imports in Colombo port and reduces truck congestion at the port gate, with an associated decrease in road transport costs and increase the revenue of SLR as a result of increased freight transportation.[9] Even though, the initial costs of these projects are massive, the long term benefits are unlimited and this will facilitate SLR to overcome from their financial crisis and problems of the current infrastructure network.

Multimodal transportation network: This is the advanced step of the intermodal transportation network and refers to the set of transport modes offering connections between origins and destinations. The improvements can be done to connect rail with other methods of transportation: road network with park and ride services for passengers in main stations, connect with airports with expanded railway lines and to connect with free trade zones to improve the services to the exporting sector of the country. Strong public-private partnerships will be the most suitable source to handle this type of projects in Sri Lanka.

---

9. A proposal has given to the government by Strategic Enterprise Management Agency (SEMA) to develop an ICD dry port implementation in some potential areas in the country.

Improving the passenger services: Improved services will increase the revenue generated in the railways. Thus, it can financially facilitate the quality improvements of the infrastructure. Responding to passenger inquires and complaints, more trains in faster schedules with fewer delays, better access to rail stations, improved safety, cleaner trains and stations, and practice of marketing skills are some strategies to increase the passenger services that will improve the financial ability of SLR for infrastructure developments.

Improving the freight services: The qualities such as the delivery time, reliability, less derailments, reduced terminal congestion, efficient management practices, less train breakdowns and reduced losses and damages should be assured to the freight users, if SLR wants to benefit through the freight transportation sector. Thus, developing funding sources for locomotives related to freight operations and developing an IT system for freight management and tracking will be useful. As railway has a strong potential than other modes of freight transportation, this can be an attractive sector to be invested in overcoming the financial issues of SLR.

Introducing information and technology to railway transportation: The introduction of new information and technology will upgrade the services provided by the rail and managing new investment projects. The opportunity can be given to a strong private IT facilitator with relevant experiences and applicable infrastructure that are ideal to the Sri Lankan railway system. Much potential are there in the signaling and communication infrastructure that should be improved through IT.

Restructuring the organisational structure and behaviour of the railway authority: Decentralising the decision-making process (worker participation in decision-making), efficient management staff, improving the speed of procurement, developing cost centres, introduction of performance related wages and perks instead of conservative labour incentive schemes and reducing unnecessary overheads will improve the performance of the railway authority thus, creates a efficient framework to run infrastructure development projects.

Competent transportation policy: The national transportation policy should not be limited to heavens in the sky and should be practical enough to implement and gain benefits. The policy should suggest an integrated strategy for every possible transportation infrastructure because an isolated strategy will end up with an utter waste of money and time.

Future Projects Planned by the SLRA

Many agreements have been signed with a Chinese company to purchase new carriages and planned to develop number of new bridges under the Austrian credit line. Also, negotiations are being continued with RITES of India based on a proposal submitted by them to upgrade the coastal line from Colombo to Matara under Indian Line of Credit. In addition, steps will be taken to construct and instal Rail Crossing Protection Systems with bell, warning light signals and automatic barrier in the year 2008.

In future, some oil tank wagons will be imported under Pakistan Line of Credit. Also, attention has been drawn towards increasing railway revenue by building shopping complexes and other trade services near crowded railway stations between Colombo and other suburban areas. Although these plans are not adequate to improve the overall quality of the railway infrastructure, this can act as a foundation in doing so. To gain maximum results, the above suggestions and recommendations can be followed by the railway authorities.

Mahinda Chinthana[10]—Short Term Future Prospects for 2008-2010

"In such a policy, provisions will be made to assign priority to public transport, and to attract passengers and goods towards larger capacity vehicles away from smaller ones and towards rail transport away from road based transport. A decade of railway development will be proclaimed, within which period a minimum of 0.5 per cent of GDP will be allocated as capital for railway development. Many long distance railway lines will be developed and expanded and new lines will be constructed to provide an island wide rail network by encouraging long distance traveling, pilgrimages and tourism sectors. In addition, an airport railway service will be

10. The proposal of policy reforms by the President of Sri Lanka.

introduced between Colombo and Katunayake to encourage the international trade" (Mahinda Chinthana).[11]

The new policy reforms of the honorable president of Sri Lanka, Mahinda Rajapaksha have suggested productive strategies to improve the existing network of transport infrastructure by giving a priority to the railways for the very first time through the national transport policy.[12] This can be a positive initiation to eliminate the railway crisis in the country as the government has understood the economic potential of the railway than before.

Long Term Future Potential of Sri Lanka Railways

We can propose that the long term future potential of Sri Lankan railways is to link with the Asian Railway Network and from there to World Railway Network. There were many global discussions and project proposals where countries tried to make some possible rail links with other countries. The Trans-Asian Railway Network was one of the main projects to create an integrated freight railway network across Europe and Asia. This was a project of the United Nations Economic and Social Commission for Asia and the Pacific in the 1960s, at the time when there was not as much shipping and air travel as today. The idea then was to have 14,000 kilometres of rail link between Singapore and Istanbul, Turkey and some further connections to Europe and Africa.

Sri Lanka was proposed to connect to the southern corridor of the Trans-Asian Railway Network in two ways. First option was to connect Colombo and port of Tuticorin in Southern India by a shipping link. The second option was to connect Talaimannar in North-Western Sri Lanka and the port of Rameshwaram in Southern India by a ferry link. Also during 2002, there was a plan to construct a bridge between Talaimannar and Rameshwaram. The bridge linking Sri Lanka and South India can be a versatile opportunity to Sri Lankan railways in expanding their network through Asian Railway Network. Even though, during 2006 Sri Lanka has signed initial agreements to connect Sri Lanka with the Trans-Asian

11. See *www.mahinda4srilanka.org*
12. See *www.treasury.gov.lk/budget2007/MahindaChintanaTenYearDevelopment Plan.pdf* and *www.groundviews.org/one-year-of-Mahinda Chintana*

Railway Network, even without the bridge, still there are no good signs of implementing this idea amidst many obstacles such as the ongoing civil wars and political disputes.

However, Sri Lanka can be greatly benefited by linking with other South Asian countries through the railway network. This will slash down the inter-country transport cost and bring people closer to each other and also will increase the multilateral tourism and trade within the region. Wider access to the market will create both new business opportunities and increased competition to the country, leading to further increases in profitability. It could be also expected to have a positive impact on private capital and labour productivity and hence, on overall economic growth. Apart from that, it will generate direct and non-direct job opportunities for Sri Lanka, which can be a good solution for the current unemployment in the country.

Concluding Remarks

Although the Sri Lankan Railways can play a vital role in the economy, the performance can be largely affected by the quality of its infrastructure because infrastructure is very important in providing satisfying services. Therefore, the railway infrastructure should be in a good quality to gather benefits of railway as an efficient transport method. Sri Lanka can promote railway transportation to make rewarding economic contributions through effective government priorities, strong private partnerships, value added services, integrated transport network and competent transportation policy.

References

Central Bank of Sri Lanka (n.d.). *Annual Reports* (various issues).

Indraratna, A.D.V. de S. and Ranasinghe Athula (2006). *Public-Private Sector Partnership in Economic Development: A Case for Sri Lanka*. Sri Lanka Economic Association (SLEA).

IPS (2005). *Sri Lanka: State of the Economy - 2005*. Institute of Policy Studies, Colombo.

Rodrigue, Jean-Paul, Brian Slack and Claude Comtois (1998). *The Geography of Transport Systems - Intermodal and Multimodal Transportation*. Chapter 03.

Klugman (2002). *A Sourcebook for Poverty Reduction Strategies*. Chapter 20 "Private Sector and Infrastructure: Overview", World Bank.

Sri Lanka Competitiveness Study USAID/ Sri Lanka (2007). *Supply Chain Management and Competitiveness in Sri Lanka*. June.

Sri Lanka Railways (n.d.). *Facts and Figures*. 1997-2006.

www.groundviews.org /one-year-of-Mahinda Chintana

www.scienceland.lk/railway

www.srilankarailways.com www.treasury.gov.lk/EPPRM/npd/pdfdocs/budget2007Mahinda ChintanaTenYearDevelopmentPlan.pdf

Annexure A-13.1

The Map of Sri Lanka Railway Network (Current and Proposed)

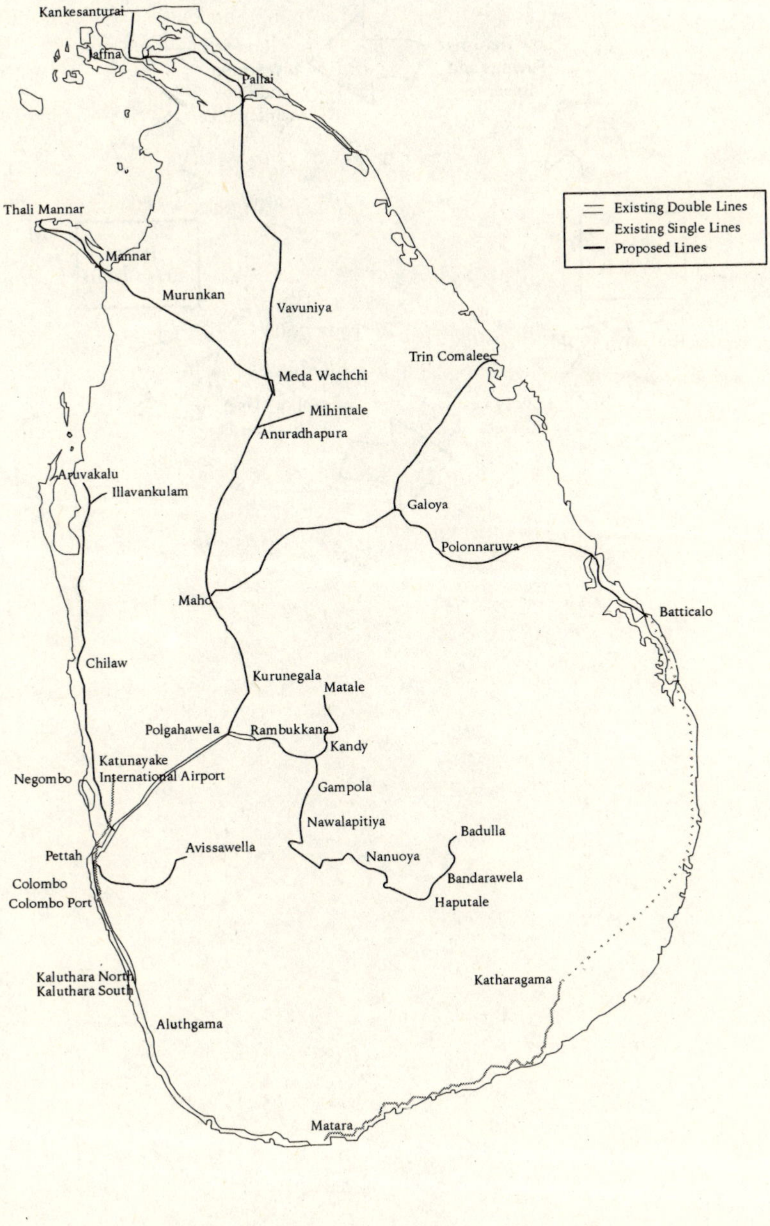

Annexure A-13.2

The Cyclic Effect of Infrastructure and Services

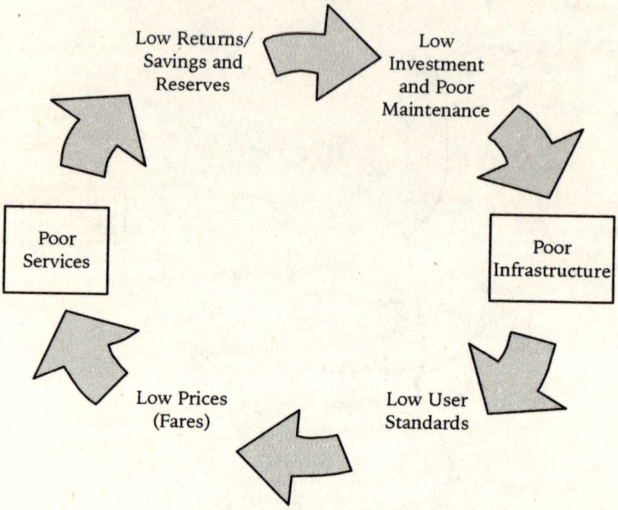

IV
Accountability, Institutions and Economic Growth

14

Do Institutions Matter for Economic Growth?

Cross-Country Experiences and Implications for Bangladesh

Sangeeta Nath

Introduction

The ultimate goal of the countries across the world has always been to achieve and maintain economic growth. Over the years, governments and policymakers have been experimenting with different measures and policies for economic growth, to bring about economic development. In the backdrop of ample evidence of wide variations in income levels across the world, average income levels in the world's richest and poorest countries differ by a factor more than 500.[1] The growth theory has highlighted physical and human capital accumulation and technological change as the determinants of economic growth. However, such determinants failed to solve the enigma of why some economies manage to accumulate and innovate more than others. Institutions in close interplay with all other probable factors actually determine the growth potential of a country. As a result, institutions surfaced as one of the important determinants of economic growth, which finally explained the discrepancies in growth between the countries. Many a time, the history of growth of the countries has adverted to the importance of the institutional foundation of an economy as a potent determining factor of economic growth and hence, accentuated the import of governance, rather good governance. Good governance is a multifaceted concept and can be examined along different dimensions.[2] It is responsible for maintaining institutional quality, which

1. Source: *World Development Indicators 2007*.

2. For example, the ability to provide basic law and order (stressed by everybody, particularly libertarians), social services to build up human capital (stressed by endogenous theorists), physical infrastructure (stressed by traditional growth theorists) or the ability to provide good economic management, all depict the different dimensions of good governance.

zeroes down to the need for government action to bring order to the market, shielding it from the variegated maladies of market failure.

The paper attempts to highlight the importance of institutional underpinnings in a society and hence, underscores the various aspects of governance, highlighting the growth-governance nexus. It further endeavours to depict the nature of the causal relationship between governance and income, using econometric models, stressing on why governance and hence institutions are important for economic growth. In addition, the governance situation in Bangladesh is discussed and some policy implications are also depicted. This paper is written in light of relevant literature reviews. For empirical analysis, Kaufmann and Kraay cross-country governance indicators and GDP statistics from *World Development Indicators 2007* are used to run bivariate and multivariate linear regression models. The paper is organised as follows: in Section 2 a glimpse of the history of development and governance is given; Section 3 highlights the significance of institutions and governance; Section 4 depicts empirical work; Section 5 describes the governance scenario in Bangladesh; some policy implications for Bangladesh are given in Section 6; lastly concluding remarks are made in Section 7.

History of Growth and Governance

With the beginning of 1990s, the development debate almost withered out in the West, mainly due to the changes in Eastern Europe and Latin America. Such changes were construed as the superiority of development models, which oriented the private sector towards exports. Market forces and economic efficiency were believed to be the best way to achieve growth, the best antidote to poverty.[3] Free-market capitalism was believed to have prevailed because it promised growth and democracy for the battered economies of Asia, Africa and Latin America. Soon gloomy manifestations of capitalist developments developed. For instance, in South Korea, with the advent of small democratic openings between 1987 and 1989, the labour force erupted in thousands of strikes during the late 1980s, undermining the country's basis of export success. Also, decades of

3. See Broad *et al.*, 1990-91.

uncontrolled industrial development left large parts of Taiwan with soil and water pollution. Furthermore, there were instances of slower growth surfacing throughout Africa, parts of Asia and Latin America, which practiced privatised adjustment. Such generalised failure of development in the 1980s produced a new wave of democratic movements, one that emphasised participation, equity and sustainability, in Africa, Asia and Latin America.

Similarly, the newly industrialised countries experienced the fastest growth rates among the developing countries over 1960-1990, only to face similar costs of high-speed, export-oriented industrialisation; the foundations of these supposed miracles of capitalist development were cracking. On the other hand, during the 1960s in Eastern Europe, the government-led "command" economies achieved higher growth rates than the countries of the capitalist world, but slowed down in the 1980s.

Moving the focus on governance alone, we can look into several country experiences pertaining to governance and development. For instance, Ukraine's living standards steadily declined during the 1990s due to weak governance in the form of ineffective rule of law, inadequate protection of property rights, widespread corruption and ill-advised policymaking serving special interests. Practical experience in many countries suggests that weak governance and slow economic development go hand in hand, while improved governance fosters development success. The scenario is similar at the sub-national level. In the city of Buenos Aires, Argentina, a participatory programme to enhance transparency in procurement brought about major improvements; in Campo Elias, Venezuela, far-reaching municipal reforms halved corruption and improved efficiency.[4]

Therefore, the lessons that can be drawn from the aforementioned experiences are:

- Communism can never be a complete failure nor can capitalism be a complete success.
- Command economies can jump-start large scale industrialisation but are unable to maximise efficiency. Such economies progress by making huge investments in productive capacity, but they cannot

4. See Kaufmann *et al.*, 2000.

produce efficiently enough to compete with the western industrialised economies.

- Command economies may propel societies through the first stages of development, but further growth into more sophisticated economies necessitates a greater role of market mechanisms.
- However, free markets are not a panacea. There must be an optimal combination of government intervention (putting the institutions right) and free market operation.
- While governance failures are widespread and costly, good governance provides significant benefits.

Growth, Institutions and Governance

The encounter between neoclassical economics and developing societies revealed the importance of institutional underpinnings in market economies, clarifying that such economics would not work, and might even generate perverse results, in the absence of adequate institutions.[5] Gradually, the importance of non-market institutions for proper functioning of the market was recognised. Scholars have discovered that over the long-term, high-quality institutions have the power to raise per capita incomes and promote growth in all parts of the world. Institutional capacity affects economic performance through allocation of resources.[6]

Hence, we find rich countries, where investors feel secure about their property rights, the rule of law prevails, private incentives are aligned with social objectives, monetary and fiscal policies are grounded in solid macroeconomic institutions, unconventional risks are appropriately mediated through social insurance and citizens have recourse to civil liberties and political representation. Poor countries are those where these arrangements are absent or are ill formed. Governance being broadly "the set of traditions and institutions by which authority in a country is exercised",[7] the responsibility of ensuring proper functioning of these institutions is

5. See Vijayaraghavan and Ward, 2001.
6. Lack of well functioning institutions may lead to inefficient investment choices by public and private sectors.
7. See *Governance Matters 2006: A Decade of Measuring the Quality of Governance*.

vested in the hands of government.[8] It is a composite measure that reflects the quality of bureaucracy, maintenance of rule of law and level of corruption in governance, rendering monetary and fiscal institutions independent, strengthening corporate governance, etc., which directly or indirectly affect the functioning of the market. These are sometimes called the "second-generation reforms", meant to overcome the apparent inefficacy of the earlier wave of reforms comprising liberalisation, stabilisation and privatisation.[9] The underlying argument is that, simple policy changes are ineffective unless they are grounded in strong institutional reforms.

Governance is quantified into six aggregate indicators: voice and accountability, political stability and absence of violence/terrorism, government effectiveness, regulatory quality, rule of law and control of corruption.[10] Policy makers and academics agree that good governance matters for economic development; the "development dividend" paid by good governance is large. According to Daniel Kaufmann, when governance is improved by one standard deviation, incomes rise about three-fold in the long run and infant mortality declines by two-thirds.[11] However, such aggregated measures of governance say very little about the specific institutional failures that bring about weak governance in a particular setting, even in the case of best cross-country governance indicators. The real challenge thus, lies in identifying and addressing these failures at the national, sub-national and corporate levels, and in understanding the key linkages between them. Enormous amounts of information is required to identify policy priorities, empower stakeholders and build political consensus for concerted and informed action to improve governance.

Empirical Evidence

Having talked about the importance of governance and hence, of institutions in promoting growth, some empirical evidence of the same can now be looked into.

---

8. Governance has three broad dimensions: political, economic and institutional aspects.
9. See Rodric, 2004.
10. A wide variety of cross-country indicators shed light on the various dimensions of governance, which are then aggregated into the aforementioned six categories. For definition of the six aggregate measures of governance, see *Governance Matters 2006: A Decade of Measuring the Quality of Governance*.
11. See *Governance Matters 2006: A Decade of Measuring the Quality of Governance*.

Data and Econometric Method

The data for per capita real GDP and GDP 1980 are taken from *World Development Indicators 2007*. For governance indicators, Kaufmann and Kraay governance indicators are used, which are measured in units ranging from about -2.5 to 2.5, with higher values corresponding to better governance outcomes. Natural logarithm of average of per capita real GDP for years 2002-2005 is used as the dependent variable (LPCGDP). Average of each of the six governance indicators (GI) for years 2002-2006 is used as one of the dependent variables. Natural logarithm of GDP of 1980 is the other explanatory variable (LGDP1980). Cross-country data for 137 countries are used (the data sheet used may be available on request).

Graphical Bivariate Representation

Governance indicators are the only explanatory variables in the six bivariate models, one for each governance indicator. Bivariate regression between log of per capita real GDP (LPCGDP) and governance indicator implies strong positive relationship between the two.

Figure 14.1

OLS Regression of Log of Per Capita Real GDP on Voice and Accountability

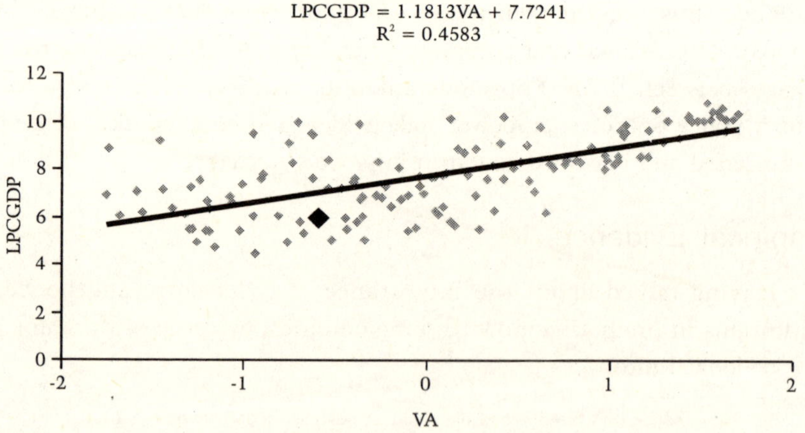

Note: The black dot indicates Bangladesh's position.

Source: Kaufmann *et al.*, 2007 for Governance Indicator and *World Development Indicators 2007* for per capita real GDP.

Figure 14.2

OLS Regression of Log of Per Capita Real GDP on Political Stability

LPCGDP = 1.1348PS + 7.8252
$R^2 = 0.4292$

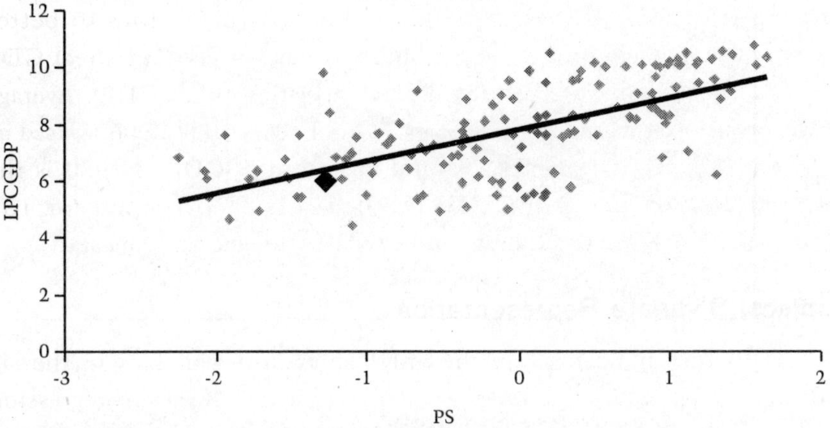

Note: The black dot indicates Bangladesh's position.

Source: Kaufmann *et al.*, 2007 for Governance Indicator and *World Development Indicators 2007* for per capita real GDP.

Figure 14.3

OLS Regression of Log of Per Capita Real GDP on Government Effectiveness

LPCGDP = 1.3906GE + 7.6664
$R^2 = 0.7386$

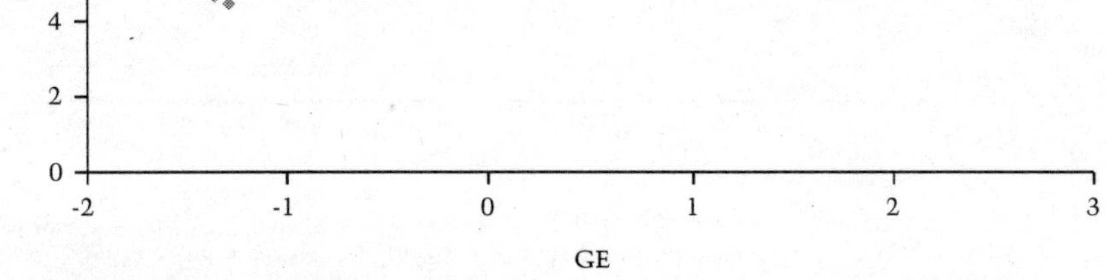

Note: The black dot indicates Bangladesh's position.

Source: Kaufmann *et al.*, 2007 for Governance Indicator and *World Development Indicators 2007* for per capita real GDP.

Figure 14.4

OLS Regression of Log of Per Capita Real GDP on Regulatory Quality

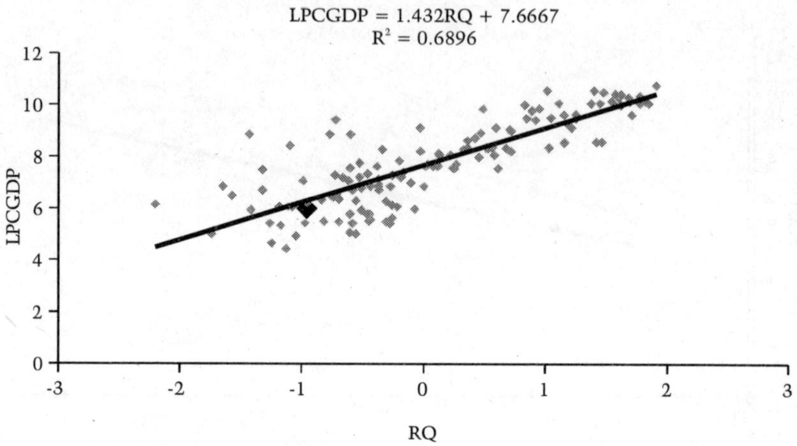

Note: The black dot indicates Bangladesh's position.

Source: Kaufmann *et al.*, 2007 for Governance Indicator and *World Development Indicators 2007* for per capita real GDP.

Figure 14.5

OLS Regression of Log of Per Capita Real GDP on Rule of Law

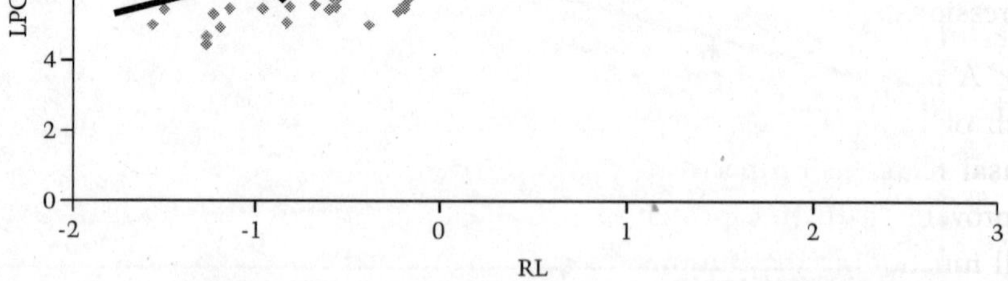

Note: The black dot indicates Bangladesh's position.

Source: Kaufmann *et al.*, 2007 for Governance Indicator and *World Development Indicators 2007* for per capita real GDP.

Figure 14.6

OLS Regression of Log of Per Capita Real GDP on Control of Corruption

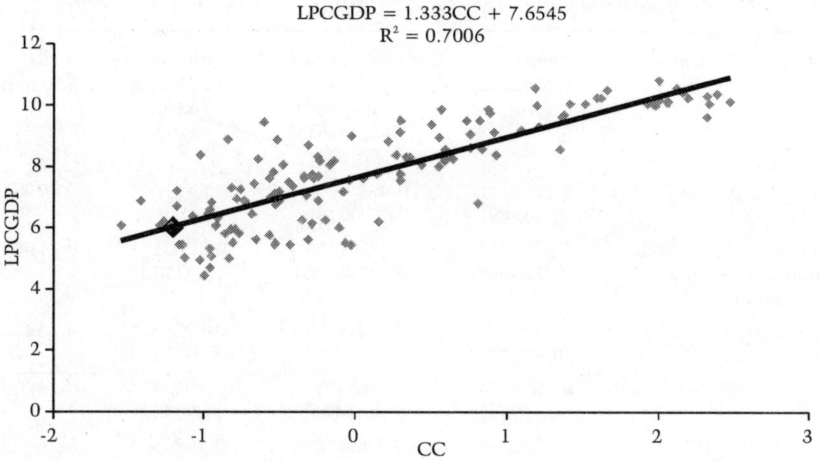

Note: The black dot indicates Bangladesh's position.

Source: Kaufmann *et al.*, 2007 for Governance Indicator and *World Development Indicators 2007* for per capita real GDP.

Multivariate Model of Cross-Country Data

In a bivariate model, a single explanatory variable (governance indicator) leaves much of the variation in per capita real GDP unexplained. Hence, six multivariate linear regression models of log of per capita real GDP (LPCGDP) on log of GDP of 1980 (LGDP1980) and each of the six aggregate governance indicators (GI) in turn are run. The cross-country model is specified as: $LPCGDP = \beta_0 + \beta_1 LGDP1980 + \beta_2 GI + \varepsilon$, where GI represents each of VA, PS, GE, RQ, RL and CC in turn, in each of the six regressions.

A positive significant relationship between per capita real GDP and each of the aggregate governance indicators is evident, which implies a causal relationship between the two; improvement in the latter leads to improvement in the former. Hence, we find well-governed countries with well functioning institutions, to have high growth rates and thus, high per capita income. Table 14.1 summarises the regression results.

Table 14.1

Regression Results of the Six Multivariate Models[12]
(Dependent Variable: Log of Per capita Real GDP, LPCGDP)

Explanatory Variables	*Constant (Standard Error)*	*Coefficient of Explanatory Variable (Standard Error)*	*Coefficient of LGDP1980 (Standard Error)*	*R-Squared*
Voice and Accountability (VA)	5.2862*** (0.36589)	0.96973*** (0.10024)	0.27116*** (0.03944)	0.59952
Political Stability and Absence of Violence/ Terrorism (PS)	4.4781*** (0.29398)	1.0961*** (0.079308)	0.37031*** (0.031437)	0.71957
Government Effectiveness (GE)	6.5731*** (0.30674)	1.2454*** (0.078846)	0.12245*** (0.033458)	0.76233
Regulatory Quality (RQ)	6.2696*** (0.31986)	1.2488*** (0.087474)	0.15639*** (0.034829)	0.73020
Rule of Law (RL)	5.9778*** (0.28789)	1.1884*** (0.074152)	0.19539*** (0.031070)	0.76679
Control of Corruption (CC)	5.9910*** (0.29135)	1.1582*** (0.073400)	0.18611*** (0.031646)	0.76201

Note: *** implies p= 0.000; ('p' shows the level of significance). No. of observations = 137

Source: Kaufmann *et al.*, 2007 for Governance Indicators and *World Development Indicators 2007* for per capita real GDP and GDP 1980.

From the table above, we can deduce the following (under *ceteris paribus*):

- For 1 standard deviation improvement in voice and accountability, per capita real GDP increases more than two-fold in the long run.[13]
- For 1 standard deviation improvement in political stability, per capita real GDP increases nearly three-fold in the long run.
- For 1 standard deviation improvement in government effectiveness, per capita real GDP increases more than three-fold in the long run.

12. Each row in the table corresponds to a single multivariate regression model. E.g. the first row corresponds to the model specified as: $LPCGDP = b_0+b_1 LGDP1980+ b_2 VA+\varepsilon$, where LPCGDP is log of per capita real GDP and VA is voice and accountability. Hence, the six rows correspond to the six multivariate models.

13. The increase in per capita real GDP is calculated by taking the exponential transformation (i.e. inverse log) of the coefficient of the governance indicator. E.g. from the first row of the table, exp (0.96973)=2.67, i.e., a more than two-fold increase in LPCGDP due to 1 standard deviation increase in VA. Other calculations are done in similar manner.

- For 1 standard deviation improvement in regulatory quality, per capita real GDP increases more than thee-fold in the long run.
- For 1 standard deviation improvement in rule of law, per capita real GDP increases more than three-fold in the long run.
- For 1 standard deviation improvement in control of corruption, per capita real GDP increases more than three-fold in the long run.

Hence, once again the importance of governance and institutional quality has been accentuated by empirical cross-country evidence.

Scenario in Bangladesh

Bangladesh continues to make endeavours to improve its overall governance environment. Despite some progress, the remaining agenda is challenging. Recognising this, the government has intensified its efforts to improve the overall governance environment. More recently, the completed Poverty Reduction Strategy Paper (PRSP) highlights good governance as a major thrust, "because everything else in the nation's life depends on it".[14] Bangladesh remains apprehensive that the price it pays for poor governance may rise to the point where it will begin to offset the beneficial impact of some of its governance successes and thus, seriously reduce the efficacy of its development efforts.

Several reforms to improve sectoral governance are already underway, mainly under three main themes: core governance, improving the investment climate through supporting sectoral governance reforms and empowering the poor. Progress on governance will be difficult without creating public demand and pressure for reform. In the coming period, it is looking more to demand side interventions and building constituencies for reform.[15]

Although the country has maintained democracy for three consecutive regimes since 1991, it has rather witnessed psuedo-democratic culture. Democracy rests on a core set of well functioning institutions, and institutional reforms have always been a weak priority for any government here. As a result targeting the people has turned out to be a "minus two"[16]

14. *Source: Governance & Public Sector Management in South Asia*, Governance in Bangladesh, 2007.
15. See *Governance & Public Sector Management in South Asia*, Governance in Bangladesh, 2007.
16. "Minus two" in the sense that the approach to target the people lacked traditions and institutions.

approach that has suffocated democracy. Furthermore, some restrictive laws in force such as the Official Secrets Act (1923), the Evidence Act (1872), the Code of Criminal Procedure (1960), the Rules of Business (1996) and the Government Servants (Conduct) Rules (1979) curtail people's right to information. The consequence has been lack of grassroots democracy, accountability and transparency leading to malfunctioning institutions.

Furthermore, governance and hence, institutional operations in the country are plagued with rampant corruption. The scenario turned out to be real grimy in terms of the business climate and confidence, which stymied the growth potential of the country. Referring to the Global Competitiveness Index by WEF, Bangladesh was ranked the last in terms of the corruption sub-index out of 104 countries and 117 countries in 2004 and 2005 respectively. Also, as per the Transparency International ranking of corruption perception index, Bangladesh has been at the bottom of the list for a number of years now. However, such a single quantitative indicator has its weakness and hence, we try to use more comprehensive and balanced measures of governance performance. Figure 14.7 shows Bangladesh's standing, in terms of the six governance indicators, relative to the other 212 countries in the world.

Figure 14.7

Cross-Country Comparison of Governance Indicators: Bangladesh (2003, 2006)

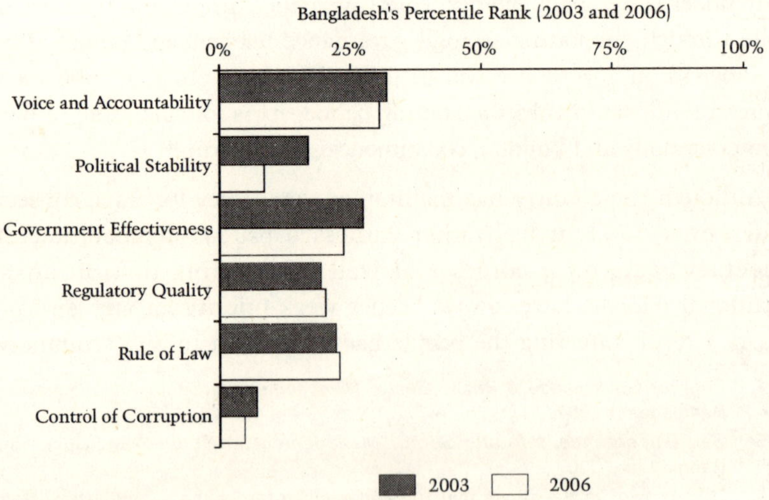

Source: Kaufmann *et al.*, 2007.

The figure shows that, despite not being the only country facing governance challenges, the difficulties Bangladesh faces are substantial. It scores worst in control of corruption followed by political stability. In terms of all the five out of six governance indicators, Bangladesh could not perform better than even 25 per cent of the 212 countries in 2006. What is more disconcerting is that the governance situation has worsened (the white bars are shorter than the grey ones in almost all the dimensions of governance). The political situation has remained highly prone to being destabilised. This fact reflects serious consequences on the country's growth performance so far and its growth potential.[17]

We can also look at Figures 14.1 to 14.6, where the position of Bangladesh is shown by the black dots. The table below summarises its relative position to OLS regression line.

Table 14.2

Governance and Per Capita Income in Bangladesh

Governance Indicators	*Position Relative to OLS Regression Line*
Voice and Accountability	Below
Political Stability	Below
Government Effectiveness	Below
Regulatory Quality	Below
Rule of Law	Below
Control of Corruption	On

What we see is that Bangladesh fares poorly in terms of its per capita income relative to almost all the dimensions of governance, in the sense that it lies below the OLS regression line. An interpretation of this may be that Bangladesh has been lagging behind in raising its per capita real GDP. Given its governance scenario, it should have had higher per capita real GDP. A rather optimistic explanation may be that the relatively low-income level is inherently robust because it is supported by sound institutions.

17. For example, fragile and cumbersome regulatory framework, a consequence of weak overall governance, raises the cost of doing business, thereby affecting the investment climate.

Policy Implications

Without binding rules and structures that govern all players, anarchy becomes commonplace. Business thereby becomes simply "casino capitalism".[18] Thus, getting the relationship right between the government departments, business organisations, civil society and market institutions is of utmost importance for instigating and sustaining growth. Developing institutions is very important for ensuring good governance. In the backdrop of the present state of affairs, it can start with the following measures.

Recalibrating Democracy

As already mentioned, Bangladesh has faltered in terms of exercising democracy. For a healthy market economy to prevail, the importance of democracy can hardly be overemphasised.[19] Whether any effort to achieve long-lasting transition to democratic, market-oriented systems would be successful or not, depends on the design and functioning of the institutional framework. People should help the current administration to take just decisions according to due process of law. Thus, the essence turns out to be that the country must find some way to stop "fly-by-night businessmen" steamrolling their way into the political arena and getting nomination from political parties. There must be accountability and transparency in all spheres of economic and social activities. However, for democracy to thrive there must be free flow of information.[20] Policy makers have often stressed the link between the flow of information and socio-economic affluence. The easier the availability of information in the state, the higher is its state of development. Bangladesh is looking forward to formulate the right to information act.

---

18. Thus, investments will turn out to be only bets that people will keep their word, that companies will tell the truth, that companies would abide by their social responsibilities, and that workers will be paid.

19. As already discussed in Section 2, experiences of the 1980s and 1990s demonstrate the fact that failure to incorporate democratic governance as a part of economic reform seriously jeopardises any reform agenda.

20. In Britain, according to freedom of information law, anyone of any nationality moving anywhere in the world, may request for information held by more than one hundred thousand public authorities and other designated non-governmental organisations in Britain, and expect an answer within 20 working days, usually free of charge.

Curbing Corruption to Support Democracy

Corruption not only economically hurts the business community and the citizens, but it also has a destabilising effect on democracy, manifested in the malfunctioning institutions and the well-being of the nation. Underdevelopment is directly related to corruption.[21] Measures are underway to combat corruption. However, a research and advocacy programme targeting at eliminating opportunities for corruption may be quite helpful for Bangladesh. At the same time, the watchdog role of the media in society can actually put a check on corruption. However, without proper access to information, the fight against corruption will always remain incomplete.

Strengthening the Role of Business Associations

Advocates for private sector and business associations in industrial nations have played a vital role in encouraging good governance and sound policymaking. Bangladesh should form a business agenda that would identify policy reforms as the highest priority for the business community and hence, specify the reforms in terms of laws and regulations, thereby making concrete suggestions for (institutional) changes.[22] The key to such agenda is people's participation. However, this once again necessitates effective access to information.

Removing Institutional Barriers to Participation

Informal sector produces legitimate products without proper permits or legal status due to lack of resources to comply with burdensome rules and regulations necessary to participate in the formal economy. In Bangladesh, the informal sector is estimated to account for 70 per cent of the official economy. A large and growing informal sector results from fundamental flaws in government process; it proves that a market hasn't been created. It is thus of grave importance that Bangladesh starts building

21. The notion has been supported by empirical evidence provided in Section 4. A positive relationship between log of per capita real GDP and control of corruption implies that better control of corruption lead to higher per capita income.

22. The Nigerian Association of Chambers of Commerce, Industry, Mines, and Agriculture (NACCIMA) coordinated economic reform using its agenda. It developed and publicised the national business agenda in the face of pressure from Nigeria's political transition and its economic crisis (Sullivan, 2002).

market institutions and instills confidence in the concerned by promoting convenient access to such institutional services.

Promoting Sound Corporate Governance

Sound corporate governance principles attack the supply side of the corruption relationship. The scandals during the Russian and Asian financial crisis have accentuated corporate governance issues as key reform issues in developing and transitional economies. Weak corporate governance can create huge potential liabilities for individual firms and collectively for society. Bangladesh must have transparent control, responsible corporate boards and shareholders' rights, efficient capital markets and accountability to promote robust corporate sector, without which, even strong economies can falter. The country will thereby enhance the faith of the public in the integrity of the privatisation process and help ensure that it realises the best return on the national investment.

Strengthening Local Governance

No Central government can work properly without strong local governance. The limited power of local government, scarce resources and limited responsibilities shrink the scope of expansion and establishment of good governance. In western democracies, local administration is a powerful organisation that effectively and smoothly governs the country. The political regimes of 1991-2006 were marked by rhetoric to strengthen local governance, but in reality no tangible progress could be seen. Local governance is important for the political development of Bangladesh. By making the people politically conscious, it will actually enable the people to establish a democratic society and administrative system. More aware citizens will better understand the needs of the wider community. Once again, right to information is a basic prerequisite to ensure wide spread awareness and accountability.

Conclusion

Across the globe, combating corruption, fostering corporate governance, reducing barriers to participation in the formal sector, creating conducive environment for proper functioning of the institutions, and ensuring democracy and participatory governance have ushered in new opportunities.

Each action serves as a focal point to push forward with pro-growth market reforms. Sound corporate governance is a prerequisite for economic growth and requires a framework of market institutions as well as sound business practices based on democratic practices. Democracy requires access to information. In ensuring all this, good governance is the cardinal thrust. Without good governance ensuring well functioning institutions, sustainable economic growth is infeasible. Hence, we find rich countries with well functioning institutions, governance and income are positively related. The state as well as the people must make concerted effort to promote governance and institutional quality to achieve economic growth.

References

Broad, Robin, John Cavanagh and Walden Bello (1990-91). "Development: The Market is not Enough," *Foreign Policy*, Paper No. 81, pp.144-162. Winter.

Kaufmann, Daniel and Aart Kraay (2002). "Growth without Governance," *World Bank Policy Research Working* Paper 2928, Washington D.C. November.

Kaufmann, Daniel, Aart Kraay and Massimo Mastruzzi (2007). "Governance Matters VI: Governance Indicators for 1996-2006," *World Bank Policy Research*, Washington D.C. Data retrieved from *http://www.govindicators.org.* June.

Kaufmann, Daniel, Aart Kraay and Pablo Zoido-Lobatón (2000). "Governance Matters: From Measurement to Action", *Finance & Development* 37(2), A quarterly magazine of IMF. June.

Rodric, Dani (2004). *Getting Institutions Right*. Harvard University. April.

Rodrik, Dani, Arvind Subramanian and Francisco Trebbi (2002). "Institutions Rule: The Primacy of Institutions over Geography and Integration in Economic Development", Harvard University, International Monetary Fund. April.

Sullivan, John D. (2002). "Democracy, Governance and the Market", *Sustainable Development, Economic Perspectives* 6(3): 28-32, Issue no 235, April. An Electronic Journal of the US Department of State.

Vijayaraghavan, Maya and William A. Ward (2001). "Institutions and Economic Growth: Empirical Evidence from Cross-National Analysis," CIT *Working Paper*, Clemson University.

WEF (2006). "Global Competitiveness Report 2006-2007", *E:\World Economic Forum -Global Competitiveness Report.htm*

———. (2005).

———. (2004).

———. (2003).

World Bank (2007). *Governance & Public Sector Management in South Asia, Governance in Bangladesh*. Washington DC: The World Bank.

———. (2006). *Governance Matters 2006: A Decade Of Measuring The Quality of Governance*. Washington DC: The World Bank.

———. (2007). *World Development Indicators 2007.* Washington DC: The World Bank.

15 Development Due to Democracy

A Myth or Reality?

Sameen Siddiqi

Introduction

Democracy as a concept is in vogue in Pakistan. From lawyers on the street to United States of America calling for "free and fair" elections, the institution of democracy seems to be the only solution of the problems of Pakistan. Political motivations aside, there is genuine belief among these promoters of democracy that democracy leads to optimal economic development, while a non-democracy does not. Some attribute cross country total factor productivity differences to institutional quality. Others link political stability with long run growth. Some certify that public allocation improves under democracy accelerating growth; others link growth as a consequence of democratically aware society. But empirical figures of Pakistan indicate that its development path has not necessarily been dictated by the kind of its governing political institutions.

This paper attempts to highlight that democratic institutions have not played a significant role in economic development of Pakistan. Pakistan has actually shown more growth in the absence of institution of democracy. If we assess economic development in terms of real GDP then Pakistan has never experienced as high growth as under military rule. It has registered an economic growth of more than 6 per cent for four consecutive years. In June 2006, Morgan Stanley listed Pakistan on a list of 25 countries displaying continued moderate to strong growth over a sustained period of time. Similarly, State Street Corporation noted that "economic growth has been helped by privatisations as well as foreign investments". Moody's Investors Service upgraded Pakistan's credit rating from B2 to B1. Exports grew from a deficit of 10.7 per cent to a surplus of 11.4 per cent in 2006. Exports accelerated under the military regime rather than under the democratic regime.

Investment has never been so high. Growth rates of 27.5 per cent in 2006 and 29.5 per cent in 2007 are unprecedented figures of total investment. Even infrastructure development has been considerable. Electricity installation jumped by 11 per cent from 15.6 in 1999 to 17.2 MW in 2000.[1] In 1999, Pakistan's debt reached 98.5 per cent of its GDP, and interest payments consumed more than half of its tax revenues. By 2005, it accounted for only 55 per cent of GDP. This scenario leads to further sub-questions. Are democratic institutions really imperative for economic development? Does the assumption of democratic institutions being accountable hold true in case of Pakistan? Democratic institutions have always been inclined to nationalism in the history of Pakistan. All military regimes in Pakistan have exhibited pro-market inclination on the other hand, and shown more growth. Does this mean that governments have failed while markets have triumphed? If democratic institutions have exhibited government failure, then should the invisible hand be allowed to rule? However, has the invisible hand truly allowed efficient allocation? If unaccountable military regimes perform better, then is the problem of unaccountability less important than theory predicts?

This paper explores each of the above sub-questions to assess the type of relationship between political institutions and economic development.

Are Democratic Institutions Really Imperative for Economic Development?

Samuel Huntington believes that governments succeed (in governing) in the presence of democracy and strong party system. He asserts there is a correlation between democracy and development. Mancur Olson in *Rise and Decline of Nations* explains that this is because the type of political institutions ultimately affects economic development. He believes "it is no accident that the countries that have reached the highest level of economic development are all stable democracies". Leblang contends that democracy indirectly helps economic growth by allowing higher levels of individual

1. The first year of General Musharraf's dictatorship.

property rights because private property rights provide incentives for production and exchange of economic goods. It is empirically clear that nations that protect property rights tend to grow faster than those that do not and that democratic societies tend to protect property rights more than other types of government. Using cross-national time-series (panel) data from 1960 to 1990, Leblang found that property rights have a positive and statistically significant impact on economic growth which proves that democracy encourages growth. Also, since democracies ensure information about the preferences of the citizens are conveyed to the policy makers, Mueller believes that the hallmark of a democracy is that it answers to questions like the quantity and quality of public goods to be provided by the government are supplied by the citizens themselves. All these arguments indicate that democracy and development go hand in hand. However, a research by Granger shows no correlation between the two. With 32 developing countries under study, only 11 showed a causal relationship. Pakistan showed none. The Granger causality test used the simple hypothesis that if X causes Y then changes in X must precede changes in Y. Despite using a different methodology, other empiricists like Gonick and Rosh also failed to establish causality between democracy and growth.

Table 15.1

Summary of the Results

Causal Direction	*Number of Countries*	*Percentile*	*Name of Countries*
Growth—>Democracy	11	34%	Costa Rica, Egypt, Guatemala, India, Israel, South Korea, Mexico, Nicaragua, Thailand, Uruguay, Venezuela
Democracy—>Growth	10	31%	Bolivia, Burma, Colombia, Ecuador, El Salvador, Indonesia, Iran, Paraguay, The Phillippines, South Africa
Feedback Relationship	3	9%	Chile, Dominican Republic, Turkey
No Relationship	8	25%	Argentina, Brazil, Haiti, Honduras, Pakistan, Panama, Peru, Sri Lanka
N=32			

Does Democracy Ensure Accountability?

As it is observed that there is no causality between democracy and development, it is natural to wonder why it should be enforced. Generally theories are provided that democracy inculcates accountability which is imperative for progress and growth. It is cited that owing to dependency of governments' stability and continuity on peoples' preferences, democratic institutions are more likely to be accountable. They become a part of the accountability chain where citizens have the responsibility to participate, especially by voting; parties have the responsibility to recruit candidates, develop policies and offer a clear direction; the legislature has the responsibility to support or defeat policies and/or governments; the president or prime minister has the responsibility to form a government; the ministers of that government have the responsibility to use their executive power in administrating and creating policies; and the public service has the responsibility to implement efficiently, effectively and impartially the policies of the elected government.

Citizens

↓

Party

↓

President/legislature

↓

Ministers

↓

Departments of government

↓

Public servants

As the democratic governments feel their performance is under scrutiny and criticism, they are compelled to be responsive to the demands of the citizens. Their control is subject to come to an end if the public ceases to tolerate corruption, which compels them to administer efficiently.

The statistics of Pakistan refute this thesis as well. According to the corruption perception index (CPI) released by Transparency International (TI), the parliamentary regime of President Musharraf after the elections in 2002, was considered to be more corrupt than his regime without parliament. Under dictatorship between 1999 and 2002, the CPI was 32.69 per cent. It more than doubled to 67.31 per cent under a parliamentary regime.[2] While one could argue that Musharraf's tenure was a "farcical" democracy, the situation was no better under credible democracies of Benazir Bhutto and Nawaz Sharif in 1990s. Five successive elected governments of these two have been dismissed on charges of corruption between end of military regime of General Zia (in 1988) and beginning of General Musharraf's rule in 1999. Yearly assessment of TI shows the extent of corruption in Bhutto's regime (1995), Nawaz Sharif's rule (1997), just before the coup (1999), under dictatorship (2002) and current caretaker government (2007). It reveals that corruption was highest in democratic regime of Bhutto and not during absolute military rule of General Musharraf.

Table 15.2

CPI Calculated for Each Type of Government[3]

Year	*1995*	*1997*	*1999*	*2002*	*2007*
CPI	2.25	2.53	2.7	2.6	2.4

Thus, Pakistan contradicts the hypothesis of negative relationship between corruption and democratic institutions. Corruption was higher in the presence of political institutions.[4]

Does Democracy Lead to Growth as a Consequence of Property Rights?

If democracy doesn't always show causality with growth nor does it ensure effective accountability then why does democracy appear as a necessary solution? Contenders argue that democratic institutions induce

2. Pakistan National Corruption Perception Survey, 2006.
3. The index ranks corruption from 0 to 10 with 10 being highly clean and 0 being highly corrupt. *www.transparency.org*
4. Explained above.

growth by strengthening property rights. Private property rights provide the incentive required for production and exchange and help to stabilise expectations about individuals' behaviour. One can present two counter arguments in this regard. Firstly, mere passing of property rights through legislation is not sufficient in a fractionalised country like Pakistan which faces both elite domination and ethnic heterogeneity. Rodrick (2000) points out that while Russia has property rights, it does not have control. Formal property rights do not count for much if they do not confer control rights. By the same token, sufficiently strong control rights may do the trick even in the absence of formal property rights. Russia today represents a case where shareholders have property rights but often lack effective control over enterprises. Town and Village Enterprises (TVEs) in China are an example where control rights have spurred entrepreneurial activity despite the absence of clearly defined property rights. As these instances illustrate, establishing "property rights" is rarely a matter of just passing a piece of legislation. Legislation in itself is neither necessary nor sufficient for the provision of the secure control rights. In practice, control rights are upheld by a combination of legislation, private enforcement, and custom and tradition. They may be distributed more narrowly or more diffusely than property rights.

In a country like Pakistan where both political and economic power lies in the hands of the same elite, existence of property rights can do little to mobilise the under-privileged and provide opportunities for growth. With the strong prevalence of a feudal system, mere legislation does little to empower the general masses and encourage development. It is also ironic that unlike Denzao and North's (1993) analysis that property rights are enforced in democracies, it was the military regimes in Pakistan who strengthened these rights by taking a pro-market approach and privatising national enterprises. This was done in recognition of government failure of the nationalising schemes of the democratic era of Bhutto. Instead of efficient allocation, nationalisation of 32 large manufacturing plants led to production decline much below the optimum levels. Cotton cloth production fell to 3.1 million square metres against a purchase of 5.2 million square metres in that decade. Fertiliser production dropped from 27.5 million tonnes to 13.2 million tonnes. Eight major industries like iron and steel, metals, heavy engineering, motor vehicle, chemicals, cement and public utilities were affected. Subsequently, domestically owned life insurance companies, privately owned banks, domestic shipping companies and firms engaged in oil distribution, vegetable oil processing, grain milling and cotton ginning were nationalised. The result was a drop of nearly 50 per cent in private investment in large-scale manufacturing between FY 1970 and FY 1973. By FY 1978, such investments were little more than one-third (in constant prices) of those in FY 1970. Private capital fled the country or went into small-scale manufacturing and real estate. Industrial output slowed considerably. Overall growth rate of manufacturing fell from 9.9 per cent to 5.5 per cent—the biggest slump in Pakistan's history. Agriculture sputtered. Organised labour demanded and received higher wages which increased production costs.

The public sector expanded greatly. In addition to the nationalisation of companies, plants were built by the government and additional public companies were created for various functions, such as the export of cotton and rice. Able managers and technicians were scarce, a situation that became worse after 1974, when many persons left to seek higher salaries in Middle Eastern oil-producing states. Labour legislation set high minimum wages and fringe benefits, which boosted payroll costs for both public and private firms. Efficiency and profits in public sector enterprises fell. Public industrial investment rose, surpassing private industrial investment in FY 1976. These economic measures undertaken by the Bhutto government proved to be ineffective because of the power of vested interests and the inefficiency of the civil administration. Inadequately planned, long-term projects that tied up the country's development resources for long periods were adopted. The attempt to achieve income redistribution failed.

Nationalisation failed both in terms of efficiency and equity, exhibited a typical case of legislative failure where allocative inefficiency that arose from excessive provision of public goods to pursue strategies designed to maximise Bhutto's chances of reelection rather than policies that would further common good. It was an easy way to appease the white collared urban employees—aroused since Ayub's regime—by guaranteeing them employment through nationalisation. It was an attempt to establish a peerless position. It was a way of rewarding his people. It was a way of rewarding the PPP leaders, their family members and supporters, the bureaucrats, workers in state-owned industries, and the employees of state-owned banks and insurance companies. PPP leaders were able to have their relatives and supporters appointed to various positions in the new industrial/commercial empire acquired by the government.[5] Nationalisation exacerbated socio-political polarisation in Pakistan. The middle classes were worse-off. The economic growth that was a major contribution of Ayub Khan came to a standstill. Such was the failure that Bhutto's own party (PPP)[6] adopted a less socialist regime in its second tenure and ventured into privatisation in 1995. Yet, the pro-market approach to address government failure did not help much either. Since accountability did not deter democracies from corruption, market allocation failed to be efficient. Having seen the outcome of nationalising policy of 1970s, privatisation was seen as the only viable option and as a panacea for economic ills.

While it was less surprising that privatisation did not exactly achieve its proposed goals, it was more surprising that the scheme failed under democratic regime. It was more fruitful under dictatorship. Leblangs' thesis that property rights lead to development proved true but it did so under military rule. Accountability did not deter corruption even in privatisation. One would expect a fair and transparent process under democracy but the privatisation of Kot Addu (KAPCO)—the largest electricity generating unit in 1995 proved to be an interesting story. According to a report by Pakistan Institute of Development Economics, there was no need to privatise an already existing big power unit which was running efficiently. Its units were either gas turbine or combined cycles which can use either oil or gas. Gas is far cheaper than oil for generating electricity and Kot Addu was mostly running on gas. However, the government decided to sell 26 per cent stake in it at a price of US$215 million. Initially, it was decided that after privatisation, KAPCO would sell electricity to WAPDA (Water and Power Development Authority) at a tariff of 5.6 US cent per kWh. Subsequently, this tariff was reduced to 4.9 US cent per kWh. WAPDA's cost of generation at Kot Addu with gas feed stock was not more than 2.5 US cent per kWh. Hence, the government received US$291 million but WAPDA became a bankrupt organisation after the sale of KAPCO. The foreign party was able to repatriate the total amount of US$291 million in the last six

---

5. *www.pakistanlink.com*

6. Pakistan People's Party under Zulfiqar Bhutto's daughter Benazir.

years but WAPDA is being forced to pay twice the cost at which it was generating electricity at KAPCO before privatisation. This was "the most senseless privatisation in Pakistan". It ruined WAPDA and its consumers all over the country are suffering because WAPDA has to pay such high rates. The electricity tariff in Pakistan which is estimated to be the highest in Asia also made industry uncompetitive in world market. Overall assessment of Asian Development Bank showed that after privatisation in 1995, only 22 per cent of the privatised units were performing better, 44 per cent performed the same and 34 per cent worse than before. The aim of improving the efficiency of units was only attained by 20 per cent of the units. On the whole, the operational efficiency not only deteriorated after privatisation but also resulted in closure of 20 units of cement, chemicals, fertilisers, oil and motors. The closure impacted the economy by causing a recession. GDP fell from above 6 per cent to 4 per cent in the post-privatisation period. Thus, market failed to yield an efficient outcome despite being employed after democratic consensus.

Table 15.3

Leadership Record in Pakistan till 1998

Government	*Economic Growth Record*	*Political Regime*	*Social Outcome*
Ayub (1958-1969)	Rapid growth	Military/autocracy	Class disparity
Z. Bhutto (1971-1977)	Decline	Socialist/populist	Uplift of masses
Zia (1977-1988)	High growth rate	Military/sacralised autocracy	Ethnic strife/ social suffocation
B. Bhutto (1988-1990)	Sluggish growth	Secular democracy	Democratic society/ chaos
N. Sharif (1990-1993)	Growth/ privatisation	Liberalised authoritarian	Social unrest/ traditional repressive tactics
B. Bhutto (1993-1998)	Growth/ privatisation	Secular democracy	Democratic society/ unrest

Economic history shows that market-oriented economic measures without corresponding liberalising social policies resulted in class disparity and an economically polarised society. Whether it was the privatisation schemes of Musharraf or those of Nawaz, the market exacerbated the schism between the elite and the poor. It marginalised the poor and concentrated power and wealth in the hands of the privileged few.

This makes one think if the introduction of democratic institutions like political rights, civil rights and freedom of press actually improve development. Have the democracies in Pakistan allowed their population to participate in public decisions or are they generally "window-dressing" used by the elite to control and sustain power?

Comparative Overview

It has been observed that development has not necessarily taken place under democracy. The authoritative regimes have been more conducive for economic growth but failed to lead to socio-economic or socio-political equality. The democratic governments neither spurred growth nor strengthened democratic institutions. During the Ayub period, economic growth was commendable but progress in the social sphere was poor. Zulfiqar Ali Bhutto's leadership gave some strength to the masses but failed to produce economic progress. The Zia era was horrendous in human and social rights although economic growth was better during the Bhutto period. Benazir Bhutto did succeed, to an extent, in creating a liberal atmosphere during her first term but economic growth slowed down measurably. Nawaz Sharif stimulated the economy with his intense privatisation but his social policies were too coercive. Bhutto's second term witnessed continuation of the economic liberalisation programmes of her predecessor and some improvement in social areas, but it also saw a rise in domestic political violence and militancy in Karachi. Wealth polarisation increased regardless of the regime type. Trends of Gini coefficient exhibit that income inequality has been unambiguously on the rise. Under Zia's dictatorship, the coefficient was 0.37. Under his presidential rule, it reduced to 0.35. Contradicting theoretical predictions, the Gini deteriorated to 0.41 during both terms of Bhutto and Sharif in the 1990s. Poverty level which started from 24.47 per cent under Zia's dictatorship, declined to 17.32 per cent in his presidential regime. Instead of showing further improvement, the democracies of 1990s exacerbated the poverty level from 22.11 per cent in 1990 to 32.6 per cent in 1999, just before the military coup. Thus, while one may argue that the poverty level has been the highest in Musharraf's era, one should not forget that the trend could be a mere extrapolation of its historical legacy. Poverty gap had been increasing even under democracy and is not a new economic woe as a consequence of military rule.

Though poverty has exacerbated, gender empowerment has definitely improved under military rule. Never before were women given power of decision-making and policy formulation of such magnitude as they have today. General Musharraf has made attempts to increase the participation by women in all tiers of the political and electoral process. Both local government bodies and parliaments must have at least a third of their seats reserved for women, by legislation. Civil service must have at least 10 per cent women representation in the bureaucracy.

In terms of human development, Pakistan has fallen much behind other countries with its level of per capita income. While its HDI has risen from 0.36 during the first democratic regime of 1970 to 0.55 under General Musharraf's regime, its ranking fell from 134 to 136 in 2005. On the other hand, its education facilities have improved considerably. Tertiary education has seen the most growth.

Conclusion and Recommendations

With such conflicting statistics, it is difficult to declare that democracy has been conducive for development of Pakistan and dictatorship has not. As there is no consistent correlation between the economic development and a particular regime, the traditional dichotomy between democracy and dictatorship cannot be applied to Pakistan. Re-institution of democracy cannot serve as a panacea to the problems of Pakistan. It will take more than improvement of political institutions to boost development in Pakistan. Democracy could actually do much worse if it is not accompanied by reformation of social institutional framework. The socio-economic gap needs to be addressed. The increasing income inequality needs to be minimised. The public needs to be motivated to exercise their political rights. Non-political institutions need to be strengthened. The civil society needs to be developed. Investment in human capital is likely to be a more effective source of growth and development than political institutions like democracy. While under no circumstance can the merits of democracy be underestimated or denied, yet it seems that Pakistan could develop much rapidly by focusing on strengthening the civil society. In essence, rather than changing the government regime, the inherent characteristics of society need to be changed at large.

References

Ali, Mukhtar Ahmad (2008). *Privatisation of Public Utilities: How is it Generating and Impacting Conflicts in Pakistan?*. Centre for Peace and Development Initiatives, Pakistan (CPDI-Pakistan).

Burki, Shahid J. (1979). *Pakistan under Bhutto: 1971-1977*. New York: St. Martin Press. p.245.

Denzau, Arthur T. and Douglass C. North (1993). "Shared Mental Models: Ideologies and Institutions", *Economic History* 9309003. EconWPA.

Economic and Social Indicators of Pakistan.

Glaeser, Shleifer and Lopez-de-Silanes (2004). "Do Institutions Cause Growth?", *NBER Working Paper* Series. *http://www.nber.org/papers/w10568*

Haque, M. Shamsul (1998). "The Paradox of Bureaucratic Accountability in Developing Nations under a Pro-market State", *International Political Science Review* 19(4): 357-372. October.

Hussain, Ishrat (n.d.). "Why Privatization is Necessary for Economic Growth in Pakistan?", *http://hdrstats.undp.org/countries/data_sheets/cty_ds_PAK.html*

Jon, S.T. Quah (1999). "Corruption in Asian Countries: Can it be Minimized?", *Public Administration Review* 59(6): 483-494. November-December.

Khan, Akhtar (n.d.). *Is Privatization Purposeful in Pakistan*. Pakistan Institute of Development Economics.

Monshipouri, Mahmud and Amjad Samuel (1995). "Development and Democracy in Pakistan: Tenuous or Plausible Nexus?", *Asian Survey* 35(11): 973-989. November. Stable URL: *http://links.jstor.org/sici?sici=00044687%28199511%2935%3A11%3C973%3ADADIPT%3E2.0.CO%3B2-J*

Omar, Azfar, Young Lee and Anand Swamy (2001). "The Causes and Consequences of Corruption", *Annals of the American Academy of Political and Social Science* 573: 42-56. *Culture and Development: International Perspectives*. January.

Rodrik, Dani (2000). "Institutions for High-Quality Growth: What They are and How to Acquire Them", *Studies in Comparative International Development* 35(3), Fall.

Siddiqui, Iqbal (n.d.). *Tariff Reduction and Functional Income Distribution in Pakistan: A CGE Model*. Pakistan Institute of Development Economics.

Uk, Heo and Alexander Tan (2001). "Democracy and Economic Growth: A Causal Analysis", *Comparative Politics* 33(4): 463-473. July. Stable URL: *http://links.jstor.org/sici?sici=00104159%28200107%2933%3A4%3 C463%3ADAEGAC%3E2.0.CO%3B2-W*

Wallis, Joe and Brian Dollery (1999). *Market Failure, Government Failure, Leadership and Public Policy*. London: Macmillian Press Ltd. July.

16 The 13th Amendment to the Constitution and Its Impact on Sri Lanka's Economic Growth

Shanuka Senerath and
Ranmini Vithanagama

Introduction

The term institution is used very generally in society, to refer mostly to business organisations. However, the term is not restricted only for profit-making organisations, as is commonly understood, but carries meanings in social, political and legal contexts as well. For example, family is a social institution, whereas a government is a political institution. However, they differ vastly from each other, both in terms of their formation, interactions, expectations and even dissolution. On the other hand, the institutions need not necessarily be those consisting of people. The very fact that institutions are of various types makes it reasonably difficult to produce a clear-cut definition for institutions. Thus, even a collection of rules and regulations can form an institution. In the light of this understanding, the political system, the legislation or bureaucracy of a country are also institutions. The bottom line however remains that whatever the type of institution, be it consisting of people or merely a set of laws and policies, be it economic, social or political in nature, it is a man-made thing.

Institutions in Economics

The neoclassical argument builds on the axiom that markets have a self-adjusting mechanism. If, according to Say's law, supply creates its own demand, then all that is produced is consumed and the market is as perfect as it could be. However, the Great Depression of 1930s seriously undermined the self-adjusting nature of the market, shaking the neoclassical utopia of non-intervention and the *General Theory* (1936) laid much emphasis on government intervention to adjust the market. Thus, the role of institutions gradually became one important facet of the framework of economics, and over time resulted in the inception of a new area of study, institutional economics.

13th Amendment to the Constitution

This research is focused on the 13th Amendment to the Constitution of the Democratic Socialist Republic of Sri Lanka, and will examine its accountability as an institution, and the contribution it has made to the economic growth of the country. The ethnic crisis raging in the North-East necessitated some long lasting solution, not only to create peace in the country, but also to stop a civil war that would later on cost many innocent lives and a lot of resources that would otherwise have been spent on development activities. Decentralisation of power was perceived to be one sensible solution, and this was to be done through the establishment of Provincial Councils (PCs), through which the government was to become closer to the people. Provincial Councils were brought into effect by the 13th Amendment to the Constitution. Accordingly, every province, or a combination of provinces as permitted by law, has to elect a PC, which is to be headed by a Chief Minister who leads the Board of Ministers. The Governor of each province is appointed by the President and is to act on the advice of the Chief Minister and holds responsibility to the PC, given that he can be removed from office upon an address passed by the PC with a 2/3rd majority.

The PC is elected for a period of five years unless dissolved earlier than that and consists of a number of members as determined by law, with a focus on the area and its population for which the PC is to be elected. The Commissioner of Elections is authorised under Section 3 of the Provincial Council Act to determine this number, taking account of the following criteria:

1. One member for every 40,000 residents in that administrative district.

2. One member for every 1000 km^2 of area in that administrative district.

In addition to the number determined thus, each province is allocated two bonus seats.

The Governor's Role

The Governor is the head of the PC and has the power to summon, prorogue and dissolve the PC in line with the related constitutional provisions. However, he is supposed to seek the Chief Minister's advice in the exercise of those powers. The Chief Minister of a PC is appointed by the Governor, according to his judgment as to who is best capable of commanding a majority in the PC. On occasions where the Governor is not required to act on the ministerial advice, he may, under the direction of the President, act on his own discretion. During an emergency situation, the President may advise the Governor to exercise his executive powers, and if the Governor fails to do so, the President has the right to assume the functions of the Governor, the administration or any other authority in the province other than the PC or to declare that the powers of the PC will be exercised by or under the Parliament authority.

The Powers and Duties of the PC

There are three lists pertaining to the manner in which powers and duties of the Parliament and PCs are allocated, namely:

(i) PC List

(ii) Reserved List

(iii) Concurrent List

Of these, the Reserved List gives details of statutes that are only to be formulated by the Parliament and the Concurrent List shows what statutes can be prepared by both the Parliament and PCs.

Reserved List

According to the Reserved List, the Parliament has the absolute right to prepare statutes related to national policy of all subjects and functions. The key areas include all matters that bring the Government of Sri Lanka into contact with the rest of the world, diplomatic, trade or consular representation, United Nations Organization, war and peace, foreign jurisdiction, entering into treaties and contracts and their implementation etc. Thus, it deals with defence and national security, industries declared as necessary for the purpose of defence, criminal investigation department etc. Moreover, foreign affairs and related legislative power lies with the Parliament.

The other major areas on which the Parliament can make laws include: justice to the judiciary and the court structure, finance in relation to national revenue, monetary policy and external resources, foreign trade, ports and harbour, airport and aviation, national transport, immigration, emigration and citizenship, elections, census and statistics, professional occupations and training, national archives and other functions that are not specified either in Lists (i) or (iii). So, the areas covered in the Reserved List are of national interest and as such are only handled at the Parliamentary level.

Concurrent List

This list includes planning, education and educational services, higher education, national housing and construction, acquisition and requisition of property, social services and rehabilitation, health, agricultural and agrarian services, animal husbandry, employment, tourism, trade and commerce, price control, environmental protection, pilgrimages etc.

PC List

The PCs have the authority to make laws that relate to the following areas: police and public order within the province, however not including national security, defence or armed forces. Planning in order to implement provincial economic plans, education and educational services, relating to schools and pre-schools only, local government, provincial housing and construction, roads, bridges and ferries within the province, social services and rehabilitation, agriculture and agrarian services, rural development, health, indigenous medicine, rest houses, pawn broking, markets, co-operatives, burials and burial grounds, provincial debt, environment protection within the province etc.

Comparing the Lists

The three lists above clearly manifest the fact that the areas allocated to the PCs are of negligible importance, compared to the reason why they were established in the first place. It is hard to imagine how power devolution could take place merely through activities that really have no bearing whatsoever on the root cause of the need to devolve power—the ethnic crisis. While the strategic areas that actually need to be dealt with in order to find a solution to the ethnic battle remain centrally at the national level, simpler and smaller areas have been allocated to the PCs, contributing very little, if at all, to the original objective that led to their inception. On the other hand, the areas that have been allowed to be handled both by the PCs and Parliament in the Concurrent List, theoretically, both the Central government and the PCs have legislative powers over them. Yet, a PC needs to take the approval of the Parliament before making a law on these subjects. On the other hand, the Parliament can make legislation with regard the Concurrent List. If the PC agrees to such legislation, it becomes law within the PCs. Even if the PCs do not agree to such Legislation, the Parliament can make such laws enforceable with $\frac{3}{4}^{th}$ majority of the Parliament.

Thus, the three lists speak for themselves that little is actually achievable from PCs to find a solution for the ethnic issue, and to contribute to regional economic growth. It is a mocking irony today that PCs have become white elephants consuming a gigantic portion of public funds, while the war is raging in the North, incurring heavy costs for the government and the country as a whole and the ethnic conflict still scourges the country, while all that had happened is the passage of time oblivious to the follies and cruelties of human nature.

PCs and the Issue of Accountability

The establishment of PCs as a means of finding a solution to the ethnic crisis cannot be called a strategically devised, or well thought-out plan. Rather, it was more of an ad hoc solution, an action taken because something, rather than nothing, should be done. After the Indo-Lanka Peace Accord was signed between Sri Lanka and India, as a result of that, PC came into existence. Not everybody has been optimistic about the new set of institutions as a means of solving the ethnic issue, as was manifested by Mrs. Sirimao Bandaranaike who sought legal action against the Amendment. Her argument was that the PCs would seriously threaten the unity of the country. However, such a possibility was ruled out in court because the Amendment was devised in such a manner that made it possible, if the need arose, to dissolve PCs altogether under a 2/3rd majority vote of the Parliament. Ironically, though, the other side of the coin questioned how feasible PCs were then as a means of addressing the ethnic crisis if they could be dissolved so conveniently. Despite this very apparent flaw, PCs were established in all nine provinces of the island. Thus, a solution that was required only for Northern and Eastern Provinces was prescribed to the whole country, depriving the people of a concentrated effort of power decentralisation only in areas where it was a pressing must. While on the one hand, the establishment of PCs covering the whole island, to some extent diluted the intensity of the focus on the ethnic issue, on the other hand, added to the expenditure of the government.

Further, the fact that the Governor who heads the PC was to be the President's choice was not an optimal decision, and created problems of accountability; s/he would naturally wish to please the President, rather than the public. By letting the President choose the Governor, it is arguable that the reigns of authority are still centralised under the façade of PCs.

Contribution of PCs to Economic Growth

Economic growth and development is a key macroeconomic objective of any country. Development is driven by purpose-oriented goals, and not ad hoc actions that arise from the impulse of the moment. Economic growth is not an overnight bloom, but a long-drawn process, and requires strategic thinking and purposive planning rather than moving with the tide. In this light, PCs do not fit into the position of an ingredient that would act as a catalyst of economic growth. This is so because, the establishment of PCs was not the result of a carefully conducted study, but of a need to take some action in the direction of peace after the Indo-Lanka Peace Accord was signed. It lacked purpose, clarity and focus and that lacking was predominant from the very launch of PCs.

Tapping on competitive advantage is the key to economic growth, and this piece of economic wisdom has gone completely amiss when the PCs were established. PCs could have been an ideal vehicle for regional economic growth, if there has been a focus on comparative advantages of each province so that such advantages can be exploited to enhance its development. For example, Jaffna has a competitive advantage over the other provinces in chilli cultivation, Central province in tea cultivation etc. An effective development strategy would be to let each province maximise its gains from its comparative advantage. The list allocated to PCs does not allow them to take any measures in these directions even if they are willing to do so. This is because the list does not entitle PCs to any decision-making at the higher level. Rather only tactical decision-making is allowed, which are not strong enough to make sure that the comparative advantages are made use of optimally to achieve provincial economic growth. For example, the PCs have the authority to recruit a labourer, but not an economist. However, economic growth requires that the PCs have the capacity to employ both of them for the different ways in which they would contribute to growth.

Further, the list only allocates areas that require day-to-day activities only such as health, administration, education and welfare. Development activities are retained at the national level. Thus, the PCs that are supposed to have a better knowledge of the advantages and disadvantages of their areas are prevented from making fruitful use of such knowledge to drive economic growth. Hence, development planning at the national level not only carries a greater chance of missing out on regional opportunities for growth but also fails to decentralise power in a meaningful way that would enhance economic growth of the country as a whole.

Even the Concurrent List acts in favour of the Parliament given that it can pass laws that affect PCs without consulting the PCs, whereas the laws made by PCs in these areas can be nullified or changed by the Parliament without the asset of PCs. Therefore, the powers of the PC, if at all are only those related to the relatively less significant day-to-day activities. Hence, PCs lack both the required capacity and the vital resources to drive regional economic growth. On the other hand, PCs consume a lot of funds for their maintenance, which is why they are tagged white elephants, consuming much and giving back virtually nothing in return. The Central government bears about 95 per cent of the maintenance cost of PCs, while the balance is self-financed by PCs. Given the large amount of funds the PCs depend on from the Central government, it is not surprising that PCs are under tight control of the latter and are short of funds to inaugurate any project to trigger economic growth even if they were bestowed with the resources and capacity to do so. The financial dependence thus created a so-called vicious cycle where PCs cannot survive without the backing of the Central government, and that backing itself tightens the actions of PCs.

Empirical evidence leads to the conclusion that PCs have not triggered any regional economic growth that has been captured by the national level figures. The GDP growth rate before 1987 i.e., before the establishment of PCs, has not witnessed any discernible rise since 1987 and proves the fact that PCs have not succeeded in enhancing regional economic growth. The GDP growth rate, which stood at 5 per cent in 1986, fell down to 1.5 per cent in 1987, slightly improving to 2.7 per cent in 1988. The relatively higher growth rate of 6 per cent in 1990 was a result of the second phase of the economic liberalisation process undertaken rather than the establishment of PCs.[1]

PCs and Decentralisation

Apart from the fact that decentralisation of power under the 13th Amendment is limited, it is also obvious that resources and opportunities also have not been decentralised satisfactorily under the PC system. For example, the vast majority of employment opportunities are centralised in the Western province. Infrastructure and other physical resources are all concentrated within the radius of the Western province. Given the nature of human beings, it is therefore natural that people flood to Colombo all the time unwilling to settle for less for education, for employment, for residence, and even for shopping.

Thus, the establishment of PCs has caused centralisation to take place all over again, resulting in a provincial imbalance where some provinces are rich with opportunities, resources, infrastructure and quality, while the others lag behind. The fact that people are attracted to areas where there are opportunities then sets in motion a vicious cycle in which prosperous provinces flourish further while those that are stagnant are neglected. This

---

1. The figures have been taken from Table 2 in Special Statistical Appendix of Central Bank Annual Report.

provincial imbalance results in a new crisis among people because some have easier access opportunities and resources while the others do not, and creates a new social gap.

Conclusion

The decentralisation of power through PCs to address the issue of ethnic crisis in Sri Lanka has not only been inadequate in that regard, but also have become a mere expense to the Central government, absorbing it to their functioning a large portion of funds, that could otherwise have been utilised for productive economic activities. The end result of an insufficiently researched on and inadequately planned out 13th Amendment is only resource wastage, with a negative impact on regional economic growth because PCs are virtually only an expense and hence, so rightfully termed a white elephant.

References

Constitution of Socialistic Republic Government of Sri Lanka (1978).

Laksman, W.D. (1997). (ed.). *Dilemmas of Development, Fifty Years of Economic Change in Sri Lanka*. Sri Lanka Association of Economists. Colombo: Karunarathna & Sons Ltd. p.647.

"Economic Progress of independent Sri Lanka 1984-1998", Central Bank of Sri Lanka.

17

Corruption: An Analysis of the Food Security Policies of India

Nayantara Sarma and Sanya Garg

Introduction

Corruption is neither a new nor an irrational phenomenon. The very fact that it has survived through the ages, from the times of the virtuous Ashoka to the present has proved its economic viability. Corruption can be defined and interpreted in many different ways, it is like an elephant—while it may be difficult to describe, it is generally easy to recognise when observed. Unfortunately, it is often difficult to observe because acts of corruption do not occur in broad daylight. The most widely used definition of corruption is the one given by the World Bank according to which, corruption is the use of public power for private benefit. For the purposes of our paper, we will focus specifically on corruption as the occurrence of rent seeking behaviour due to misalignment of incentives, lack of accountability and paradoxical government policies.

Why Does Corruption Occur?

Misalignment of Incentives

It occurs when rational individuals work towards maximising their own utility which is in contradiction to the objectives set by the governing institution. There is scope for such misalignment when forces (other than demand and supply) which distort the market come into play. These distortions move the market outcome away from the optimum free market outcome.

Lack of Accountability

In large bureaucratic organisations, where monitoring is not always feasible and is a drain on resources, individuals have a greater motive to work around the system. Due to a general sense of impunity, such behaviour goes unnoticed and unchecked. Thus, the system itself becomes vulnerable to acts of corruption ranging from petty bribes to large scale manipulation. Institutions set up to ensure accountability also become redundant as the structural setups of these very organisations make them prone to corruption. The problem is further compounded by an asymmetry of information biased towards the holders of greater market power. Whereas the other side of the equation, namely the public, which is less aware or informed become nothing more than sitting ducks!

Paradoxical Government Policies

The Directive Principles of State Policy direct the Government to formulate policies geared towards the twin objectives of development with equity. However, development is often sacrificed for greater equity. This leads to policies which are not necessarily economically sound and instead of greater equity, lead to stunted development.

Why is Corruption Rational?

The basic premise of all economic theory is the assumption that all individuals are rational and profit maximising. When only the free market forces prevail, the market price and quantity adjust such that total welfare is maximised. On the other hand, when policy instruments like price ceilings and floors are introduced, the market outcome moves away from the optimum. Such distortions lead to deadweight loss, i.e., the loss of welfare resulting from contraction of the market which prevents realisation of optimum welfare. When distortions occur, there is opportunity for rational profit maximising individuals to capture part of the market and divert a certain portion of the welfare in their favour (See Figure 17.1).

Case Study—Food Security Policies in India

Food security has always been a major cause for concern in India. This is an issue wrought with heated economic and political debates. The scale of operations being massive gives rise to a correspondingly massive level of corruption. This issue is all the more critical as it is inseparably linked to the welfare of Indians belonging to the low and medium income categories. There is no greater scam in India at this time than the so called "food subsidy". Although the Government is spending about Rs.10,000 crore in a year on "food subsidy", half of India's children are still chronically undernourished. If this isn't Government failure then what is?

Figure 17.1

Market Distortions and Opportunities for Rent Seeking

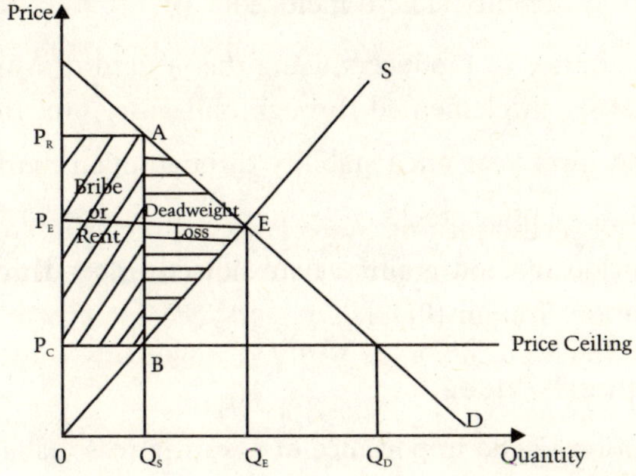

P_E = Free Market Price — Q_E = Eqquilibrium Quantity at P_E

P_C = Price Ceiling — Q_S = Quantity Supplied at P_C

Q_D = Quantity Demanded at P_C — P_RABP_C = Rent

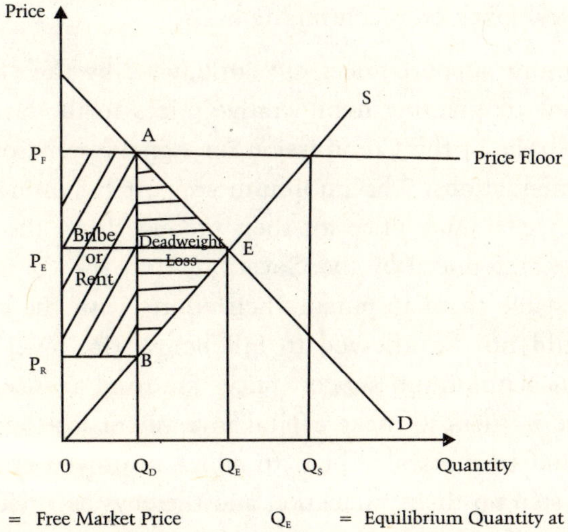

P_E = Free Market Price — Q_E = Equilibrium Quantity at P_E

P_F = Price Floor — Q_D = Quantity Demand at P_F

Q_S = Quantity Supplied at P_F — P_FABP_R = Rent

Government intervention in food grain markets in India began in a big way in the mid 1960s. It was meant to create a favourable incentive environment for the adoption of new technology based on high-yielding varieties of wheat and rice. The new technology provided a ray of hope to tackle the problems of food shortage and hunger. Several measures were initiated to achieve the dual objectives of raising food production and improving food availability. These included:

- Price assurance to producers using the system of Minimum Support Prices (MSP) implemented through obligatory procurement.
- Inter and intra year price stability through open market operations.
- Maintaining buffer stocks.
- Distribution of food grains at subsidised prices through the Public Distribution System (PDS).

Minimum Support Prices

In recognition of the importance of assuring reasonable produce prices to the farmers, motivating them to adopt improved technology and to promote investment by them in farm enterprises, the Agricultural Prices Commission (currently known as the Commission for Agricultural Costs and Prices) was established in 1965 for advising the Government on agricultural prices policy on a continuing basis.

The minimum support prices are announced by the Government of India with a view to ensuring remunerative prices to the farmers for their produce on the basis of the Commission for Agricultural Costs and Prices (CACP) recommendations. The minimum support prices are perceived by the farmers as a guarantee price for their produce from the Government. These prices are announced by the Government at the commencement of the season to enable them to pursue their efforts with the assurance that the prices would not be allowed to fall below the level fixed by the Government. Such minimum support prices are fixed at incentive level, so as to induce the farmers to make capital investment for the improvement of their farm and to motivate them to adopt improved crop production technologies to step up their production and thereby their net income.

Determination of MSP

In formulating the recommendations in respect to the level of minimum support prices and other non-price measures, the Commission takes into account, apart from a comprehensive view of the entire structure of the economy of a particular commodity or group of commodities, the following factors: cost of production, trends in market prices, demand and supply, effects on general price level and cost of living and effect on issue prices and implications for subsidy.

Public Distribution System (PDS)

Historically, the objectives of the PDS have been:

- Maintaining price stability,
- Raising the welfare of the poor (by providing access to basic foods at reasonable prices to the vulnerable population),
- Rationing during situations of scarcity, and
- Keeping a check on private trade.

In 1997, the Government introduced targeting in the PDS in the form of the Targeted PDS or TPDS. The TPDS aims to target the poorest of the poor or specifically, divide the entire population into below poverty line (BPL) and above poverty line (APL) categories, based on the poverty line defined by the Planning Commission for different states for 1993-94.

Buffer Stocks

In addition to the requirements of wheat and rice under the TPDS, the central pool is required to have sufficient stocks of these in order to meet any emergencies like drought or failures of crop, as well as to enable open market intervention in case of price rise. Therefore, the minimum stocks that should be available in the central pool are announced at the beginning of each quarter of the year.

Open Market Sales Scheme (OMSS)—Domestic

The FCI on the instructions from the Government, has been resorting to sale of food grains i.e., wheat and rice, at predetermined prices to the open market from time to time to achieve the objectives as under:

- To enhance the supply of food grains especially during the lean season and thereby, to have a healthy and moderate influence on the open market prices.
- To offload the excess stocks in the central pool and to reduce the carrying cost of food grains to the extent possible.
- To save the food grains from deterioration in quality and to use food grains for human consumption.
- To release valuable storage space for stocks procured during the ensuing marketing season of wheat/rice.

Problems Arising Out of Food Policies in India

The MSP is not only determined keeping in mind the cost of production but other extraneous factors as well. This has led to a disproportionate increase in the MSP of wheat and rice as compared to the free market prices that would have prevailed without intervention, creating scope and opportunity for corruption (Refer to Table 17.1).

Table 17.1

Prices of Wheat

(Rs. Per quintal) for 2000-01	*Procurement Prices (MSP)*	*PDS Prices*	*OMSS Prices*
Tamil Nadu	580.00	830.00	853.00
Delhi	580.00	830.00	749.00
Haryana	580.00	830.00	730.00
Punjab	580.00	830.0	730.00
Uttar Pradesh	580.00	830.00	770.00
Kerala	580.00	830.00	857.00
Karnataka	580.00	830.00	850.00
Bihar	580.00	830.00	796.00
Orissa	580.00	830.00	829.00
Gujarat	580.00	830.00	802.00
Maharashtra	580.00	830.00	817.00

The procurement operations of the FCI and various associated state agencies are not very transparent. High variations in procurement from different states suggest an appalling level of corruption (Refer to Table 17.2).

Table 17.2

Procurement of Wheat and Rice

Year/State	*2000-01 (Wheat)*	*2000-01(Rice)*
Punjab	94.24	69.35
Haryana	44.98	14.76
Uttar Pradesh	15.45	11.13
Rajasthan	5.38	NA
Uttaranchal	0.00	0.42
Delhi	0.00	NA
Himachal Pradesh	0.00	NA
Total (North Zone)	160.05	95.66
All India	163.56	212.68
% North Zone to All India	98	45

- Current accumulations of buffer stocks have far exceeded the norms (Refer to Table 17.3). According to Jean Dreze, the sacks of food grains lying in Government godowns now are enough, if laid out in a row, to take us to the moon and back, and back to the moon again. This is clearly a Government failure which is increasing the fiscal deficit.

Table 17.3

Food Stocks

Food Grains in mn tonnes	*Actual Stocks*	*Norms*	*Excess Stocks*
2000 – January	31.4	16.8	14.6
2000 – April	21.7	15.8	5.9
2000 – June	42.2	24.3	17.9
2000 – October	40.0	18.1	21.9
2001 – January	45.7	16.8	28.9
2001 – April	44.7	15.8	28.9
2001 – June	60.4	24.3	36.1
2001 – October	58.3	18.1	40.2

- Storage costs of excess grain exceed the expenditure on agriculture, rural development and on irrigation and flood control taken together. These costs are funded by the government, thereby, creating incentives for procurement authorities to misrepresent information.
- Total monetary value of petty corruption in the PDS is estimated to be Rs.358 crore per annum by Transparency International.

- Ration shop dealers, distribution agents and other intermediaries divert PDS food to the black market. According to the Planning Commission, 36 per cent of PDS wheat and 31 per cent of PDS rice is appropriated by private parties at the all India level (Refer to Table 17.4). The price differences (Refer to Table 17.1) encourage rent-seeking behaviour amongst PDS officials who divert food stocks into the black market.

Table 17.4

Diversion of Food Grains

States	*Diversion of Wheat (%)*	*Diversion of Rice (%)*	*Literacy Rates (%)*
Tamil Nadu	24	33	73.47
Delhi	53	53	81.82
Haryana	53	44	68.59
Punjab	69	40	69.95
Uttar Pradesh	46	49	57.36
Kerala	28	23	90.92
Karnataka	30	18	67.04
Bihar	44	64	47.53
Orissa	39	54	63.61
Gujarat	23	21	69.97
Maharashtra	26	30	77.27

- The major criticism of the TPDS has been that it has wrongly excluded a large number of deserving persons and families. The question is whether the official poverty line represents a very low level of absolute expenditure, and if so, whether it excludes a larger section of the population who experience low and variable incomes. These doubts are raised by the fact that other parameters such as nutritional criteria show that a much larger proportion of the population is food insecure.

India's Food Security Policies—An Analysis

There are innumerable rent-seeking opportunities implicit within the very structure of the institutions set up to deliver food security. The corruption in the PDS ranges from petty bribes for procuring ration cards to large scale diversion of food stocks. At each stage, the welfare distribution gets further skewed against the targeted population.

The paradox of the Indian food security problem is that we have immense food mountains on one hand and the largest population of undernourished in the world on the other hand. This procurement often amounts to more than 15 per cent of total output of rice and wheat. Effectively, this creates perverse incentives for the market: private participation in food grains has reduced as private traders choose to buy from the Government (through OMSS) rather than directly from the farmers in the lean months. Although the Government heavily subsidises food prices, consumers still have to pay an inflated price, reducing the supply amount because a sizeable stock of food grains are kept away from the market, thus and pushing up the prices as compared to what would have prevailed without Government intervention. Fundamentally, the overall effect of the food subsidy is more spectacular in transferring money to farmers (mostly from rich agricultural states in Punjab and Haryana) than in transferring food to the undernourished millions.

Given below is a graphical analysis using the effects of the Government's food grain procurement and distribution policies.

Figure 17.2

Impact of Government Intervention in the Grain Market

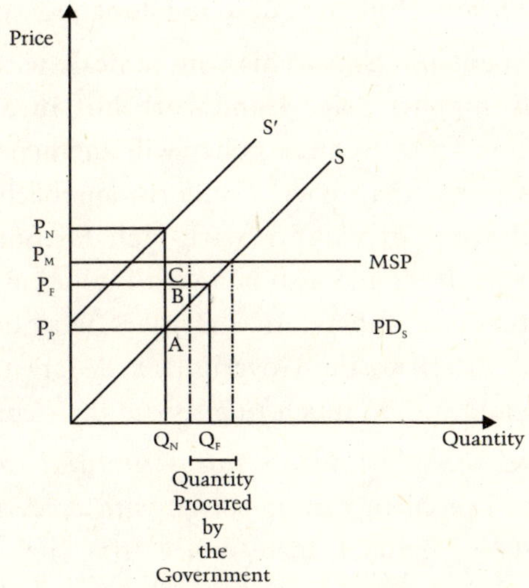

P_F	:	Price in Free Market without Government Intervention
P_P	:	PDS Price
P_M	:	Minimum Support Price
P_N	:	Price Prevailing in the Market After Procurement
Q_F	:	Quantity Exhanced without Intervention
Q_N	:	Quantity in the Market at P_N
P_MCBP_F	:	Rent Generated During Procurement
P_FBAP_P	:	Rent Generated During Through the PDS

As can be seen from Figure 17.2, government procurement operations shift the market supply curve from S to S′ which pushes up the market price from P_F to P_N. Thus, consumers (who are not covered by the PDS) have to pay a higher price than they would have paid without procurement. At the same time, rent-seeking opportunities are generated as shown in the figure.

A Framework For Improvement

This section of the paper deals with certain suggestions to improve the food security paradigm as it exists in India today. However, we acknowledge that the efforts must be holistic and multi-pronged.

1. *Release excess buffer stocks*: If the Government releases the stock of food grains held in godowns presently above the norm levels, the supply in the economy will increase and push down prices to such an extent that food grains will become affordable to a larger number of people. The new concern that now arises is to ensure that farmers maintain their levels of income despite falling prices.
2. *Target procurement methods*: This can be dealt with by continuing the minimum support price framework but in a more rational manner. A targeted procurement policy will augment the incomes of poorer farmers rather than have a uniform approach which leads to skewed distribution of welfare with rich farmers deriving the maximum benefit. It should also be taken into account that most of the BPL farmers are subsistence farmers who do not generate enough surplus to sell to the Government. A targeted procurement policy, thus, would not do much to alleviate their condition.
3. *Reallocate food subsidy towards infrastructural investment*: The above mentioned problem can be solved with a revision of the food subsidy allocated to the FCI. Instead of issuing such a hefty subsidy, we propose to direct some of these funds towards better irrigation facilities and research and development of better yield varieties. However, such a move will not be immune to corruption.
4. *Panchayat control*: If the responsibility of food security was transferred from the state and Central governments to the grassroots level, there would be greater accountability. The social set-up in a

rural scenario is such that there are more efficient mechanisms of procuring and distributing food grains. We propose a common pool of grains procured and distributed by the *panchayat* according to need. Such micro level operations would ensure optimum targeting.

5. *Promote literacy and awareness*: Information is more easily dispersed through informal channels as compared to bureaucratic channels. With reference to Table 17.4, we find that in states with higher levels of literacy, there is less diversion of grains. Further, in a village setting, there is greater transparency and hence, greater accountability. The Right to Information Act also empowers the public. This proves the significance of the role played by information in any market.
6. *Free market solution:* In the long run, if the comprehensive policy solutions mentioned above are undertaken, we can see an eventuality where the need for Government intervention will be eliminated on its own. With increasing supply (after release of excess stocks) which leads to decreasing price differentials, the scope and incentive for corruption will automatically decline. An overall fall in prices of food grains will make the basic levels of nutrition affordable to a larger populace of the currently undernourished, eventually removing the need for the PDS. With the targeted procurement system and more judicious investment in agriculture, ultimately the incomes of the poorer will be augmented to such an extent that there will be no need to support farmers' incomes any longer with MSP. Here, the theoretical difference between consumers and suppliers should be blurred. The welfare of both parties will be amplified and there will be no deadweight loss in the economy. Thus, removal of market distortions will remove corruption as well as lead to a better outcome for the whole economy.

In Figure 17.3, the supply curve (of wheat) which had shifted to S' due to procurement by the government, shifts towards the right to S'' after the proposed release of excess buffer stocks in the market. This shift brings about a fall in the market price from P_N to P_N'. Hence, the market price comes closer to the free market price that would have prevailed without government intervention. One can also notice a decrease in the rent seeking opportunities as marked in the figure.

Figure 17.3

Eliminating Rents by Releasing Excess Stocks

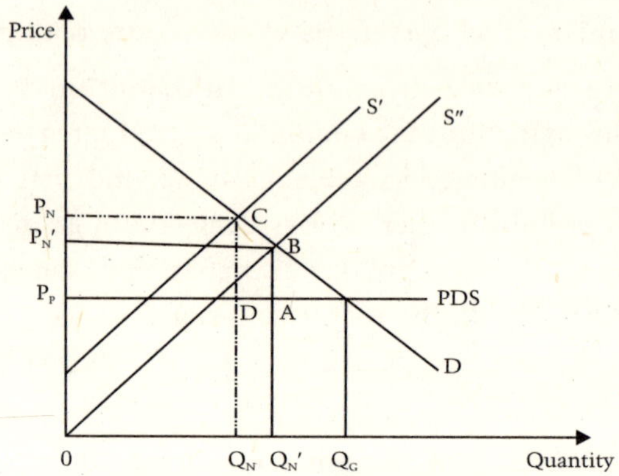

P_N	:	Market Price after Procurement
P_P	:	PDS Price
Q_N	:	Quantity in the Market after Procurement
P_N'	:	Market Price after Proposed Release of Buffer Stocks
Q_G	:	Quantity Supplied under PDS by the Government
$P_N'BAP_P$	:	Scope for Corruption after Proposed Release of Buffer Stocks
P_PDCP_N	:	Scope for Corruption after Procurement

Generalisation

Corruption is a widespread phenomenon and the tools to tackle it should likewise, be far reaching in their effect, yet precise in their attack. What is the purpose of the case study and, in fact, of our whole paper? Like the solutions proposed above, the purpose is multi-pronged. Firstly, we have proved (as indeed, have many others before us) that corruption is rational and hence, not an aberration for the rational person. Secondly, by the means of our case study, we have attempted to show that corruption cannot be treated effectively, unless it stops being rational. Thirdly, we have proposed some case-specific policy remedies which make corruption an economically unattractive option. But these remedies can be generalised to be applicable to the larger problem of corruption.

The first lesson is that as soon as market distortions enter the picture, corruption becomes possible if not inevitable. So, the best alternative would be to remove all of these distortions and let the free market do its job unhindered. But many might see problems with putting so much of trust in free market mechanisms which do not take into account equity or social development objectives. In such situations, it is best to weed out as many supply constraints as possible and ensure that the distribution of gains is, in reality, equitable. This reduces at least a part of the deadweight loss incurred as a result of market distorting instruments and brings the market closer to the free market ideal, thereby, reducing the scope for corruption. Another generalisation which can be made is that the nearer is the working of any institution to the grassroots level, the lesser is the scope for corruption. This is because of the fact that an institution working closely with and for the people (who are the consumers of the goods or services this institution has to offer), has greater accountability, thus, reducing the scope for corruption. Another very important deterrent to corruption is information. Most market failures occur due to the problem of imperfect and asymmetric information. This makes it very difficult to discern corruption, and further, makes it very difficult to prevent corruption. Thus, a better market structure which ensures at least symmetric, if not perfect information can greatly reduce the incidence of corruption.

References

Basu, Kaushik, Patrick Emerson (1968). "The Economics and Law of Rent Control", *Policy Research Working Paper.*

Basu, Kaushik, Sudipto Bhattacharya, Ajit Mishra (1992). *Notes on Bribery and Corruption.* August 1992, pp.349-359.

Dreze, Jean (2001). "Starving the Poor", originally published in *The Hindu*, 26 and 27 February.

———. (2004). "Democracy and the Right to Food", *Economic and Political Weekly.*

Sanyal, Amal (2004). *Economica* 71: 155-168.

Tanzi, Vito (1998). "Corruption around the world", *IMF Staff Papers* 45(4) (December).

The Food Corporation of India (2000). *High Level Committee Report on Long Term Food Policy*, November, *http://fciweb.nic.in/*

The Food Corporation of India, Annual Report, 2004-05.

18 Privatisation of Banks in Pakistan

A Detailed Analysis

Amna Khan

Introduction

The debate on the role of government in financial systems is not a new one. While one side of it advocates active government control to direct savings towards productive sectors, the other side opposes it on the basis of causing lower economic efficiency. The first view is based on Gerschenkron's thesis that advocates active government control of strategic sectors to achieve economic development. Realising it, governments in developing countries focused on increasing ownership of banks and other financial institutions to direct the financial resources towards key sectors (Khalid, 2006). It was thought that by active government participation, resources could be allocated in an efficient manner and towards productive sectors that have a potential for growth but need financial assistance. Economic literature is full of various studies that sought to empirically analyse the effect of an active government involvement in banking and financial sector. The main aim of these studies was to determine if there is any relationship between the privatisation in this sector and economic efficiency. I will be discussing only a few studies here.

Barth *et al.* (2001) used cross-country data of 60 countries and concluded that state ownership of banks is negatively associated with bank performance and overall financial sector development. Another study by La Porta *et al.* (2002) finds evidence that government ownership of banks is associated with slower financial development, lower economic growth and lower growth of productivity (Khalid, 2006); Otchere (2003) compares the pre- and post-performance of privatised banks. The author, however, did not find any significant improvement in the banks' post-privatisation performance (Khalid, 2006).

Similarly, an analysis of economic performance both before and after privatisation was done by Asian Development Bank, and is cited in a working paper of Pakistan Institute of Development Economics (PIDE) written by Dr. Akhtar Hassan Khan. It showed that only 22 per cent of the privatised units were performing better than in pre-privatisation, 44 per cent were approximately the same and about 34 per cent were performing worse than before. Hence, efficiency of the units was attained by only one-fifth of the units.

However, if we only look at the banking sector, two banks improved in efficiency and two remained the same. So efficiency in financial sector was increased in 50 per cent of the units. These studies show a mix trend of the efficiency level after privatisation and no conclusive argument can be made about it. After discussing the broad economic literature regarding effectiveness of privatisation, I will now move to discuss the case of Pakistan and the rationale for privatisation and how that was accompanied by changes in institutional structures. The institutional analysis will be followed by two case studies of MCB and ABL, the two banks that were privatised, to analyse the micro-level effect of privatisation. I will then use the CAMELS approach to compare the macro-level analysis of privatised and public banks The effects of privatisation on equity will be discussed after it. Lastly the policy lessons from privatisation will be discussed.

Rationale for Privatisation in Pakistan

In the decade of 1970s, the government of Pakistan moved from private ownership to public ownership to achieve equitable distribution of wealth and to promote the interest of the poor. However in 1990s, especially after the collapse of Soviet Union, the governments in developing countries started to reconsider the policy of nationalisation. It soon became apparent that rather than benefiting the poor, the nationalised industries were a drain on economic resources as large amounts were spent on financing the losses of these enterprises. Almost 100 billion a year was spent to finance the losses (Hussain, 2005). Similarly, jobs in such enterprises were not allocated on the basis on merit of managerial skills but rather as a prize to supporters of the political parties (Hussain, 2005). Ishrat Hussain, Governor of State Bank cites one example of the inefficiency of state enterprises. Pakistan Telecommunication Company Limited (PTCL) could only instal 3 million telephone connections in Pakistan over the course of 50 years while under the environment of deregulation and private sector, 6 to 7 million mobile phones were given in a single year of 2004. Under these conditions, the government started a move towards privatisation to achieve economic efficiency and equitable distribution of wealth by maintaining broad based equity. Privatisation was not restricted to any one sector. However, I will be focusing on banks alone.

According to a report presented at the World Bank, IMF and Brooking Institution conference presented by the governor of State Bank of Pakistan, the nationalised commercial banks were characterised by the following features: "high intermediation costs, overstaffing and over branching, huge portfolio of non performing loans, poor customer services, undercapitalisation, poor management, averse to lending to SME and undue interference in lending, loan recovery and personal issues." With these features at play, the inefficiency of the financial institution was obvious and the government sought to correct it using the tool of privatisation. A Privatisation Commission was set up to provide an institutional framework to accompany privatisation. By March 2004, share of state ownership of banks was reduced to 18.6 per cent and share of private sector banks increased to 76 per cent (Table 18.1) (Hussain, 2004). Some institutional factors were also important that allowed privatisation to take place. The process of privatisation was completed in the military regime of General Pervez Musharaf and could have been difficult in an elected government as they would be under pressure not to downsize or close the loss-making branches (Hussain, 2004). Similarly, Pakistan had a pool of capable bankers working in international banks. They were brought in and used in restructuring of the three privatised banks. If these bankers were not available, restructuring banks could have been very difficult and would have had a negative effect on efficiency (Hussain, 2004).

Table 18.1

Post-Privitisation Structure of Banking Sector (March 2004)

Banks	No.	Assets		Deposits		Equity	
		Amount (Rs. Bill.)	Share %	Amount (Rs. Bill.)	Share %	Amount (Rs. Bill.)	Share %
State Owned	4	518.8	18.6	379.3	20.1	22.5	17.2
Private	20	1840.3	66.0	1292.3	68.5	92.8	70.9
Foreign	13	278.4	10.0	198.0	10.5	26.7	20.4
Specialised Banks	3	149.8	5.4	16.1	0.9	-11.1	-8.5
Total	40	2787.2	100	1885.6	100	130.9	100

Source: Hussain, Ishrat (2004). "The role of state-owned financial institutions: Policy and practice", World Bank, IMF. Washington. 27 Apr. 28 Jan. *<unpan1.un.org/intradoc/groups/public/documents/APCITY/UNPAN020760.pdf>*

Privatisation and Bank Performance: Two Case Studies

Now I will be discussing the case studies of Muslim Commercial Bank (MCB) and Allied Bank Limited (ABL) to determine the micro level effect of privatisation. MCB was the first bank to be privatised. A look at the financial indicators reveals that there is a marked improvement in the bank's performance (Table 18.2). The growth of assets increased to 28.3 per cent. Similarly, deposits as a percentage of nationalised commercial bank increased to 26.5 per cent in 1994 from 17.6 per cent in 1994—an increase of 51 per cent. Advances also showed similar trend and they increased from 17.7 per cent in 1994 to 26.7 per cent and non-profitable loans decreased from 18.1 per cent to 11.3 per cent in 2003. If we take the net non-profitable loans ratio for the bank, it comes close to 2 per cent while the non-profitable loans (NPL) ratio of the entire banking system is 5.5 per cent. Profitability has also increased from 0.2 per cent to 0.8 per cent. These financial indicators suggest that the bank became more efficient after privatisation (Hussain, 2004).

Table 18.2

Financial Indicators of MCB

Year	Assets	Deposits	Advances	NPLs
1994	18.1	17.6	17.7	18.1
1997	21.5	20.8	21.9	11.6
2000	18.02	18.3	21.5	14.4
2003	28.3	26.5	26.7	11.3

Source: As in Table 18.1.

The next case study that I will discuss is of ABL. Financial indicators reveal that growth of assets, deposits and advances have only been marginal. However, there is an alarming rate of increase in NPL (Table 18.3). It increased from 16.6 per cent in 1994 to 43.8 per cent in 2003. It is worth pointing out that in 1994, NPL of MCB were higher in 1994 (18.1 per cent) than of ABL (16.6 per cent). However, this situation was reversed in later years as the new management in MCB was able to reduce NPLs and the new management in ABL was responsible for an increase in NPLs. Because of the high percentage of non-performing loans, the profitability of ABL fell drastically and the bank made huge losses between the years 2000-2002 (Hussain, 2004).

Table 18.3

Financial Indicators of ABL

Year	*Assets*	*Deposits*	*Advances*	*NPLs*
1994	9.6	9.8	10.9	16.6
1997	10.4	10.6	12.5	17.9
2000	11.7	13.0	14.2	29.4
2003	12.2	14.3	11.2	43.8

Source: As in Table 18.1.

Private *versus* Public Sector Banks: A CAMELS Approach

After analysing the micro-level efficiency of the banks, I will be comparing the public sector banks with the private sector banks using CAMELS approach which is widely used to analyse the performance of the banking industry. Umer Khalid, an analyst in the research department of the State Bank of Pakistan, used it to determine the efficiency levels in both public and privatised sector banks from 1990 to 2002. The first ratio that is discussed is capital adequacy ratio which observes the capacity of the bank to anticipate unexpected shocks. It is measured by comparing capital with liability. Analysis reveals that in public sector banks, it has been continuously falling, indicating that capital is being eroded from the public base. In 1997, it was negative as United Bank Limited (UBL) and Habib Bank Limited (HBL) made huge losses. The subsequent increase in that ratio can be explained by the fact that State Bank injected capital into UBL to make it capable of being privatised (Khalid, 2006). Privatised banks consisted mainly of ABL and MCB with UBL joining them in 2002. However, that is the last year that is being covered in this analysis and hence, does not have any substantial impact on the ratios of privatised banks. Capital-liability ratio for privatised banks is lower that that of public banks. This can largely be explained by the incurrence of heavy losses by ABL as discussed in the case study above (Khalid, 2006). The next ratio discusses asset quality which can be explained by the ratio of non-performing loans to total loans. In case of public banks, the ratio of non-performing loans have been continuously increasing and the main reason that is attributed to such higher percentage of NPLs is that many loans were granted on the basis of political patronage. Also, State Bank prescribed higher disclosure in 1997 which forced these banks to reveal the true picture. After hitting a high point of 32.4 per cent in 1999, it started to decline slowly (Khalid, 2006).

In case of privatised banks, we can see that the ratio of non-performing loans to total loans is less than the public sector ratio throughout the period in consideration. However, it is continuously rising over the period and this can be attributed to the accumulation of NPLs in the portfolio of ABL (Khalid, 2006). Management soundness needs to be discussed next. Analysis of it is relatively subjective. However, we will use the ratio of earning per employee to determine the efficiency of the management. In case of the public banks, earning per employee is continuously increasing from 0.4 million in 1990 to 1.9 million in 2002. This can be largely explained in terms of the reduced workforce that resulted from the voluntary separation scheme which reduced workforce from 99954 to 81079 between 1997 to 1999 (Khalid, 2006).

Earnings per employee also increased in privatised banks; from a mere 0.3 million per employee, it reached 1.6 million per employee in 2002. So, the earnings per employee has been rising for both the private sector and the public sector banks (Khalid, 2006). Earning and profitability is the next feature to be discussed. We commonly use the two ratios of return on assets (ROA) and return on equity (ROE) to compare the profitability of banks. In case of public sector banks, ROA increased till 1993 but then started to fall sharply becoming negative from 1996-1998. This can be explained in terms of a higher proportion of non-performing loans and a fall in proportion of earning assets. On one hand, the revenues were falling and on the other hand, the expenses were increasing. This led to a sharp fall in ROA (Khalid, 2006).

In case of privatised banks, the ROA also remained low ranging from a negative 1.5 to a highest 0.4. This can largely be explained in terms of the huge losses incurred by the ABL which offset any profits earned by MCB. However, the ratios started to improve from 2002 (Khalid, 2006). ROE is the ratio of net profit to total equity. In case of public banks, this has also showed a declining trend and became negative in period from 1996 to 1998, improving only after fresh capital was injected by the government (Khalid, 2006). In case of private banks, it has showed a mix trend. It increased during early nineties but then became negative in 2000-01, rising again in 2002. The negative value of this ratio in 2000 is due to the huge incurrence of losses by ABL in this period (Khalid, 2006).

The last ratio that I will discuss now is liquidity and sensitivity to market risk. It measures an institution's exposure to interest rate risk, exchange rate risk, equity price risk and country risk. It can be calculated by comparing loans to deposit ratio. In case of the public banks, it fell over the period covered, suggesting that the banks were gaining liquidity. In case of privatised banks, it has been rising suggesting that there might be liquidity problems if the management is not careful enough (Khalid, 2006).

Concluding this analysis, it becomes apparent that there has not been a marked improvement in financial indicators of most privatised banks. A look at the case studies discussed earlier shows that this is due to the poor performance of ABL. However, this study ended at 2002 when the process of privatisation was still going on so we must view it with a little caution (Khalid, 2006).

While it is true that privatisation resulted in employment based on merit, the overall efficiency did not increase in banks across board. We can see this in the financial analysis just discussed. This result is compatible with the study of Naqvi and Kemal which concludes that privatisation was neither a necessary nor a sufficient condition for efficiency (Khan, 2008).

Equity Implications of Privatisation

After discussing the efficiency of privatised banks, we will now discuss other issues that have more to do with equity. Privatisation was thought to benefit economy through its influence on the fiscal impact. Privatisation increased revenues from sale proceed of nationalised industry. The strain on fiscal budget was also removed as after privatisation, the government did not finance the losses of banks. However, it must also be noted that taxes paid to the government were doubled after nationalisation (Khan, 2008). Moreover, if these nationalised firms are making a profit then they are giving a return to government that is higher than market return. Privatisation of such profit-making firms will have an adverse effect on the budget (Khan, 2008). Privatisation also resulted in a change of labour composition of banks. While it lead to downsizing of workforce by 11101 workers out of a total of 39277 (Hussain, 2004) in the three major banks (HBL, UBL and NBP), after privatisation was completed, the banking sector has expanded from 105000 workers to 114000 workers (Hussain, 2005). The pattern has changed from low and unskilled workers to a more productive and skilled workforce. It is hard to make a statement about welfare implications here as it is a zero sum game. Those that lost their jobs due to privatisation are losers in such policymaking and those that gained jobs on merit and productivity are winners. More productive workers and efficient management is also one reason that could explain efficiency in MCB.

With privatisation, competition has also increased in the banking and financial sector. This has reduced the interest rate from 21 per cent to 5 per cent in just a few years (Hussain, 2004). Loans can now be borrowed at a much cheaper rate and to engage in any productive activity that requires huge financing is easy now.

Privatisation also resulted in closure of 1646 loss-making branches of nationalised commercial banks, mostly in rural areas (Hussain, 2004). Although from efficiency perspective it makes absolute sense to close such branches, it has negative implications if viewed from the equity perspective. The rural-urban divide intensifies and the rural and far off areas such as in Baluchistan and NWFP have less access to the financial market now. Here is the efficiency-equity tradeoff and we can see that although interest rate has fallen significantly, financial services are not available to all.

Privatisation led to rent-seeking behaviour as well as pointed out by many analysts. Although one of its aims was to reduce corruption in nationalised industry, it led to excessive rent-seeking activity on a higher level. The units were sold without checking the creditworthiness of the buyers. For example, the Schon Group was given three units, National Fibre, Pak China and Quaidabad Woolen Mills. All these were closed after privatisation. The consultants of the Asian Development Bank commented that the privatisation process was not transparent and Schon Group was able to access other bids before submitting their own (Khan, 2008). The Privatisation Commission also did not act when they were unable to pay the first instalment. Similarly, Bankers Equity Limited (BEL) was also closed after privatisation as billions of depositor's money was lured away (Khan, 2008). Closure of a leading financial institution had a strong negative impact on the financial market.

Conclusion

The examples above suggest that in order for privatisation to succeed, several factors are important that deserve special attention for future policy formulation. Firstly, privatisation should be a transparent process which should allow equal opportunity to all investors and should not fall victim to crony capitalism. The valuation of assets should be carefully done and firms should not be sold at throw away prices (Khan, 2008). As in examples discussed above, lack of transparent process led to closure of three units and loss of investor's deposits in the BEL example. This issue is extremely important as it damages the investment and financial environment of the country. The second important thing is the sequence and timing of privatisation. It should not be done over a short period of time as the private sector might not have enough resources to pay the correct price of the nationalised industry. This may make private investment shy and lead to a reduction in investment rates (Khan, 2008). The investment climate of the country must also be kept in view. Privatisation after September 11, 2001 was not a good idea as international investment climate slumped and investors' confidence suffered sharply. It had a more pronounced effect in Pakistan especially as it has a long border with Afghanistan (Khan, 2008). Similarly, laws should be created to guarantee that people buying nationalised industry are not doing so to sell the real estate but rather they plan to engage in productive activity. This is important to safeguard loss of jobs and output in form of their closures (Khan, 2008). Another pre-privatisation activity that was seen was that of recapitalisation of public sector banks by injection of new equity of Rs. 30 billion to UBL to cover for its NPLs and to make it capable of being privatised. After pouring such huge amount of money into UBL, it was sold to Abu Dhabi and Best Way Group for a mere 12.35 billion. Therefore, while the proceeds from privatisation in second period were 34.7 billion, the net proceeds are only 4.7 billion, which is a trivial amount when compared to the capital outlay (Khan, 2008). The analysts should have engaged in a careful analysis of cost and revenue to determine the correct costs of such industry. Another result can be drawn from privatisation by looking at the case study of MCB and ABL that were discussed earlier. MCB was sold to a group of strategic investors who have turned the bank around and have made it highly efficient by improving all of the financial indicators while at the same time have introduced new products for increased customer satisfaction. ABL on the other hand was not transferred to a strategic investor but rather its control was given to its employees. This did not have the desired effect on the performance of the bank. By looking at all these reasons, it becomes clear that for privatisation to succeed, not only should it be done at the right time but also in the right way to achieve maximum gain. Also, the effects of privatisation are not so clear cut as assumed by many and any absolute judgment on it only reveals the shortsightedness of the researcher.

References

Barth, James, Gerard Caprio, and Ross Levine (2001). "Banking Systems around the Globe: Do Regulation and Ownership affect Performance and Stability?", NBER Conference Report, University of Chicago.

Hussain, Ishrat (2005). "Why Privatisation is Necessary for Economic Growth in Pakistan?", Karachi. 12 Aug. 28 Jan. 2008 <*www.bis.org/review/r050829c.pdf*>

———. (2004). "The Role of State-Owned Financial Institutions: Policy and Practice", World Bank, IMF. Washington. 27 Apr., 28 Jan. <*unpan1.un.org/intradoc/groups/public/documents/APCITY/UNPAN020760.pdf*>

Khalid, Umer (2006). "The Effect of Privatization and Liberalization on Banking Sector Performance in Pakistam", *SBP Research Bulletin* 2(2006): 403-425. 6 Feb. <*http://www.sbp.org.pk/research/bulletin/2006/vol2num2/Privatization_Liberalization_of_Banking_Sector_in_Pakistan.pdf*>

Khan, Akhtar H. (2008). "Is Privatization in Pakistan Purposeful?" PDR. 4 Feb. <*www.pide.org.pk/pdf/psde%2018AGMIs%20Privitization%20in%20Pskitan%20Purposeul*

Otchere, Isaac (2003). "Do Privatized Banks in Middle- and Low-Income Countries Perform Better than Rival Banks? An Intra-Industry Analysis of Bank Privatization", Presented at *World Bank Conference on Bank Privatization*, Nov. 20-21.

Porta, Rafael La, Florencio Lopez-De-Silanes and Andrei Shleifer (2002). "Government Ownership of Banks", *Journal of Finance* 57(1): 265-301. American Finance Association.

Annexure Table A-18.1

Post-Privitisation Structure of Banking Sector (March 2004)

Banks		*Assets*		*Deposits*		*Equity*	
		Amount	*Share*	*Amount*	*Share*	*Amount*	*Share*
	No.	*(Rs. Bill.)*	*%*	*(Rs. Bill.)*	*%*	*(Rs. Bill.)*	*%*
State Owned	4	518.8	18.6	379.3	20.1	22.5	17.2
Private	20	1840.3	66.0	1292.3	68.5	92.8	70.9
Foreign	13	278.4	10.0	198.0	10.5	26.7	20.4
Specialised Banks	3	149.8	5.4	16.1	0.9	-11.1	-8.5
Total	40	2787.2	100	1885.6	100	130.9	100

Source: Hussain, Ishrat (2004). "The Role of State-Owned Financial Institutions: Policy and Practice", World Bank, IMF. Washington. 27 Apr., 28 Jan. *<unpan1.un.org/intradoc/groups/public/documents/APCITY/UNPAN020760.pdf>*

Annexure Table A-18.2

Financial Indicators of MCB

Year	*Assets*	*Deposits*	*Advances*	*NPLs*
1994	18.1	17.6	17.7	18.1
1997	21.5	20.8	21.9	11.6
2000	18.02	18.3	21.5	14.4
2003	28.3	26.5	26.7	11.3

Source: Hussain, Ishrat (2004). "The Role of State-Owned Financial Institutions: Policy and Practice", World Bank, IMF. Washington. 27 Apr., 28 Jan. *<unpan1.un.org/intradoc/groups/public/documents/APCITY/UNPAN020760.pdf>*

Annexure Table A-18.3

Financial Indicators of ABL

Year	*Assets*	*Deposits*	*Advances*	*NPLs*
1994	9.6	9.8	10.9	16.6
1997	10.4	10.6	12.5	17.9
2000	11.7	13.0	14.2	29.4
2003	12.2	14.3	11.2	43.8

Source: Hussain, Ishrat (2004). "The Role of State-Owned Financial Institutions: Policy and Practice", World Bank, IMF. Washington. 27 Apr., 28 Jan. *<unpan1.un.org/intradoc/groups/public/documents/APCITY/UNPAN020760.pdf>*